THEY WERE
MAGNIFICENT GAMBLERS
IN
WWII'S TOUGHEST GAME

All I could hope for was to save my own skin. Every flak post in the area was alerted by now. Dazzled by the showers of tracer I crouched down and instinctively moved my head about as if to avoid the bullets. I felt I was going to be hit any second and crash helplessly like the Hurricanes. Taking my life in my hands, I got right down to the deck, feinting violently to left and right. Too late I saw the obstacle—a row of poplars along a canal. I banked instinctively, putting on full left rudder. With a terrifying crash which reverberated through the fuselage, and a jolt which nearly wrenched the stick out of my hands, my starboard wing caught the tree-tops . . . Dazed by the shock, paralyzed by fear, that fearful physical fear which twists your guts and fills your mouth with gall, I felt my muscles liquify . . . Losing my head I pulled the stick back . . . during the few seconds that my climb lasted I was hit five times—a shell exploding in my left aileron, three bullets in my elevator, and another through one of the blades of my propeller . . .

THE BANTAM WAR BOOK SERIES

This is a series of books about a world on fire.

These carefully chosen volumes cover the full dramatic sweep of World War II. Many are eyewitness accounts by the men who fought in this global conflict in which the future of the civilized world hung in balance. Fighter pilots, tank commanders and infantry commanders, among others, recount exploits of individual courage in the midst of the large-scale terrors of war. They present portraits of brave men and true stories of gallantry and cowardice in action, moving sagas of survival and tragedies of untimely death. Some of the stories are told from the enemy viewpoint to give the reader an immediate sense of the incredible life and death struggle of both sides of the battle.

Through these books we begin to discover what it was like to be there, a participant in an epic war for freedom.

Each of the books in the Bantam War Book series contains a dramatic color painting and illustrations specially commissioned for each title to give the reader a deeper understanding of the roles played by the men and machines of World War II.

THE
BIG SHOW

SOME EXPERIENCES OF A FRENCH
FIGHTER PILOT IN THE R.A.F.

PIERRE CLOSTERMANN,
D.S.O., D.F.C.

Translated by Oliver Berthoud

With a Foreword by
Marshal of the Royal Air Force
Sir John Slessor
G.C.B., D.S.O., M.C.

*This low-priced Bantam Book
has been completely reset in a type face
designed for easy reading, and was printed
from new plates. It contains the complete
text of the original hard-cover edition.*
NOT ONE WORD HAS BEEN OMITTED.

ᑭ

THE BIG SHOW
*A Bantam Book / published by arrangement with
Chatto and Windus, Ltd.*

PRINTING HISTORY
*First published 1951 in Great Britain
by Chatto and Windus, Ltd.
10 printings through 1972
Bantam edition / March 1979*

*Drawings by M. Stephen Bach.
Maps by Alan McKnight.*

ISBN 0-553-12658-X

---

*Bantam Books are published by Bantam Books, Inc. Its trade-
mark, consisting of the words "Bantam Books" and the por-
trayal of a bantam, is Registered in U.S. Patent and Trademark
Office and in other countries. Marca Registrada. Bantam
Books, Inc., 666 Fifth Avenue, New York, New York 10019.*

PRINTED IN THE UNITED STATES OF AMERICA

TO *Jacques Remlinger, my old companion, in memory of the two hundred sorties which we flew together.*

TO *Commandants Mouchotte and Martell, of 341 "Alsace" Squadron, and to all my comrades of the Free French Air Force, who gave their lives for France.*

TO *my fellow Pilots of the R.A.F. who also died in order that France should be free.*

TO *you all—to whom we owe so much, and who are so soon forgotten—I dedicate with a full heart these pages which you have lived . . .*

FOREWORD

*By Marshal of the Royal Air Force
Sir John Slessor, G.C.B., D.S.O., M.C.*

If anyone has ever doubted that the French Air Force can produce flying crews of first-class quality, let them read this book. As a fighter pilot and junior commander with a record of 420 operational sorties, first in the famous "Alsace" squadron of the Free French Air Force in Britain and then with R.A.F. units, Pierre Clostermann was second to none. His book is first class —a modest, unflinching record of the real thing. No false glamour, no bravado, no glossing over nor undue exaggeration of the grim facts of air warfare as all operational pilots know them. As he says himself, "it is a record of the daily life of every fighter pilot," in a wide variety of jobs—Sweeps and Bomber escorts over France in '43; close defence of the Fleet base at Scapa; beating up V-I sites; the Normandy landing and the land-air war on the Continent right through to the bitter end.

It is a magnificent story, and makes one proud, not only of those French boys who fought so gallantly and gaily with us, but of the Royal Air Force with which they served.

If ever we have to fight again, which God forbid, it will be good to remember that "L'Armée de l'Air" is alongside us, with good men and true like Clostermann and his friend Jacques Remlinger, Mouchotte and Martell, Boudier and de Saxe and the hundreds of other gallant Frenchmen who shared our trials and our triumphs in those grim years.

break put. The bastards are dgin about.

Three thousand feet .... boats a figure, pu-
.... home to town and ... until always ....
the rim of the cumulus .... silhouette of the
German fighter.

"........ then ....!" I said to myself, ...

CONTENTS

PART III
COMMANDS IN THE R.A.F.

CONTENTS

PREFACE

For four years my parents and I—their only child—
were separated by many thousands of miles. Between
London and Brazzaville the mails were erratic, and any
reference in letters to military matters was heavily cen-
sored. It was possible to send them a monthly air-
letter, but that was too cramped for any description of
my life in England with the Free French and the R.A.F.
Yet I did want to make my father and mother understand this new life and the mingled feelings it aroused,
a life that was unforeseen, often harsh but deeply
satisfying. I wanted them to live it with me, day by day,
even if I did not come back to describe it myself.

So every evening I used to write down for them the
events of the day in a fat Air Ministry notebook,
stamped "G.R." In an old envelope, stuck to the cover,
I put my will; it was rather an absurd gesture, for General de Gaulle's "mercenaries" had no goods and chat-
tels to dispose of except their faith in France and their
uncertain dreams of home. On the flyleaf I wrote: "In
case I should be killed or posted missing, I want this
book to be sent to my father, Captain Jacques Clostermann, French Headquarters, Brazzaville. 10.3.1942."
This notebook went with me everywhere, crumpled by
the weight of my parachute in the cockpit, stained with
tea in the mess, or beside me at Dispersal during the
long, dull hours of readiness. From the Orkneys to
Cornwall, from Kent to Scotland, from Normandy to
Denmark through Belgium, Holland and Germany,
these notes—by the end of the war they filled three
books—were always with me.

Fate, so cruel to most of my friends, decreed that

I should survive 420 sorties and that one day I should be able to tell my father, in my own words, the story of those four years. The notebooks remained unread for two years. In that time, with the other few survivors of the Free French Air Force, I had the painful task of visiting the families of our friends who had not come back and giving them the bitter consolation of hearing of their sons' deeds. We also met a number of Frenchmen who had no idea of what had happened on the other side of the Channel, and who—in some cases—didn't want to learn. But equally we knew that there were many who were trying to find out, in the hope perhaps of being reminded of their own hopes and loyalties.

It is for them that this book is published. Change the dates and a few minor details and it is a record of the daily life of every fighter pilot. Any of my comrades could produce similar episodes by looking through his log-books.

I ask the reader not to expect a work of literature. I simply jotted down day by day the impressions, the fleetingly caught incidents so sharply imprinted on my memory. It would require a remarkable talent to reproduce with truth and at the same time with literary grace the life of a fighter pilot in the last war. It is precisely because they are *true,* because they were written in the flush of action, that I have made no attempt to retouch these notes.

PIERRE CLOSTERMANN

Pierre Clostermann D.F.C.

PART ONE

PILOT WITH THE "ALSACE" SQUADRON

OPERATIONAL TRAINING UNIT IN WALES

1942

The high Welsh hills, half-drowned in mist, glided to left and right of the railway line. We had passed Birmingham, Wolverhampton and Shrewsbury buried in greasy soot. Without exchanging a word, Jacques and I gazed indifferently at the depressing landscape, washed by an incessant drizzle, the dirty enervating mining towns crawling up the valleys, each one crushed by a pall of grey smoke anchored to the housetops, so dense that the wind, blowing in icy gusts, could not move it.

Our fellow-passengers gazed curiously at our navy-blue, gold-buttoned French uniforms. The pilot's brevet of the "Armée de l'Air" gleamed proudly on our breasts, with the wings of the R.A.F. over our left pockets.

Barely a fortnight before we had still been pilots under training at the R.A.F. college at Cranwell, dragging round manuals on navigation and armaments and thick books full of notes.

All that was only a memory now. In a few hours, perhaps, we would be flying a Spitfire, thus clearing the last hurdle that separated us from the great arena.

A few minutes more and we reached Rednal, No. 61 O.T.U.*—for a conversion course on Spitfires before a squadron posting.

Suddenly Jacques pressed his face to the window:

"Look Pierre, there are our Spitfires!"

Sure enough, as the train slowed down alongside an

---

*Operational Training Unit.

airfield, a damp ray of sunshine succeeded in piercing the fog, revealing twenty or so aircraft lined up along a strip of tarmac.

*   *   *

The great day had come! It had snowed all night and the airfield was dazzling white beneath the blue sky. Heavens, how good to be alive! I filled my lungs with the icy air and felt the snow crunch under my feet, soft and yielding like an oriental carpet. It brought back many memories. The first snow I had seen for so long.

*   *   *

At the door of the flight-hut, where you shelter between flights, my instructor was waiting for me, smiling.

"How do you feel?"

"O.K., Sir," I replied, trying to hide my emotion.

All my life I shall remember my first contact with a Spitfire.

The one I was going to fly bore the markings TO-S. Before putting on my parachute I stopped a moment to gaze at it—the clean lines of the fuselage, the beautifully streamlined Rolls-Royce engine: a real thoroughbred.

"You've got her for one hour. Good luck!"

This thunderbolt was mine for an hour, sixty intoxicating minutes! I tried to remember my instructor's advice. Everything seemed so confused. I strapped myself in, trembling, adjusted my helmet, and still dazed by the mass of instruments, dials, contacts, levers, which crowded on one another, all vital, and which one's finger must not fail to touch at the psychological moment, I got ready for the decisive test.

Carefully I went through the cockpit drill, murmuring the ritual phrase, BTFCPPUR—Brakes, Trim, Flaps, Contacts, Pressure (in the pneumatic system), Petrol, Undercarriage and Radiator.

Everything was all set. The mechanic closed the door behind me and there I was, imprisoned in this metal monster which I had got to control. A last glance.

"All clear? Contact!"

I manipulated the hand pumps and the starter buttons. The airscrew began to revolve slowly, and suddenly, with a sound like thunder, the engine fired. The exhausts vomited long blue flames enveloped in black smoke, while the aircraft began to shudder like a boiler under pressure.

When the chocks were removed I opened the radiator wide, for these liquid-cooled engines over-heat very rapidly, and I taxied very carefully over to the runway, cleared by snow-ploughs, jet black and dead straight in the white landscape.

"Tudor 26, you may scramble now, you may scramble now!" Over the radio the control tower authorized me to take off.

My heart was thumping in my ribs. I swallowed the lump in my throat, lowered my seat and with a clammy hand I slowly opened the throttle. At once I felt myself swept up by a cyclone.

Snatches of advice came back to me.

"Don't stick the nose too far forward!"

In front of me there was only a slight clearance between the ground and the tips of the enormous airscrew which was going to absorb all the power from the engine.

Timidly I eased the stick forward, and, with a jolt that glued me to the back of my seat, the Spitfire started forward, then moved faster and faster while the airfield swept by on either side with increasing speed.

"Keep her straight!"

I ruddered frantically to check incipient swings.

Suddenly, holding my breath, and as if by magic, I found myself airborne. The railway line passed by like a flash. I was vaguely aware of some trees and houses, which disappeared indistinctly behind me.

I quickly raised the undercarriage, closed the transparent hood of my cockpit, throttled back and adjusted the airscrew pitch for cruising.

Phew! Drops of sweat ran down my forehead. But instinctively my limbs reacted like the well-regulated levers of an automaton. The long, tedious months of training had prepared my muscles and reflexes for just this minute.

How light she was on the controls! The slightest pressure with hand or foot and the machine leapt into the sky.

"Good heavens! Where am I?"

The speed was such that the few seconds which had elapsed had been enough to take me half a dozen miles from the airfield. The black runway was no more than a streak of soot on the horizon.

Timidly I hazarded a turn, passed over my base again and turned to left and right. I eased the stick back slightly and I climbed to 10,000 feet in the twinkling of an eye.

Gradually the speed went to my head and I got bolder. Moving the throttle the fraction of an inch was enough to unleash the engine.

I decided to try a dive. Gently I eased the stick forward—300, 350, 400 m.p.h. The ground seemed to be hurtling towards me in a terrifying way. Scared by the speed I instinctively moved the stick back, and suddenly my head was driven into my shoulders, a leaden weight pressed my backbone down and crushed me into my seat, and my eyes blurred.

Like a steel ball falling on a marble block the Spitfire had bounced on the elastic air and, as straight as a rod, had shot up into the sky.

As soon as I had recovered from the effects of centrifugal force I hastened to throttle back, as I had no oxygen and the machine was still climbing.

Over the radio I heard Control calling me back. Christmas! an hour already! Everything seemed to have happened in one second.

Now I had to land.

I opened the radiator wide, throttled back, changed to fine pitch, opened my hood, raised the seat, and began my approach.

Once again I started to panic. The enormous engine in front of me with its broad exhaust pipes blotted out the whole runway. Blinded, my head kept in by the terrific pressure of the air, I was a prisoner in my cockpit.

I lowered the undercarriage and the flaps. The runway drew near at frightening speed. I would never succeed in putting her down. The airfield seemed to be getting simultaneously narrower and closer. Stick back, back desperately. The machine touched down with a loud metallic jolt which reverberated in the fuselage and —I felt her awkwardly rolling on the tarmac.

A touch of left brake, then a touch of right, and the Spitfire came to a standstill at the end of the runway. The throb of the engine ticking over was like the beating of a winded race-horse's flanks.

My instructor jumped up on the wing, helped me off with my parachute, smiling at my pale, drawn face.

I took a couple of steps, staggered, and had to hold on to the fuselage.

"Good show! You see, nothing to worry about!"

All the same, if only he knew how proud I felt. At last I had flown a Spitfire. How beautiful the machine seemed to me, and how alive! A masterpiece of harmony and power, even as I saw her now, motionless.

Softly, as one might caress a woman's cheeks, I ran my hand over the aluminum of her wings, cold and smooth like a mirror, the wings which had borne me.

Going back to the hut, my parachute on my back, I turned again and dreamt of the day when, in a squadron, I would have a Spitfire of my own, to take into combat, which would hold my life within the narrow confines of its cockpit, and which I would love like a faithful friend.

*   *   *

Those were, at O.T.U., two arduous winter months.

Course succeeded course, flying hours accumulated rapidly, aerial gunnery exercises over the snow-covered Welsh hills quickly mounted up in my pilot's log-book.

Not without losses and tragedies, however. One of our Belgian comrades' Spitfires exploded in mid-air during an aerobatics practice. Two of our R.A.F. friends came into collision and were killed before our eyes.

Then Pierrot Degail, one of the six Frenchmen on the course, crashed one misty evening into an ice-covered hill-top. It took two days to reach the debris through the snow. His body was found in a kneeling position, his head in his arms, like a sleeping child, by the side of his Spitfire. Both his legs were broken and, unable to move, he must have died of cold during the night.

The burial ceremony, with military honours, was moving in its simplicity. Jacques, Menuge, Commailles and I carried the coffin, wrapped in the tricolour. God, how sad and weighed down we were, under the thin icy rain. The slow procession, one by one, before the pit filled with the sound of shovelfuls of British soil falling on the poor kid.

After five weeks at Rednal we spent the last three weeks of our training at Montford Bridge, a small satellite airfield lost in the hills.

Without interruption, as soon as the weather cleared somewhat, we flew. Formation exercises in threes, fours, twelves, emergency take-offs, dog-fight practice, air-firing, course on tactics, on aircraft recognition, on elocution for speaking over the RT*, etc.

The cold was appalling. We lived in Nissen huts which had no insulating walls and keeping warm was a real problem. I used to go with John Scott, the baby of our team, who shared a room with me, and "borrow" coal from a dump by the railway. John was very particular about his appearance, and it was a comic sight to see him, precariously balanced on barbed wire, passing greasy blocks of anthracite held distastefully between the thumb and forefinger of a carefully gloved hand.

Then followed the Homeric business of lighting the diminutive stove which had the task of warming our hut. Pints of petrol—filched from the bowser—were necessary to excite the faltering enthusiasm of the damp coal and the wet wood. One fine evening, I remember, the stove, saturated with petrol vapour, blew up and

---

*Radio telephony.

Jacques, John and I were transformed into Zulu warriors of the darkest hue.

New Year's Eve came and went, very quiet and slightly sad in that remote corner. Then came the day of posting. Commailles, Mengue and I were to leave for Turnhouse in Scotland to join 341 Squadron, Free French Fighter Squadron "Alsace," then in process of formation. Jacques, John and Aubertin were leaving for 602 Squadron in Perranporth.

The die was cast. The real war was beginning. At last!

THE "ALSACE" SQUADRON

Three young Sergeant Pilots disembarked in Edinburgh.

The world was theirs. They glanced absent-mindedly at the "Princess of the North" bathed in sunlight, though she had adorned herself with a resplendent snowy mantle.

They were very tired. They had just crossed the whole of England diagonally from south-west to north-east. An exhausting night in the train, with charges in the dark, jostling on damp platforms, mist forming haloes round screened lamps, the panting of engines, the thronging crowd of uniforms.

"The train for Leicester, please?"

Dazed by the noise, dragging their heavy kit-bags, they had vainly searched for seats in crowded coaches with people sleeping on top of each other—smell of soot, of sweat, of stale tobacco smoke.

The coaches had started moving. Then the alarming syncopated wail of the sirens.

"Air-raid on! Lights, please, lights, please!"

The jamming on of brakes, the hiss of compressed air, the impact of the buffers jolting the dazed passengers, thin blue lights extinguished. A quarter of an hour. Half an hour. One hour of cold and silence. A few flashes in the sky. The distant hum of engines. Vague gleams of light on the horizon, showing up for a moment the silhouettes of factories or chimney stacks. Then the sirens again.

"All clear!"

A blast on a whistle, the squeaking of rusty chains, more jolts—the engine skidding and racing. Vague impressions, drowned in an exhausting and uncomfortable twilight sleep.

*   *   *

The bus stopped in front of the airfield guard-room. Miraculously, all fatigue disappeared.

"Turnhouse!" cried the conductor.

We saw great hangars camouflaged with green and brown stripes, the low buildings of the messes, the wooden dispersal huts scattered round the big tarmac runways which quartered the grassy surface of the ground. A few aircraft here and there.

The S.P. corporal on duty examined our papers, our identity cards, and had us escorted to the Sergeants' mess.

Slightly cold greeting from the Station Warrant Officer.

"French squadrons? I haven't seen anybody yet."

Good heavens! Perhaps it was a ghost fighter squadron? We began to sing a different tune. A utility truck deposited us with our baggage in front of a big, gloomy building. Dead silence. A smell of mildew, a large empty dormitory—iron beds, small grey cupboards. Not a soul about. The first impression was disconcerting. Where was the cosy, animated squadron bar, where were the gay, noisy comrades whom our imagination had showed us greeting us with open arms?

"Nom de Dieu! On ne peut plus dormir tranquille ici!"

The voice made us jump—an honest-to-goodness

French voice, and from Paris, judging by the accent.

And right at the far end of the room in a dark corner we made out a shape, lying on a bed and smoking a cigarette. Navy-blue uniform, gold buttons—a Frenchman! He got up languidly.

"Why, it's Marquis!"

We looked at each other and laughed. We four *were* 341 Squadron.

* * *

The days passed, and the "Alsace" Fighter Squadron took shape.

Commandant Mouchotte,* one of the first to join the F.F.F., was to be in command. A tall, dark, slim man, with piercing eyes and a voice that snapped and admitted of no argument, but was followed by a warming, friendly smile. The kind of man for whom you get yourself killed without discussion, almost with pleasure.

Then Lieutenant Martell, who was to be my flight-commander, a blond giant with broad shoulders and enormous feet, and magic hands that handled a Spitfire with incredible power and flexibility.

Lieutenant Boudier—Boubou—a little wisp of a man behind a big pipe, with a heart of gold. He was an ace, with seven Jerries to his credit already. He commanded the other flight.

Then the pilots started arriving one by one, from the four corners of England, after tearing themselves away from the four corners of occupied France to come and fight. A natural selection brought about by will-power and patriotism; every social class, but an élite.

De Bordas, under a gay and carefree exterior, hid the tragedy of the loss of his best friend, killed at his side near Dieppe; Bouguen, a stiff-necked Breton; Farman,

---

*The French ranks, which were often retained, were as follows:

Commandant	"	"	"	"	" Squadron Leader
Capitaine	"	"	"	"	" Flight Lieutenant
Lieutenant	"	"	"	"	" Flying Officer
Sous-Lieutenant	"	"	"	"	" Pilot Officer
Adjudant	"	"	"	"	" Warrant Officer
Sergent Chef	"	"	".	"	" Flight Sergeant

bearer of a name famous in the French air arm; Chevalier, calm, coldly determined; Lafont, one of the veterans of the G.C.1* in Libya; Girardon, one of our rare regular officers, full of banter and dry humour; Roos, who hid his bashfulness and his kind heart under a surly exterior; Mathey, who had crossed the Pyrenees on skis to join Free France; Savary, the poet of the party, subtle and cultured; Bruno, an experienced pilot and a wag; Gallet, his bosom friend, also a veteran from the heroic days with the G.C.1 in Libya; Pabiot, from the "Ile de France" Squadron, who just wanted to continue the fight.

Gradually the team built up, and still they continued to come.

De Mezillis, from Brittany, who had lost an arm with the "Lorraine" Squadron in Libya and, by an incredible effort of will, had learnt to fly with his artificial arm; Béraud, the "steady type" of the gang, a sensible and studious pilot, whom you always went and consulted before you did anything silly; Laurent, meticulous, scientific, enthusiastic; Mailfert, that priceless practical joker; Leguie, another Breton, as phlegmatic as any Anglo-Saxon; Raoul Duval, hero of sensational escapes, a regular to his finger tips; Borne, friendly, self-effacing and discreet; Buiron, "Bui-Bui and his pipe" to his friends; De Saxe, a walking skeleton who feared neither God nor the Devil.

* * *

One fine day, with a noise like thunder, our Spitfires arrived. Our English fitters took them over and we cleaned them up. Lorraine crosses appeared on the fuselages, with the markings of 341 Squadron, N and L.

Under the energetic leadership of Mouchotte and thanks to the experience of Martell and Boudier, the team of friends became a redoubtable combat formation. The planes were incessantly in the air—shooting, combat formation, dog-fight exercises, scramble practice.

---

*Groupe de Combat 1—Fighter Squadron 1.

The British were amazed at how fast the unit got into shape and generously admitted that it certainly was an exceptional one.

One month later the "Alsace" Squadron was posted to the Biggin Hill Wing. It was an honour, how great an honour we did not perhaps completely realize at the time. Biggin Hill, south of London, was the base with the highest number of victories to its credit and was reserved for the most select squadrons of the R.A.F.

To go there we were to be equipped with Spitfire IX's, with Rolls-Royce Merlin 63 engines with two-stage superchargers, British aero technique's last word, parsimoniously distributed to a few outstanding units.

To celebrate the event suitably we threw a monster party for the Turnhouse personnel, from Group Captain Guinness, the Station Commander, to the last mechanic. I watched Mouchotte, in a corner, looking very calm but a little bit sad. I knew what he was thinking. He was wondering with bitterness in his heart how many of the kids in his squadron would survive to the end. Death had already struck. De Mezillis had been killed last week, when the wings of his Spitfire folded up in a dive. And only the day before Commailles and Artaud had crashed, the wrecks of their two aircraft interlocked, during a combat exercise.

MY FIRST BIG SHOW OVER FRANCE

We were still "in readiness." All was calm in the Biggin Hill sector and the morning wore slowly on. Wrapped in blankets, the mechanics lay drowsily under the dew-covered wings of the Spitfires.

Time was hard to kill. In a corner of the Dispersal but a gramophone was grinding out an old favourite,

while Martell, Mailfert, Girardon, Laurent, Bruno, Gallet and I played a desultory game of Monopoly. Outside under the window, Jacques and Marquis, covered
with grease, were fitting an enormous engine to a
motor-cycle frame which they had dug up God knows
where.

The telephone rang. Everyone looked up, with tense
faces.

"Early lunch for pilots. There's a show on!" shouted
the orderly from the booth. A very important sweep
must have been laid on for early afternoon and the mess
was preparing a special early lunch for the pilots taking
part. Mouchotte had been warned and arrived at once,
together with Boudier.

"Martell, detail your section, you provide Red 2 and
Boubou will provide Red 3 and 4."

We crowded round the board, studded with twelve
nails on which would shortly hang twelve metal Spitfire
silhouettes, each bearing a name. The squadron battle
order was posted after a few moments' discussion between the two flight commanders.

	Cdt. Mouchotte.	
Lt. Boudier.	Sgt. Ch. Bruno.	Lt. Martell.
Sgt. Remlinger.	Lt. Pabiot.	Sgt. Clostermann.
S-Lt. Bouguen.	S-Lt. De Bordas.	Lt. Béraud.
Sgt. Marquis.		Sgt. Mathey.
	Reserve: Sgt. Ch. Gallet.	

Those left out muttered restlessly among themselves.

Rendezvous in the Intelligence Room at 1230 hours.
Mouchotte went off in his Hillman utility with Martell
and Boudier, while the other pilots piled into the mess
truck. Quick meal with the pilots of 611; soup, sausages
and mash. You could feel a certain apprehension in the
air all the same. For most of us this was our first big
operational flight, and it would probably take us far
inside the enemy zone.

I felt very nervous. I was curious, and anxious at the
same time, to know how I would react in the face of
danger, a rather morbid wish to know what fear felt
like—real fear, the fear of man, alone, face to face

with death. And yet there remains deeply rooted, the old scepticism of the civilized human being; the routine of work, travel in comfort, the humanities, city life —all this, in truth, leaves very little room for a realization of mortal danger or for any testing of purely physical courage. However, I would have liked to get right inside the mind of that Canadian from 611 Squadron, whose first operational flight this was far from being. He calmly asked the W.A.A.F. waitress for a second helping of mashed potatoes, while I was having difficulty in swallowing my first. And Dixon and Bruno, discussing football without pause, what were they thinking about, deep down?

It was at that moment, by association of ideas, that a certain Thursday at the Croix Catelan came back to me. I was keeping goal for my school football eleven, Nôtre Dame de Boulogne. The Albert de Mun centre-forward, a hefty chap who must have weighed at least 12 stone, had caught our backs off their guard and slipped past them. There was only one way of preserving my goal intact: to dive at his feet. Instinctively, I hurled myself forward with arms outstretched. Then, a fraction of a second before getting my hands to the ball, I twisted sideways. I was frightened of getting hurt by the studs on my opponent's boots. I was frightened, and the goal was duly scored. Ought I to be dreading a purely physical reaction of the same kind this afternoon? This sudden glimpse into the past finally killed my appetite.

It was 12:35.

*　　*　　*

"Come on chaps. Briefing!"

We moved in small silent groups towards the Intelligence Room. First, a room cluttered up with photos, maps, easy chairs, technical papers and confidential Air Ministry publications. In a corner a small low door gave access to the briefing room down a few steps. The atmosphere caught you by the throat the moment you put your foot inside the door. The first thing you saw was the big map of our sector of operations, completely covering the wall behind the platform; south-east En-

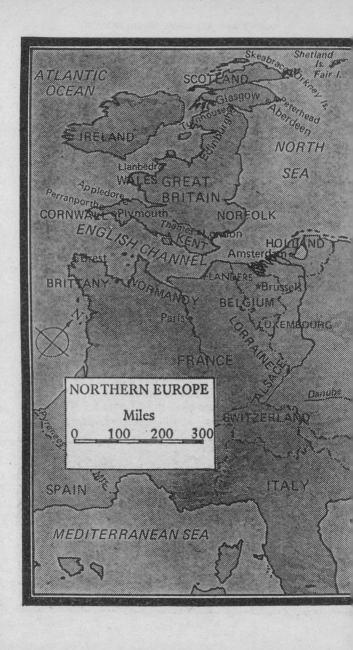

gland, London, the Thames, the Channel, the North
Sea, Holland, Belgium, and France as far west as
Cherbourg. On the map a red ribbon joined Biggin Hill
to Amiens, turned back through Saint-Pol, and returned
via Boulogne to Dungeness—our route for the day's
sortie.

The pilots pushed in and found themselves somewhere to sit, amid the muffled stamping of flying boots
and the scratching of matches. Smoke began to curl up
from cigarettes held in nervous fingers. From the ceiling
hung models of Allied and German aircraft. On the
walls were pinned photos of Focke-Wulfs and Messer-

Focke-Wulf 190

schmitt 109's taken from every angle, with diagrams
giving the corresponding aiming deflections. The vital
battle slogans were posted everywhere.

"The Hun is always in the sun."

"Wait to shoot till you see the whites of his eyes."

"Never go after a Jerry you have hit. Another will
get you for certain."

"It's better to come back with a probable than to be
shot down with the one you've confirmed."

"Look out! It's the one you don't see who gets you."

"Don't dream about your popsie. If you don't see the
Hun who is going to get your mate, you are a criminal."

"Silence on the radio. Don't jam your RT channel!"

"If you are brought down over enemy territory, escape. If you are caught, keep your trap shut."

The navy-blue French uniforms stood out among the
blue-grey battle-dress of the British and Canadians, but
the same hearts beat beneath them all. A sound of

brakes was heard outside. Doors banged. Everyone got up noisily. Group-Captain Malan, D.S.O., D.F.C., and Wing Commanders Al Deere and De La Torre came in, followed by Mouchotte and Jack Charles, O.C. 485 Squadron. Malan leaned against the wall in a corner, De La Torre and Al Deere went up on the platform.

"Sit down, chaps," said De La Torre. Silence. He started to read Form D in his monotonous voice:

"This afternoon the Wing is taking part in Circus No. 87. H hour is 1355 hours. Seventy-two Flying Fortresses will bomb Amiens Glissy airfield.

"Close escort will be provided at 16,000 feet, by 7 Wings, i.e. 14 squadrons of Spitfire V's. The Wing from Kenley will provide advanced support and will operate at 20,000 feet in the vicinity of the target at H hours minus 5 minutes. Medium cover will be assured by 24 Spitfire IX's from West Malling and the 2 Wings of Spitfire IX's from Northolt will provide top cover at 29,000 feet.

"Two diversions have been laid on: 12 Typhoons escorted by 24 Spitfires will dive-bomb Poix airfield at H minus 20 minutes, i.e. at 1335 hours. Twelve Bostons escorted by 36 Spitfires will bomb the docks at Dunkirk to H minus 10 minutes, after a feint on Gravelines. The diversions will have the effect of taking the German Radar's attention off the Flying Fortresses while they form up and of dispersing, at least we hope so, the efforts of the enemy fighters.

"The Biggin Hill Wing is to operate in the region of Amiens from H plus 5, i.e. 1400 hours, to cover the return of the Forts.

"The order of battle of the Luftwaffe relevant to this operation is as follows: 60 Focke-Wulfs available at Glissy—you'll probably have about 40 of them in the air. One hundred and twenty Messerschmitt 109 F's, and Fw 190's at Saint Omer and Fort Rouge. You'll probably see a few of them coming back from Dunkirk where the Bostons will have drawn them. The 40 Fw 190's from Poix, stirred up by the Typhoons, will probably be the first to intervene over Amiens, but by the time you get there they will already have had a bone to pick with the escort proper. It seems probable that your immediate opponents will be the 60 Fw's from Rosière en Santerre, those from Glissy if they can get into the air before the bombing attack and, inevitably, your old friends the Abbeville Boys, whom you will be glad to see again.

"You will be controlled over the objective by Appledore, on frequency C, call-sign Grass Seed. Zona will control you on B up to that time. You will be the only formation on frequency C, so no interference to worry about.

"I am now going to hand over to Wing Commander Deere, who is going to lead the show."

In a calm, measured voice, contrasting with his tough and dare-devil appearance, Al Deere gave us our final flying instructions:

"I shall lead 485 Squadron, whose call-sign will be Gimlet. My personal call-sign will be Brutus. René will lead 341, call-sign Turban. We shall take off in squadron formation from the north-south runway. Start up engines at 1320 hours for Turban and 1322 hours for Gimlet. Take off at 1325 hours. I will orbit base so that you can form up and at 1332 I shall set course.

"We will stay at zero feet until 1350, then we shall climb at full throttle so as to cross the coast at a minimum of 10,000 feet, and we shall rendezvous over Amiens, if all goes well, at 25,000 feet. On the way out Turban will fly 2,000 yards to my right. As soon as we gain height Turban will keep 2,000 feet above us and slightly to the rear. When we reach Amiens we will turn 90° port and steer a course of 047° for 5 minutes, unless Appledore gives us other instructions. In principle we will fly for 35 minutes on our auxiliary tanks. When I give the signal "drop your babies," you will take up battle formation.

"Absolute RT silence is compulsory until I give that signal. We are going to fly at sea-level for 18 disagreeable minutes, so as not to be picked up by the German Radar—we can't have some clot wrecking the whole show by shooting off his mouth unnecessarily. If you have trouble and want to return to base, waggle your wings, pass over on to D frequency, but don't use it unless you are really in serious trouble. Otherwise, for Christ's sake, keep your trap shut.

"Now a final bit of advice. If your drop-tank doesn't come off, warn your leader and go home. It's useless trying to go on with that extra drag. You'll either handicap everyone else or you'll lag behind and be shot down as sure as fate.

"Give clear indications of the whereabouts of suspicious aircraft in relation to me by means of the clock code,* speaking slowly and clearly and giving your call-sign. If there's a scrap, keep together, and if things get very sticky, keep in pairs at least, that's essential. No. 2's must never forget that they are responsible for covering their No. 1. Always break towards the enemy. And mind your oxygen.

"If things go wrong, the direct course home is 317°. If you are lost somewhere over France and short of petrol, call Zona on frequency B. If you are more than half-way back across the Channel and in difficulties, but capable of getting back to base, warn Tramline on frequency A. If you can't get back to the coast, bale out after calling "May Day" on frequency D with, if possible, a transmission for a fix. As always, everything possible will be done to fish you out quickly.

"Don't forget to switch on your I.F.F.† as soon as you take off, and check your sights. Empty your pockets properly.

"Synchronize your watches; it is exactly 12 hours 51 minutes 30 seconds . . . one . . . two . . . three . . . it is 12 hours 52 minutes zero seconds. Keep your eyes open, and good luck!"

While Deere was speaking, the pilots had been scribbling the essential gen straight on to the skin of the backs of their hands: times, homing course, radio frequencies, etc. Then a rush for the door and the waggons.

---

*The clock code—normal way in the Services of indicating position relative to oneself. 12 o'clock is straight in front, 6 o'clock is behind 5 o'clock is behind and slightly to the right, and so on.
†Identification Friend or Foe.

The weather was superb, and for three days the sun had been unusually bright for the time of year. At the Dispersal everyone made a bee-line for his locker. I carefully emptied my pockets—no revealing bus tickets must be left, no addressed envelopes which might give away my airfield to the Hun. I took off my collar and tie and put on a silk scarf instead. I drew the thick white regulation pullover over a sheepskin waistcoat. I pulled on over my socks thick woollen stockings up to my thighs. Then on top of those my fleece-lined boots, tucking in my trousers. I slipped my hunting knife into the left boot, my maps into the right. I loaded my Smith and Wesson service revolver and passed the lanyard round

Smith and Wesson .38

my neck. In the pockets of my Mae West were my "escape kit" and my emergency rations.

My fitter came for my parachute and dinghy, to place them in the seat of the aircraft, together with my helmet, whose earphones and mask the electrician would connect to the radio and the oxygen bottles.

1315 hours. I was already installed, firmly fixed to my Spitfire NL-B by the straps of my safety harness. I had tested the radio, the sight and the camera gun. I had carefully adjusted the oxygen mask and verified the pressure in the bottles. I had armed the cannon and the machine guns and adjusted the rear-vision mirror.

Tommy was wandering round the aircraft with a screw-driver, getting the detachable panels firmly fastened. My stomach seemed curiously empty and I was beginning to regret my scanty lunch. People were busy all round the field. In the distance Deere's car stopped by his aircraft, under the control tower. He was wearing a white flying suit and he slipped quickly into his cockpit. The fire crew took up their positions on the running boards of the tender, and the medical orderlies in the ambulance. The hour was approaching.

1319 hours. Deep silence over the airfield. Not a movement anywhere. The pilots had their eyes glued on Mouchotte who was consulting his watch. By each aircraft a fitter stood motionless, his finger on the switch of the auxiliary starter batteries. Another stood guard by the fire extinguishers lying on the grass at the ready. My parachute buckle was badly placed and was torturing me, but it was too late to adjust it.

1320 hours. Mouchotte glanced round the twelve Spitfires, then began to manipulate his pumps. A rasping rattle from the starter, then his propeller began to turn. Feverishly I switched on.

"All clear?—switches ON!"

Kept in perfect trim, my Rolls-Royce engine started first shot. The fitters rushed round, removing chocks, dragging batteries away, hanging on to the wing tips to help the aircraft pivot. Mouchotte's NL-L was already taxi-ing to the northern end of the field.

1322 hours. The engines of 611 were turning and the 12 Spitfires beginning to line up on either side of Deere's in a cloud of dust. We lined up behind them in combat formation. I took up my position, my wing tip almost touching Martell's. I was sweating.

1324 hours. The 26 aircraft were all ready, engines ticking over, wings glinting in the sun. The pilots adjusted their goggles and tightened their harness.

1325 hours. A white rocket rose from the control tower. Deere raised his arm and the 13 aircraft of 611 Squadron started forward. In his turn Mouchotte raised his gloved hand and slowly opened the throttle. Eyes fixed on Martell's wing tip, and my hands moist, I fol-

lowed. The tails went up, the Spitfires began to bounce
clumsily on their narrow undercarriages, the wheels left
the ground—we were airborne.

I raised the undercart and locked it, throttled back
and adjusted the airscrew pitch. We swept like a whirlwind over the road outside the airfield. A bus had
stopped, its passengers crowding at the windows. I
switched over to the auxiliary tanks and shut the main
tank cocks. Handling the controls clumsily and jerkily,
I contrived to keep formation. The Spitfires slipped
southward at tree and roof-top level in a thunderous
roar which halted people in the streets in their tracks.
We jumped a wooded hill, then suddenly we were over
the sea, its dirty waves edged with foam and dominated
on the left by Beachy Head. A blue hazy line on the
horizon must be France. We hurtled forward, a few
feet above the water.

Some disconnected impressions remain vividly im-
pressed on my memory—a British coastguard vessel
with its crew waving to us; an Air Sea Rescue launch
gently rocking with the swell and surrounded by a
swarm of seagulls.

Out of the corner of my eye I watched the pressure
and temperature—normal. I switched on my reflector
sight. One of the 611 aircraft waggled its wings, turned
and came back towards England, gaining height. Engine trouble, probably.

1349 hours. Over the radio we would hear in the far
distance shouts and calls coming from the close escort
squadrons—and suddenly, very distinctly, a triumphant: "I got him!" I realized with a tightening of the
heart that over there they were already fighting.

1350 hours. As one, the 24 Spitfires rose and climbed
towards the sky, hanging on their propellers, 3,300 feet
a minute.

France! A row of white cliffs emerged from the mist
and as we gained height the horizon gradually receded
—the estuary of the Somme, the narrow strip of sand
at the foot of the tree-crowned cliffs, the first meadows,
and the first village nestling by a wood in a valley.

Fifteen thousand feet. My engine suddenly cut out

and the nose dropped violently. With my heart in my mouth and unable to draw breath I reacted instinctively and at once changed to my main petrol tanks. My auxiliary was empty. Feeling weak about the knees I realized that through lack of experience I had used too much power to keep my position and that my engine had used proportionately more fuel. A second's glide, a sputter, and the engine picked up again. At full throttle I closed up with my section.

"Brutus aircraft, drop your babies!" sounded Deere's clear voice in the earphones. Still considerably shaken, I pulled the handle, hoping to God that the thing would work . . . a jerk, a swishing sound, and all our 24 tanks fell, fluttering downwards.

"Hullo, Brutus, Zona calling, go over Channel C Charlie."

"Hullo, Zona, Brutus answering. Channel C. Over!"

"Hullo, Brutus. Zona out!"

I pressed button C on the V.H.F.* panel. A crackling sound, then the voice of Squadron Leader Holmes, the famous controller of Grass Seed:

"Hullo, Brutus leader, Grass Seed calling. There is plenty going on over target. Steer 096°—zero, nine, six. There are 40 plus bandits 15 miles ahead, angels† 35, over to you!"

"Hullo, Grass Seed. Brutus answering. Steering 096°. Roger out."

Mouchotte put us in combat formation:

"Hullo, Turban, combat formation, go!"

The three sections of four Spitfires drew apart. Below to my right the Gimlets did the same.

"Brutus aircraft, keep your eyes open!"

We were at 27,000 feet. Five minutes passed. The cloudless sky was so vast and limpid that you felt stunned. You knew that France was there, under the translucent layer of dry mist, which was slightly more opaque over the towns. The cold was painful and breathing difficult. You could feel the sun, but I could not make out whether I was being burnt or frozen by

*Very high frequency.
†Altitude expressed in thousands of feet.

its rays. To rouse myself I turned the oxygen full on. The strident roar of the engine increased the curious sensation of being isolated that one gets in a single-seater fighter. It gradually becomes a sort of noisy but neutral background that ends up by merging into a queer kind of thick, heavy silence.

Still nothing new. I felt both disappointed and relieved. Time seemed to pass very slowly. I felt I was dreaming with my eyes open, lulled by the slow rhythmical rocking movement up and down of the Spitfires in echelon, by the gentle rotation of the propellers through the rarefied and numbing air. Everything seemed so unreal and remote. Was this war?

"Look out, Brutus leader, Grass Seed calling. Three gaggles of 20 plus converging towards you, above!"

Holmes' voice had made me jump. Martell now chimed in:

"Look out, Brutus, Yellow One calling, smoke trails coming 3 o'clock!"

I stared round and suddenly I spotted the tell-tale condensation trails of the Jerries beginning to converge on us from south and east. Christ, how fast they were coming! I released the safety catch of the guns.

"Brutus calling. Keep your eyes open, chaps. Climb like hell!"

I opened the throttle and changed to fine pitch, and instinctively edged closer to Martell's Spitfire. I felt very alone in a suddenly hostile sky.

"Brutus calling. Open your eyes and prepare to break port. The bastards are right above!"

Three thousand feet above our heads a filigree pattern began to form and you could already distinguish the glint of the slender cross-shaped silhouettes of the German fighters.

"Here they come!" I said to myself, hypnotized. My throat contracted, my toes curled in my boots. I felt as if I were stifling in a strait-jacket, swaddled in all those belts, braces and buckles.

"Turban, break starboard!" yelled Boudier. In a flash I saw the roundels of Martell's Spitfire surge up before me. I banked my aircraft with all my strength,

opened the throttle wide, and there I was in his slipstream! Where were the Huns? I dared not look behind
me, and I turned desperately, glued to my seat by the
centrifugal force, eyes riveted on Martell turning a
hundred yards in front of me.

"Gimlet, attack port!"

I felt lost in the mêlée.

"Turban Yellow Two, break!"

Yellow Two? Why, that was me! With a furious
kick on the rudder bar, I broke away, my gorge rising
from sheer fear. Red tracers danced past my windshield . . . and suddenly I saw my first Hun! I identified it at once—it was a Focke-Wulf 190. I had not
studied the photos and recognition charts so often for
nothing.

After firing a burst of tracer at me he bore down on
Martell. Yes, it certainly was one—the short wings, the
radial engine, the long transparent hood: the square-cut
tail-plane all in one piece! But what had been missing
from the photos was the lively colouring—the pale
yellow belly, the greyish green back, the big black
crosses outlined with white. The photos gave no hint of
the quivering of the wings, the outline elongated and
fined down by the speed, the curious nose-down flying
attitude.

The sky, which had been filled with hurtling Spitfires,
seemed suddenly empty—my No. 1 had disappeared.
Never mind, I was not going to lose my Focke-Wulf. I
was no longer afraid.

Incoherent pictures are superimposed on my memory—three Focke-Wulfs waggling their wings; tracers
criss-crossing; a parachute floating like a puff of smoke
in the blue sky.

I huddled up, with the stick hugged to my stomach
in both hands, thrown into an endless ascending spiral
at full throttle.

"Look out! . . . Attention! . . . Break!"—a medley of
shouts in the earphones. I would have liked to recognize a definite order somewhere, or some advice.

Another Focke-Wulf, wings lit up by the blinding
flashes of its cannon firing—dirty grey trails from ex-

hausts—white trails from square wing tips. I couldn't make out who or what he was firing at. He flicked—yellow belly, black crosses. He dived and fell like a bullet. Far below he merged into the blurred landscape.

Another one, on a level with me. He turned towards me. Careful now! I must face him!

A quick half-roll, and without quite knowing how, I found myself on my back, finger on firing button, shaken to the marrow of my bones by the roar of my flame-spitting cannon. All my faculties, all my being, were focused on one single thought: I MUST KEEP HIM IN MY SIGHTS.

What about deflection?—not enough. I must tighten my turn! More . . . more still . . . more still! No good. He had gone, but my finger was still convulsively pressed on the button. I was firing at emptiness.

Where was he? I began to panic. Beware, "the Hun you haven't seen is the one who gets you!" I could feel the disordered thumping of my heart right down in my stomach, in my clammy temples, in my knees.

There he was again—but a long way away. He dived, I fired again—missed him! Out of range. Raging, I persisted . . . one last burst . . . my Spitfire quivered, but the Focke-Wulf was faster and disappeared unscathed into the mist.

*   *   *

The sky had emptied as if by magic. Not one plane left. I was absolutely alone.

A glance at the petrol—35 gallons. Time to get back. It was scarcely a quarter past two.

"Hullo, Turban, Yellow Two. Yellow One calling. Are you all right?"

It was Martell's voice from very far away.

"Hullo, Yellow One, Turban Yellow Two answering. Am O.K. and going home."

I set course 320° for England, in a shallow dive. A quarter of an hour later I was flying over the yellow sands of Dungeness. I joined the Biggin Hill circuit. Spitfires everywhere, with wheels down. I wormed my way in between two sections and landed.

As I taxied towards Dispersal I saw Tommy, with arms raised, signalling and showing me where to park.

I gave a burst of throttle to clear my engine and switched off. The sudden silence dazed me. How odd to hear voices again undistorted by the radio.

Tommy helped me out of my harness. I jumped to the ground, my legs feeling weak and stiff.

Martell came striding towards me, and caught me round the neck.

"Good old Clo-Clo! We really thought you had had it!"

We went over to join the group by the door round Mouchotte.

"Hey, Clo-Clo, seen anything of Béraud?"

Béraud, it appeared, must have been shot down.

Bouguen's aircraft had been hit by two 20 mm. shells. 485 Squadron had brought down two Focke-Wulfs. Mouchotte and Boudier had severely damaged one each.

I was now voluble and excited. I told my tale, I felt light-hearted, as if a great weight had been lifted from me. I had done my first big sweep over France and I had come back!

That evening, in the mess, I felt on top of the world.

FIRST SUCCESSES

Another day that smelled of powder. We bolted our lunch.

Briefing at 1430 hours.

That afternoon our objective was the airfield at Triqueville. It was going to be bombed in force by two waves of 72 Marauders.

Triqueville, near Le Havre, was the hide-out of one

of the best Jerry fighter wings—the famous "Yellow-Nose" Richthofen outfit. According to our information they had recently been re-equipped with the latest model Focke-Wulf, the 190 A-6, fitted with a more powerful engine and, it was said, flap settings which enabled them to do very tight turns.

All the Richthofen pilots were hand-picked. They were commanded by one of the aces of the German Air Force, Major von Graff, and with their new machines they had specialized—with a good deal of success—in attacks on our day bombers.

Bombing them on the ground and wiping out their airfield had of course already been tried. But every time they had taken off before the attack and landed unperturbed on one of their three satellite fields—Evreux/Fauville, Beaumont-le-Roger, or Saint-André.

This game had gone on for four months and the R.A.F. wanted to finish the business to-day, especially as the American Marauder H.Q. had given out that they would refuse to fly any more sorties in that sector unless the Richthofen crowd were polished off.

This afternoon, therefore, Triqueville and the other three airfields were going to be bombed simultaneously.

As for us, should the Jerries already be in the air, we were going to intercept them at all costs and teach them a good lesson.

Sure, but there was probably going to be the hell of a scrap.

*   *   *

At Dispersal a disappointment was in store for me—I was not down for the sweep. I made a scene, stamped, shouted it was unfair, made quite an exhibition of myself, in fact. Like a good scout, and also for the sake of peace and quiet, Martell allowed himself to be persuaded and took me as his No. 2.

My bad luck still held. We had scarcely left the English coast behind when my jettison-tank gave out—probably a vapour-lock in the feed pipes.

Damn! I knew perfectly well that this show might take us a long way south of Le Havre, as far as Rouen or Evreux. After the fight—if there was one—I might well be distinctly short of fuel.

To hell with common sense. I was staying on!

The Channel was covered with mist, but 3,000 feet up the weather was marvellous. No trace of a cloud. Already, halfway between Le Havre and Rouen, you could distinguish under the layer of fog the Seine crawling like a big silver snake.

* * *

Breaking the silence, the controller's voice in the radio sounded very excited:

"Hullo, Turban Leader, Donald Duck and his boys are up already and climbing hard. Can't give you very definite information yet!"

Donald Duck was the cover-name given to von Graff. Some humorist in the I. Branch must have nicknamed him that because, it appears, he spoke through his nose like his namesake, Walt Disney's creation.

The old bastard was up to all the tricks and knew that the best defence was attack. If we let him slip through our fingers, the Maurauders would once again catch a packet!

Mouchotte, leading the wing on this show, was, as usual, perfectly self-possessed:

"O.K. Zona, message received and understood. Turban leader out." Then for our benefit, "Turban and Gimlet, open your eyes!"

I noticed with a certain amount of anxiety that Martell, leading our section, was imperceptibly drawing away from the rest of the squadron and beginning to climb. Soon we could only see the rest of the Turbans as bright dots lost in the blue of the sky.

"Come up a bit, Yellow Section!"

Mouchotte, calling us to order, was interrupted by a yell from the Gimlets, flying 3,000 feet above us to the right:

"For Christ's sake break, Gimlet aircraft!"

It was old Donald Duck, who had been waiting for us to pass him, tucked away in the sun with his gaggle of pirates. The 485 boys had nearly fallen for it and

it was only by chance that one of the New Zealanders
had seen them coming. He had warned them now and
they turned to face Donald Duck as he swooped down
at 450 m.p.h.

Everything happened in a flash. At the S O S from
485 Mouchotte went into a climbing turn with Red and
Blue Sections to go and help. So we found ourselves
all on our own, 5,000 feet below the main scrap.

Martell made us turn to the left and we climbed to
take part in the battle. Suddenly I saw a dozen Focke-
Wulfs coming out of the sun straight down on top of us.

"Focke-Wulfs eleven o'clock, Yellow!"

Led by a magnificent Fw 190 A-6 painted yellow
all over and polished and gleaming like a jewel, the
first were already passing on our left, less than a hundred yards away, and turning towards us. I could see,
quite distinctly, outlined on their long transparent cockpits, the German pilots crouching forward.

"Come on, Turban Yellow, attack!"

Martell had already dived straight into the enemy
formation. Yellow 3 and Yellow 4 immediately lost
contact and left us in the middle of a whirlpool of yellow noses and black crosses. This time I did not even
have time to feel really frightened. Although my stomach contracted, I could feel a frantic excitement rising
within me. This was the real thing, and I lost my head
slightly. Without realizing it I was giving vent to incoherent redskin war-whoops and throwing my Spitfire
about.

A Focke-Wulf was already breaking away, dragging
after him a spiral of black smoke, and Martell, who
was not wasting any time, was after the scalp of another. I did my best to play my part and back him up
and give him cover, but he was far ahead and I had
some difficulty in following his rolls and Immelmann
turns.

Two Huns converged insidiously on his tail. I opened
fire on them, although they were out of range. I missed
them, but made them break off and make for me. Here
was my opportunity!

I climbed steeply, did a half roll and, before they

could complete the 180° of their turn, there I was—within easy range this time—behind the second one. A slight pressure on the rudder and I had him in my sights. I could scarcely believe my eyes, only a simple deflection necessary, at less than 200 yards range. Quickly I squeezed the firing-button. Whoopee! Flashes all over his fuselage. My first burst had struck home and no mistake.

The Focke-Wulf caught alight at once. Tongues of flame escaped intermittently from his punctured tanks, licking the fuselage. Here and there incandescent gleams showed through the heavy black smoke surrounding the machine. The German pilot threw his plane into a desperate turn. Two slender white trails formed in the air.

Suddenly, the Focke-Wulf exploded like a grenade. A blinding flash, a black cloud, then debris fluttered round my aircraft. The engine dropped like a ball of fire. One of the wings, torn off in the flames, dropped more slowly, like a dead leaf, showing its pale yellow under-surface and its olive green upper-surface alternately.

I bellowed my joy into the radio, just like a kid:

"Hullo, Yellow One, Turban Yellow Two, I got one, I got one! Jesus, I got one of them!"

The sky was now full of Focke-Wulfs, brushing past me, attacking me on every side in a firework display of tracer bullets. They wouldn't let me go; a succession of frontal attacks, three-quarters rear, right, left, one after the other.

I was beginning to feel dizzy and my arms were aching. I was out of breath too, for manoeuvring at 400 m.p.h. a Spitfire whose controls are stiffened by the speed is pretty exhausting work—especially at 26,000 feet. I felt as if I was stifling in my mask and I turned the oxygen to "emergency." All I could feel was a hammering in my damp temples, my wrists and my ankles.

My Spitfire was standing up to it valiantly. We made an integral whole together, like a rider and his well-trained steed, and the engine was giving of its utmost. I blessed Rolls-Royce, all the engineers and mechanics who, with loving care, had drawn, constructed and assembled this enormous precision instrument.

Defending myself to the best of my ability, and economizing on my ammo, I fired away at any Focke-Wulfe passing within range. Out of the corner of my eye I saw Martell settling the hash of a second Jerry, whose tail-plane floated off.

My somewhat crazy manoeuvring brought me immediately above a Focke-Wulf and I promptly dived down on him vertically, without worrying about anything else. I saw his outline getting bigger in my sights, short wings, yellow cowling and fuselage tapering off towards the tail. Through the transparent cockpit I glimpsed the white smudge of the pilot's face turned up towards me.

Two short bursts and I was on the mark. The cockpit flew into fragments and my shells chewed up the fuselage just behind the pilot. Carried away by the speed I was still going straight for him. Instinctively I pushed the stick forward, banged my head horribly against the bullet-proof windshield, but avoided a collision by a hair's breadth.

I pulled brutally out of my dive and saw my Jerry gliding down on his back, a trail of black smoke issuing from the engine. A dark shape detached itself from the fuselage, twirled through the air, followed the aircraft for a space as if tied to it by an invisible string, and then suddenly blossomed forth into a big ochre-coloured parachute, which remained suspended in space while the Focke-Wulf continued its last flight.

*   *   *

I was flabbergasted. I had shot down two Huns! Two Huns! I was at the same time bursting with pride and trembling with suppressed jitters, my nerves all jangled.

What about Martel? What had happened to him? He would again think I had left him in the lurch. The sky was empty. Although I was beginning to get used to it, I was again taken by surprise by the phenomenon of this sudden disappearance of every aircraft. The Focke-Wulfs, who had perhaps had enough, were diving towards their base and already merging into the countryside, 10,000 feet below me.

All gone . . . except one! Looking up, I could see, far above me, one Spitfire—Martell's, probably—and that notorious yellow Focke-Wulf. It was a fascinating display—the whole gamut of aerobatics; Immelmann turns, flick rolls—the whole shoot. But neither could gain an inch on the other. Suddenly, as if by common accord, they turned and faced each other. It was sheer madness. The Spitfire and the "190," firing with everything they had, charged each other head-on. The first to break would be lost, for he would inevitably expose his machine to the other's fire.

With bated breath I saw, at the moment when the collision seemed imminent, the Focke-Wulf shudder, shaken by the impact of the shells, then all at once disintegrate. The Spitfire, miraculously scatheless, flew through a shower of flaming debris, falling like rain.

*   *   *

Martell and I returned together, but I was very short of juice and had to land at Shoreham to refuel. I was still so excited and overwrought that I nearly pranged on landing. The airfield was very short for a Spitfire IX and I had to brake hard, practically collapsing my undercart.

I taxied up to the bowser near the control tower, switched off and jumped down with a very superior air, as if one could read on my face that I had just shot down two enemy planes.

I could not resist ringing up Biggin Hill from the Watch office—partly to let them know that I was safe and sound, but mostly for the pleasure of announcing in an off-hand manner (with a covert glance round the people in the office):

"Oh, by the way, I bagged a couple of Focke-Wulfs!"

Slightly childish, perhaps, but not at all disagreeable.

*   *   *

I did my first victory roll over Biggin Hill in almost solemn mood. Martell confirmed my first success. He had seen the Focke-Wulf set on fire. The second would probably be confirmed by the film.

*   *   *

I could not sleep all night and in the Sergeants' mess I bored everybody to tears with the constantly repeated story of my fight.

This show had been a success for the "Alsace" Squadron. Boudier had brought one Jerry down and Mouchotte and Bruno had fired on one together. Mouchotte, very decently, had awarded it to his No. 2. 485 had brought three down. By a miracle, apart from seven aircraft damaged, we had sustained no losses.

On the evening of the 27th July we received a telegram:

"To the Alsace and 485 boys stop nine for nought is pretty good score stop keep it up stop."

WINSTON CHURCHILL

To complete the picture, we heard over the German radio three days later that Major von Graff, Iron Cross with swords, oak-leaves and diamonds, had been wounded in the course of a heroic combat against an enemy force very superior in numbers!

After this confirmation of Martell's victory over the yellow Focke-Wulf, the poor chap had to stand an impressive number of drinks all round.

COMMANDANT MOUCHOTTE
FAILS TO RETURN

27th August, 1943

The third show that day! The heat at Biggin Hill was stifling.

Briefing took place after tea. It was going to be an interesting sweep all right: four waves of 60 Flying Fortresses, each going to bomb a wood south-west of Saint-Omer, at 20 minute intervals. A German armoured division on manoeuvres had been reported there. Our Wing was to provide the sole escort for the first formation of American bombers; i.e. 24 Spitfires in all (12 from 341 Squadron, and 12 from the New Zealand Squadron, No. 485).

As an escort, it was a bit thin. The strategists of 11 Group had decided that the Luftwaffe would not in fact have time to concentrate on the first box and that the main scrap would probably be with the second and third waves, which were going to be strongly escorted.

Taking part in the operation would be two squadrons of Spitfire XII's from Tangmere, eight squadrons of Spit VB's and the Hornchurch and Kenley Wings, together with a squadron of Spit VI's—117—due to follow directly behind us at high altitude. In addition four Thunderbolt squadrons from the American 8th Air Force were taking part as a strategic reserve.

When we got back from Dispersal the notice board had the final details up. I was Commandant Mou-

chotte's No. 2. Start up engines at 1803 hours. Take off
and set course Hardelot at 1805 hours. There we were
to meet the Forts at 18,000 feet at 1840 hours.

My old kite NL-B was by the Commandant's NL-L.
Everything was ready, my parachute on the wing, my
helmet slung round the control column and my gloves
stuffed in between the throttle and the pitch-control
lever.

I settled in. A last look at the instruments. Tommy
stuck his arm into the cockpit to set the camera-gun
switch. He checked the runners of the hood. All set: oil
temperature 40° C., radiator 10° C., trimmer tabs in
position. I tested the sights.

It was close that day and I was stifling, trussed up
in my Mae West, my parachute harness and my safety
straps.

Commandant Mouchotte was beginning to strap himself in. For the first time since I had known him he had
put on his uniform tunic over his white pullover. I
heard Pabiot remark on it as he passed.

"Oh!" answered Mouchotte with a laugh. "You
never know. I want to look my best when I make my
bow."

Six o'clock less 2 minutes. I saw his emaciated figure
slip into the cockpit and, before putting on his helmet
and his oxygen mask, he did a thumbs-up and smiled
his irresistible friendly and encouraging smile at me.

1803 hours. The engines roared into life one after
the other.

*   *   *

In the middle of the Channel I sensed that things
were going badly.

"Hurry up, Turban Leader, the Bib Boys are about
to be engaged!"

Hell! The strategists had boobed. Not only were
the Huns reacting, but on top of that the Forts, prover-
bially late, were 5 minutes early. They were flying
desperately round and round in circles between Boulogne and Calais, not daring to commit themselves
further south without an escort.

We accelerated, 2,600 revs. and plus 6 boost, and climbed.

At last I spotted the Forts in the distance, in impeccable formation as usual. Nothing abnormal at first sight, except possibly the pyramid of flak rising from Boulogne.

The controller was beginning to get on our nerves:

"Twenty-five Huns, over Abbeville, 15,000 feet, climbing."

"Thirty plus over Saint-Omer, 20,000 feet, going west."

"Fifteen plus 10 miles south of Hardelot, no height yet."

"Forty plus 5 miles from the Big Boys, 25,000 feet, about to engage."

The whole Luftwaffe was in the air to-day! Things were going to get warm.

We were almost immediately above Griz-Nez, at 22,000 feet when suddenly I saw the Jerries. About thirty Focke-Wulfs, in line astern, 900 yards above the Forts, were beginning to dive two at a time, and the mass of bombers lit up in a thousand points of fire— German explosive bullets striking, or Colt machine guns firing back. Higher up, lost in the light, you could guess there was a whole swarm of Focke-Wulfs, revealed from time to time by the flash of a wing catching the sun.

Calmly, as if on a training flight, Mouchotte began to give his orders:

"Come up, Gimlet Squadron!" to 485, thus placing them so as to cover us from any attack from the sun.

"Turban and Gimlet, drop your babies!"

We duly switched over to our main tanks and dropped our supplementary tanks.

All was ready for the battle. With my thumb I released the safety catch of the guns and switched on the sight.

An electric current seemed to animate the whole squadron and the 12 Spitfires began to waggle their wings and swing to left and right restlessly. Everyone kept their eyes open.

The radio started getting jittery:

"Hullo, Turban Leader, 6 aircraft at 9 o'clock above!"

"Hullo, Turban Leader, Yellow One calling, about 10 Focke-Wulfs at 4 o'clock above!"

It was Captain Martell's calm voice. You could feel that he was hugging himself at the prospect of the big scrap coming.

We were now a good 20 miles inside France. To the left and below, the Fortresses were enveloped in a confused mass of Focke-Wulfs—about a hundred of them. So much the worse for them, nothing we could do about it. If it wasn't for us, there would be two hundred. We were keeping the rest at a respectful distance by our presence—but not for long!

"Turban, Red Section, break port!"

The sudden shout in the earphones pierced my eardrums. A glance to the left showed an avalance of twenty or thirty Fw 190's tumbling down on us out of the sun. The first three were already 900 yards behind me, on my tail.

"Turban Squadron, quick, 180 port, go!"

A Hun opened fire; the tracers passed 15 yards from my wing tips. Decidedly unhealthy. I opened the throttle wide, pulled desperately on the stick to follow Mouchotte who was doing a very tight turn and climbing almost vertically.

I had pulled too hard. The engine cut out for one precious second and I hung there, with my nose in the air, while the first Huns began to flash like thunderbolts in between our sections.

My engine picked up, with a terrific jerk, but too late; I had lost contact with my section, whom I could see 100 yards farther up, climbing in a spiral. Couldn't be helped. I did a wide barrel roll, which brought me within 100 yards of a Focke-Wulf at whom I let loose a long burst of 20 mm. with 40° correction.

Missed him!

A tight turn, to break away to the left, and I found myself parallel with two other Huns—two magnificent, brand-new glistening "190's," their cowlings painted red and their big fascinating black crosses standing out on the ochre and olive-green of the fuselage. Whang! Three others passed like lightning a few yards below me, wagging their stubby yellow wings.

Not too good! Up above me it was still less good. I could hear various people shouting over the radio. Captain Martell was handling his section in masterly fashion. Commandant Mouchotte's detached voice was trying to get the two squadrons to join up. There were shouts for help, New Zealanders yelling like demons, a few highly seasoned Parisian oaths.

I began to struggle like one possessed, twisting and turning in every direction. I blacked out and my oxygen mask, dragged down by the g,* skinned my nose. I practically dislocated my neck keeping an eye on all the frightful jumble of aircraft passing within range.

Suddenly I found myself in a relatively clear bit of sky. Spitfires and Focke-Wulfs swirled all around. Four vertical trails of heavy black smoke that hung in the air without dissipating marked the fatal trajectory of 4 aircraft, whose debris blazed on the ground, scattered in the meadows 27,000 feet below.

Parachutes began to blossom on every side.

Why no reinforcements? What was the controller waiting for? Twenty-four against 200 didn't give us much chance.

Paradoxically, we got along quite well for a time. There were far too many Focke-Wulfs, and they got in one another's way. All the same, our retreat was cut off.

It would have been suicide to fly for more than 30 seconds without a violent turn first one way and then the other. What got me down was that, with so many Huns all round me, I wasn't shooting a single one down.

At last an opportunity presented itself. Two Spitfires were diving hell for leather after a Focke-Wulf. Unnoticed another Hun slipped on to their tail and

---

*g = centrifugal force, measured in multiples of the force of gravity.

fired. I could see the whiffs of smoke from his four cannon. Two New Zealanders evidently—lots of guts, but less sense. I tried to warn them:

"Look out, the two Spits following that Hun! Break!"

It was a bit vague, but I hadn't been able to read their markings. I turned quickly on my back, a glance to left and right. I attacked the rear Fw 190 from three-quarters rear. Just as I opened fire he saw me and broke right, diving.

I had made up my mind I'd get him. The air-speed indicator went up and up—420, 430 m.p.h. I pressed the firing button and the recoil of the guns made my Spit shudder. The Hun jigged about but I had him well in the sights—5 degrees correction, range 200— Bang! Bang! Bang! Bang! I fired in short bursts. Three explosions on the right wing between the fuselage and the black crosses.

We were now doing over 450 m.p.h. A shell on his cockpit, whose perspex hood flew off and passed within a few feet of my aircraft. I was now gaining on him and went on firing at less than 100 yards. I distinguished the pilot's face turning round, looking like some queer insect with his flying goggles over his eyes.

We levelled out, and the chase went on. I pressed on the multiple button and this time fired all my guns at once—two cannon and four machine guns—to have done with it. Two shells exploded simultaneously just behind the engine and the cockpit belched forth a cloud of black smoke. The pilot disappeared. Slowly the Focke-Wulf turned over on its back. We were only 1,000 feet up. Roads and villages passed below our wings. Flames now gleamed through the smoke—the blow had been mortal. We went on down still further. A church steeple went by on a level with me. I had to throttle right back to avoid getting in front of my Hun. I had exhausted my ammunition and every time I pressed the button I heard nothing but the whistle of compressed air and the breech blocks clanking away.

But I had got him! At appalling speed the Focke-Wulf, still on its back, hit the ground and slid, scattering incandescent fragments everywhere, leaving a trail of blazing fuel, hurtled through two hedges and crashed against a road bank in a dazzling shower of sparks.

Fascinated, I only pulled out in the nick of time to avoid a row of telegraph poles. Climbing up in spirals at full throttle I cast a last look down. The petrol-sodden grass formed a fiery crown around the charred skeleton of the Focke-Wulf and the oily smoke swept by the wind drifted heavily towards the village of Hazebrouck.

But I hadn't finished yet: I had to get back to England. Quickly I pinpointed my position: I was to the east of the forest bordering Saint-Omer airfield. I began to breathe again, but not for long. Up there the battle still went on. The radio told me that Buiron had shot down a Hun.

*   *   *

A few seconds later I heard, for the last time, Commandant Mouchotte's voice, calling:

"I am alone!"

What a hell of a fight for a wing-leader—particularly the Biggin Hill leader—to find himself isolated!

*   *   *

Things were still going badly above me, as I soon saw. I had just discreetly set course for England when a bunch of Focke-Wulfs decided to take an interest in my poor isolated Spitfire which seemed so ill at ease.

Stick right back, 3,000 revs., plus 20 boost, I climbed desperately, followed by the Fw's—two to the right, two to the left, a few hundred yards away. If I could reach the second stage of my supercharger before being shot down I would diddle them.

Six thousand feet. You need about 2 minutes at full throttle to reach 13,000 feet. In the present circumstances you might just as well have said 2 centuries.

Twelve thousand five hundred feet—I felt the sweat trickling down the edges of my oxygen mask and my right glove was absolutely sodden.

A roar, and my blower came into action before they could get into firing range. In desperation one of them sent me a burst but without touching me. I now easily drew away from them and was saved for the time being.

On the coast just above Bologne I succeeded in catching up with four Spitfires in impeccable defensive formation. I drew near cautiously, announcing my presence. I identified them as NL-C, NL-A, NL-S, and NL-D, evidently Yellow Section, and Martell authorized me over the RT to join them.

For five more minutes the Germans went on attacking us. If this went on much longer, we had had it, as we would never have enough fuel to reach the English coast—and the Germans knew it.

Suddenly the sky filled with "contrails"—a hundred perhaps, in fours, coming from the north. It was the Thunderbolts, at last. Still, better late than never, and they certainly saved our bacon.

The Focke-Wulfs, also short of ammunition and with tanks practically dry, did not insist. They all dived down and disappeared in the rising evening mist.

*   *   *

We landed on the first airfield on the coast—Manston. Chaos reigned supreme there. The Luftwaffe's reaction, in such an unfrequented sector, had disagreeably surprised everyone. Aircraft were simply piling up. A Fortress had crashed in the middle of the runway. The Thunderbolts, disregarding all the rules, were landing cross and down wind. The perimeter of the field was cluttered up with Spitfires, Typhoons and aircraft of every sort waiting for the bowsers. The poor ground-control chaps were rushing about with their yellow flags, firing red Verey lights in all directions, trying to park the aircraft from each flight all together.

We came across a few of our mates. Fifi had stood his Spitfire on its nose properly and it looked pretty comic, with its tail in the air and its propeller buried in the ground.

We counted heads—only ten. Commandant Mouchotte and Segt. Chef Magrot were missing. We hung on the telephone. Biggin Hill had no information, the controller had lost all trace of Mouchotte, and none of the emergency fields had reported his arrival. Not much hope now, for his tanks must have been empty for the last quarter of an hour at least.

It was a tragic blow, and the world no longer seemed the same.

* * *

When we took off to return to Biggin the sun was beginning to slip down to the sea and, on the horizon, low mist hung over the battlefield where we had left two of our comrades.

We landed with navigation lights on, and we could make out a silent group in front of Dispersal. All the personnel of the squadron were there—those who had not flown to-day, the fitters, Group Captain Malan, Wing Commander Deere, Checketts—anxiously waiting for fresh news, a scrap of information, anything on which to build hope.

Commandant Mouchotte, Croix de Guerre, Compagnon de la Libération, D.F.C. . . . For us he had been the pattern of a leader, just, tolerant, bold and calm in battle, the finest type of Frenchman, inspiring respect whatever the circumstances.

RADAR AT DAWN

26th September, 1943—4 a.m.

I groped my way out of my room, and made for the mess, where a sleepy W.A.A.F. served me with eggs and bacon. When I came out again the sky was still dark and a few stars twinkled in the glacial air. I could hear the roar of an engine over by the Dispersal. Probably the ground crews warming up my Spit.

On my way down I called in at the Intelligence Room for the final gen on my mission.

I was to leave on my own on a calibration flight for the radar stations which controlled us. From the English coast I had to set a straight course of 145 degrees, gaining the maximum height meanwhile, which would bring me over Beauvais at about 33,000 feet. Then I had to come up as far as Saint-Omer and give in clear over the radio my position in relation to given landmarks.

My only chance of coming through without any bother was to get a move on, to dawdle as little as possible on the way, so as to reduce to the minimum the possibility of interception by a superior enemy force.

When I took off by the light of the flare path and began to climb on my course it was still pitch dark. I could dimly see the vague phosphorescence of my instruments and the blue flames, punctuated by red sparks, vomited by my exhausts.

I climbed hard and fast and crossed the English coast at about 22,000 feet. The fog was concentrated in the narrow valleys in long milky trails. The atmosphere was so calm that I could distinguish in the shadows, over there in the distance, the smoke of a train near Dungeness, motionless, as if anchored to the ground. The Channel was but an indistinct opaque mass with a vague silver hem along the cliffs. Not a cloud anywhere.

I climbed through the darkness embracing the earth towards the now luminous sky and the dimming stars.

Suddenly, without any transition, I plunged like a diver into full golden light. The wings of my Spitfire turned crimson. I was so dazzled that I had to lower my smoked glasses over my eyes. Beyond Holland, far away over there on the left, the sun emerged like a molten ingot from the inert leaden mass of the North Sea.

Beneath my wings was night—I was alone, 30,000

feet up in the daylight. I was the first to breathe in the warm life of the sun's rays, which pierce the eyeball like arrows. In France, in England, in Belgium, in Holland, in Germany, men were suffering in the night, whilst I, alone in the sky, was the sole possessor of the dawning day—all was mine, the light, the sun; and I thought with calm pride: all this is shining only for me!

Moments such as these compensate for many a sacrifice and many a danger.

* * *

I crossed the French coast on a level with Dieppe, and a few minutes later I had arrived over Beauvais. I could vaguely make out the airfield at Beauvais-Tillé and Mont Saint-Adrien surrounded by the forest of Fouquencies.

"Hullo, Dagger 25, Dagger 25, Piper calling. Orbit please, orbit please. A for able!"

A for able was the code-word for Beauvais. Control was ordering me to circle while they calibrated their instruments. It was very cold in spite of the sun and I began to feel drowsy as I mechanically went on flying.

"Hullo, Dagger 25, Piper here, what are your angels?"

The note of urgency perceptible in the controller's voice made me jump. A glance at the altimeter: 30,000 feet.

"Hullo, Piper, Dagger answering, angels X for X-ray."

Something must be up for the controller himself to ask me to break the compulsory RT silence.

A minute passed.

"Hullo, Dagger 25, Piper here. Steer 090 degrees—zero, nine, zero."

This time I twigged. There must be a suspicious aircraft somewhere about and the controller wanted to identify me for certain on his radio-location screen. I looked around me, waggled my wings to check on the blind spots—everything seemed quiet enough. If the Hun was above me he would doubtless, in this freezing cold, be leaving a condensation trail.

"Hullo, Dagger 25, Piper calling. Look out, you are being shadowed by a Hun. Look out at 5 o'clock!"

I immediately turned my head in the direction indicated and, sure enough, glimpsed a small brilliant dot slipping into a layer of cirrus cloud. It was too far for me to be able to identify him. If it was a fighter I was going to keep a discreet eye on him, keeping to my course in the meantime so as to make him commit himself. I switched on my reflector sight and released the safety catch of my guns.

Three minutes, and the dot had become a cross, about 2,500 feet immediately above me. At that height it was probably one of the new Messerschmitt 109 G's. He waggled his wings . . . he was going to attack at any moment, thinking I had not seen him. In a trice solitude, poetry, the sun, all vanished. A glance at the temperature and I pushed the prop into fine pitch. All set. Let him try it on!

Another minute crawled by. By dint of staring at my opponent my eyes were watering.

"Here he comes!"

The Hun embarked on a gentle spiral dive, designed to bring him on my tail. He was about 600 yards away and not going too fast, in order to make certain of me.

I opened the throttle flat out and threw my Spitfire into a very steep climbing turn which enabled me to keep my eyes on him and to gain height. Taken by surprise by my manoeuvre, he opened fire, but too late. Instead of the slight 5° deflection he was expecting, I suddenly presented him with a target at 45°. I levelled out and continued my tight turn. The "109" tried to turn inside me, but at that height his short wings got insufficient grip on the rarefied atmosphere and he stalled and went into a spin. Once again the Spitfire's superior manoeuvrability had got me out of the wood.

For one moment I saw the big black crosses of the

"109" standing out on the pale blue under-surface of his wings.

The Messerschmitt came out of his spin. But I was already in position, and he knew it, for he started hurling his machine about in an effort to throw off my aim. His speed availed him nothing, however, for I had profited by his previous false move to accelerate and now I had the advantage of height. At 450 yards range I opened fire in short bursts, just touching the button each time. The pilot of the "109" was an old fox all the same, for he shifted his kite about a lot, constantly varying the deflection angle and line of sight.

He knew that my Spitfire turned better and climbed better, and that his only hope was to out-distance me. Suddenly he pushed the stick forward and went into a vertical dive. I passed on to my back and, taking advantage of his regular trajectory, opened fire again. We went down fast, 470 m.p.h., towards Aumale. As I was in line with his tail the firing correction was relatively simple, but I had to hurry—he was gaining on me.

At the second burst three flashes appeared on his fuselage—the impact visibly shook him. I fired again, this time hitting him on a level with the cockpit and the engine. For a fraction of a second my shell bursts seemed to stop the engine. His propeller suddenly stopped dead, then disappeared in a white cloud of glycol bubbling out of the exhausts. Then a more violent explosion at the wing root and a thin black tail mingled with the stream gushing from the perforated cooling system.

It was the end. A tongue of fire appeared below the fuselage, lengthened, licked the tail, and dispersed in incandescent shreds.

We had plunged into the shadows ... a glance at my watch to fix the time of the fight—twelve minutes past five.

As for the Messerschmitt, he had had it. I climbed up again in spirals, watching him. He was now nothing but a vague outline, fluttering pathetically down,

shaken at regular intervals—an explosion, a black
trail, a white trail, an explosion, a black trail, a white
trail.... Now he was a ball of fire rolling slowly
toward the forest of Eu, burning away, soon scattered
in a shower of flaming debris, extinguished before
they reached the ground.

The pilot had not baled out....

"Hullo, Dagger 25, Piper calling, long transmission
please. Did you get that Hun?"

"Hullo, Piper, Dagger 25 answering and transmitting for fix."

"Got him all right. One ... two ... three ... four
... I am getting short of juice. May I go home?"

"O.K. Dagger 25. Steer 330 degrees—three, three,
zero. Good show!"

The petrol was getting low in my tanks and the
sun was climbing on the horizon. This spot was going
to get unhealthy. Time I was getting back. I set
course for England.

ATTACHED TO
THE R.A.F.

PART TWO

ATTACHED TO THE EAR

"CITY OF GLASGOW" SQUADRON

28th September, 1943

It was with rather a heavy heart that I left Biggin Hill and took my leave of the "Alsace" Squadron, with whom I had fought my first battles and where I had met comrades whose patriotism, dash, and skill in combat made me proud to be a Frenchman.

As the truck passed the guard-room I saw the Tricolour floating in front of Dispersal disappear among the trees.

Forewarned by Jacques, I had got rid of most of my kit. All the same, I was as usual cluttered up with suitcases, a parachute bag which seemed filled with lead (that blasted chute and its dinghy seemed to weigh a ton!), my revolver belt and cartridge pouches, my Irvine jacket—I presented a curious sight to the travellers gazing through the windows of their train while I stood on the platform waiting for mine.

At Ashford a lorry picked me up and a few minutes later I entered 125 Airfield.

Jacques introduced me. I met the whole charming band of pirates of the air who composed 602 "City of Glasgow" Squadron—Scotsmen, Australians, New Zealanders, Canadians, one Belgian, two Frenchmen and a few Englishmen.

The squadron leader was an Irishman called Mike Beytagh, with a pink boyish face, a great drinker, a fine pilot and a good commanding officer.

The two flight commanders were both phenomenal types, each in his own way; "A" flight commander had worked his way up in record time from Sergeant to Flight Lieutenant by sheer dash and courage. He was

6 feet 4 inches, as strong as an ox and always wore a gap-toothed grin. His name was Bill Loud. The other, Max Sutherland, was a typical English Public School product, complete with tooth-brush moustache; he was an ex-heavyweight champion of the London police. I was to be in his flight. A nice chap, slightly immature, inclined to be moody, capable of the most mulish obstinacy, as of the most extreme generosity. None the less an excellent pilot, very experienced and as brave as a lion. We were to become fast friends.

After Biggin Hill, with its comforts and its glamourous status of world's premier fighter base, 125 Airfield gave a rather country-cousin impression. But it had an atmosphere of friendliness and jauntiness and of living with no thought for the morrow. 602 had been one of the brightest stars in the Battle of Britain but had been relegated to a secondary position for the two following years. It had then been one of the first units to be transferred to the Tactical Air Force and for some months had been moving up again under the impulse of Beytagh's drive.

The R.A.F. was to provide units to support the invasion of the Continent in close co-operation with the Army. To this end 602, with a dozen other squadrons, had been submitted to an intensive process of preparation: ground-level attack, machine-gunning of tanks, tactical reconnaissance, dive-bombing, etc.

Finally these units had been sent to airfields to complete their training. For four months the pilots had been living under canvas, learning to refuel, rearm and camouflage their aircraft and defend them, Tommy-gun in hand—leading, in fact, a real "Commando" life.

Operating from fields similar to those which could be constructed in a few hours by the Engineers (two or three meadows joined up into a landing strip by laying steel mesh on the ground), Squadrons 602, 132, 122, 65 and a few others were at the same time participating in the current R.A.F. offensive. Equipped with Spitfire V-D's (technically, L.F.V's) with clipped wings, these squadrons carried out close support missions for Marauders, Mitchells and Bostons.

602 shared Airfield 125 with another Spit unit, 132 "City of Bombay" Squadron, commanded by an old friend, Squadron Leader Colloredo-Mansfield, and an anti-tank Hurricane Squadron, No. 184. The airfield was on the sandy spit of Dungeness, and it was quite a pleasant spot in the glorious September sunshine.

Out tents were set up in an orchard. The atmosphere was delightful, more that of a holiday camp or a picnic than anything else. You could stuff yourself with enormous sweet, juicy apples by just sticking your arm out through the tent flap. They may not have been quite ripe, but the open air and our youthful digestions allowed us to survive without discomfort. We ate out of doors or, when it rained, in a barn, all the pilots in a crowd together. I had no mess-tin and no "irons," and so I used Jacques'.

Naturally I bunked in his tent too, shared with a Belgian—Jean Oste—and an absolutely charming Englishman called Jimmy Kelly, who was to become one of my best friends. He used to shout with rage whenever anyone started talking French. We slept on camp beds and we washed in the river—the water was very cold, and so we washed as little as possible.

The great problem was lighting. Candles were too dangerous because of the hay covering the floor. We were provided with storm lanterns from R.A.F. stores, but they never worked. When there were matches, there was no wick. When a wick had been unearthed (usually scrounged from the tent next door), there was no paraffin. When we had finally collected all the necessary and lit up with enormous care, the whole shoot would usually go up in flames, followed by a stampede and a battle with foam extinguishers. The whole tent would get a rocket from the squadron leader and finally undress by the light of a cigarette lighter or the stars.

In the morning we were awakened by a soldier with a can of boiling hot tea who made such a racket that everybody was up in five seconds, tearing barefoot across the grass, mug in hand. After that we went to fetch water from the river in more or less watertight canvas buckets, washed extremely perfunctorily, slipped on a dirty battle-dress and flying boots, wound a scarf round our necks and galloped off to the mess for eggs and bacon, a cup of coffee, and a slice of bread baked in the farm nearby.

Then a crazy drive round the field in jeeps, as many as twelve precariously clinging onto each, tearing at full speed across the fields, jumping the ditches and crashing through the hedges.

Quickly we removed the camouflage nets from our aircraft, warmed up and checked over the engines, and prepared for the first show of the day.

Such was the daily life in my new squadron.

*   *   *

"Clipped, cropped, clapped" was the magnificent description of the Spitfire V-D invented by that great humorist in the squadron, Tommy Thommerson.

"Clipped" for its clipped wings. In order to increase its speed and its lateral manoeuvrability, the Vickers engineers had reduced the Spitfire's wing span by about four feet by suppressing the wing tips, which rounded off the ellipse of the wing so harmoniously.

"Cropped" for its Merlin 45M engine. It was only a Rolls-Royce Merlin 45 with a supercharger turbine reduced in diameter, allowing the power to be stepped up, below 3,000 feet, and 1,200 h.p. to 1,585 h.p. As the volume of supercharged air was much reduced however, the power curve fell rapidly from 8,000 feet up, until at 12,000 feet it produced only about 500 h.p. On top of that, these engines, artificially pushed up to plus 18 boost, had a very reduced life.

"Clapped"—which is self-explanatory—expressed the general opinion among pilots of the Spitfire V-D. For though extremely fast at ground or sea-level (350 m.p.h. straight and level) they became lumps of lead at 10,000 feet, the height at which we had to operate on our escort missions. The square wings also made them lose the Spit's main advantage, the ability to turn tight.

Our confidence in these machines was only limited —a feeling which was more or less justified by the fact that the airframes had all done about 300 hours and, graver still, the engines 100 to 150 hours. It is not always amusing to cross the Channel there and back twice a day on a single-engined aircraft of this sort! To cap all, the cannon only carried sixty shells each (as against 145 in the Spitfire IX!).

If one remembers that even in 1941 and 1942 Spit V's were easily outclassed by Focke-Wulf 190's, my very qualified enthusiasm can be imagined when Sutherland informed me that we were going to have to carry out another five or six sweeps on Spit V-D's before celebrating the arrival of our brand-new IX-B's.

THE MUNSTERLAND BUSINESS

The Germans, in war-time, raised obstinacy to the level of a national virtue. When Providence adds luck to this attribute, certain situations arise which defy logic. The *Munsterland* will certainly go down to prosterity as a symbol of Teutonic stubbornness, and of British obstinacy too, if it comes to that.

The *Munsterland* was a fast ultra-modern cargo ship of 10,000 tons equipped with oil-burning turbine engines. She had been surprised in a Central American port by Pearl Harbor and had made for Japan. There she had loaded a precious cargo of rubber and rare metals and had then calmly sailed for Germany again.

Fortune favours the brave, and, by a series of incredible circumstances, she had succeeded in slipping through the air and naval patrols and making Brest. She was immediately photographed and dive-bombed 3 hours later by 24 Typhoons. Towards 6 p.m. on the same day, 32 strongly escorted Mitchells attacked her, still without appreciable results.

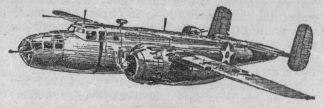

B-24 Mitchell

In the course of the night she made for Cherbourg at full speed and was again photographed as soon as she made port. A study of the prints showed that everything was ready for her to be discharged. Three flak ships from Havre and two from Saint-Malo had anchored off the Pelée at dawn and sizeable light and heavy flak units were in position.

Extremely unfavourable meteorological conditions led to the failure of a raid laid on at about eight in the morning.

Without medium bombers it was difficult to cope with a problem of this magnitude. The Beaufighters could not intervene as the lay-out of Cherbourg harbour did not lend itself to a torpedo attack. The Bostons might at a pinch have tried a low-level bombing attack, but the powers that be could really not send them in to be slaughtered at 250 m.p.h.

The weather was getting worse—rain, fog, low cloud.

*   *   *

At 0845 the flying personnel of the Wing were urgently summoned to the Intelligence Room. 602 and 132 were put at immediate readiness.

First Willie Hickson, in a speech improvised for the occasion, reminded us that the *Munsterland*'s cargo was of vital importance to German industry. The thousands of tons of latex she carried, suitably mixed with the synthetic leuna product, would enable no fewer than 22 armoured divisions to be equipped and maintained for two years. The special metals would be precious for

German metallurgists producing jet engines. In addition the Kriegsmarine must not be allowed to get away with the moral fillip of such a flagrant breach of the blockade.

Thirty-six Typhoons equipped with 1,000 lb. delayed action bombs were to force an entry into the bay and try to sink the *Munsterland* or set her on fire.

A special dispensation of Command had bestowed the delightful task of escorting them on 602 and 132 Squadrons. Our rôle would consist in neutralizing the flak ships with cannon and machine-gun fire and then covering the operation against the important German fighter forces massed in the Cotentin peninsula in case of need.

To increase our radius of action the Wing would put down at Ford, where the refuelling of the aircraft had been arranged, and from there we would take off again for the rendezvous with the Typhoons, over Brighton at zero feet.

Wing Commander Yule, prospective leader of the operation, reminded us briefly that flak ships were normally armed with four quadruple automatic 20 mm. mountings, and with four or eight 37 mm. guns, also automatic. The last P.R.U.* photos had revealed, along the mole linking the six forts of the roadstead, at least 190 light flak guns, probably reinforced and very active since our client's arrival.

In principle the two squadrons would split up into six sections of four which would each look after a flak ship, in order to reduce them to silence for the few seconds necessary for the passage of the Typhoons. After that, they were free to take such offensive action against any fighter formations as might be necessary.

Obliging to the end, Command had decided to lay on a special Air Sea Rescue service, the fast launches of which would be strung out between Cherbourg and the British coast along our track.

Even for the most enthusiastic amongst us, this last arrangement looked suspiciously like belated remorse

---

*Photographic Reconnaissance Unit.

on the part of Command and had a sinister implication which considerably chilled the atmosphere.

The last preparations before we took off were carried out in silence. Only Joe Kestruck made a disillusioned remark to the effect that every time the Navy made a balls of a job, the poor bloody R.A.F. had to clear up the mess. At Ford there was the usual panic about tire-bursts and flat starter batteries. Luckily Yule's long experience of advanced airfields had led to the provision of three reserve aircraft per squadron and at 0950 hours 602 and 132 took off at full strength.

I was flying as Blue 4, next to Jacques who was Blue 3, in Ken Charney's section.

On our way to the rendezvous we passed three Bostons whose task was to scatter, over a stretch of 20 miles towards Cape de la Hague, strips of tin-foil designed to jam the German radar. Thanks to this, and to the mist, we would probably reach the entry to Cherbourg without being picked up too much.

We joined up with the Typhoons at house-top level over Brighton and set off obliquely for Cherbourg, skimming the grey sea.

I loathe flying so low as that with all the paraphernalia of supplementary tanks and cocks. Somewhere or other there is always liable to be an air-lock, enough to make the engine cut out for just the fraction of a second necessary to send you slap into the drink at 300 m.p.h.

We flew through belts of opaque mist which forced us to do some very tricky I.F.* a few feet above the sea, which of course we could not see. The Typhoons, in spite of the two 1,000-lb. bombs under their wings, were setting a cracking pace and we had a job to keep up with them.

Obsessed by the idea of seeing the red light on the instrument panel going on (indicating a drop in the flow of petrol to my carburettor), I began to sweat from head to foot. What would it be like when the flak started?

*   *   *

*I.F. = instrument flying.

1015 hours. The fog thickened and it started to pelt with rain. Instinctively the sections closed up to perserve visual contact.

Suddenly Yule's calm voice broke the strict RT silence:

"All Bob aircraft drop your babies, open up flat out, target straight ahead in sixty seconds!"

Freed of its tank and drawn by the 1,600 h.p. of its engine, my Spitfire leapt forward and I took up my position 50 yards on Jacques' left and slightly behind him, straining my eyes to see anything in the blasted fog.

"Look out, Yellow Section, flak ship, 1 o'clock!"

And immediately after Frank Wooley, it was Ken Charney who saw a flak ship, straight in front of us!

"Max Blue attacking 12 o'clock!"

A grey mass rolling in the mist, a squat funnel, raised platforms, a mast bristling with radar aerials—then rapid staccato flashes all along the superstructure. Christ! I released the safety catch, lowered my head and nestled down to be protected by my armour plating. Clusters of green and red tracer bullets started up in every direction. Following Jacques, I went slap through the spray of a 37 mm. charger which only just missed me—the salt water blurred my windshield. I was 50 yards from the flak ship. Jacques in front of me was firing; I could see the flashes from his guns and his empties cascading from his wings.

I aimed at the bridge, between the damaged funnel and the mast, and fired a long, furious continuous burst, my finger hard on the button. My shells exploded in the water, rose towards the water line, exploded on the grey black-striped hull, rose higher to the handrails, the sandbags. A wind-scoop crashed down, a jet of stream spurted from somewhere. Twenty yards—two men in navy-blue jerseys hurled themselves flat on their faces—10 yards—the four barrels of a multiple pom-pom were pointing straight between my eyes—quick— my shells exploded all round it. A loader carrying two full clips capsized into the sea, his legs mown from under him, then the four barrels fired; I could feel the vibration as I passed a bare yard above—then the smack of the steel wire of the aerial wrenched off by my wing as I passed. My wing tip had just about scraped the mast!

Phew! Passed him.

My limbs were shaken by a terrible nervous tremor, my teeth were chattering. Jacques was zigzagging between the spouts raised by the shells. The sea was seething.

Half a dozen belated Typhoons passed to my right like a school of porpoises, bearing down on the hell going on behind the long granite wall of the breakwater.

I skimmed over a fort whose very walls seemed to be belching fire—a curious mixture of crenellated towers, modern concrete casements and Thirty Years' War glacis.

We were now in the middle of the roadstead—an inextricable jumble of trawler masts and rusty wrecks sticking out between the battered quays. The weather seemed to have cleared a little—look out for Jerry fighters! The air was criss-crossed with tracers, lit up by flashes, dotted with black and white puffs of smoke.

The *Munsterland* was there, surrounded by explosions, flames and debris. Her four masts bristling with derricks and her squat funnel well aft emerging from the smoke. The Typhoon attack was in full swing, bombs exploding all the time with colossal bursts of fire and black clouds of smoke, thickening as they drifted away. A Typhoon vanished into thin air in the explosion of a bomb dropped by one in front. One of the enormous harbour cranes came crashing down like a house of cards.

* * *

"Hullo, Bob leader, Kenway calling—there are Hun fighters about, look out!"

What an inferno! I was close to Jacques, who was gaining height in spirals, making for the layer of clouds. Two Typhoons emerged from a cumulus, a few yards from us, and I just stopped myself in time from firing at them. With their massive noses and clipped wings they looked uncannily like Focke-Wulfs.

"Break, Blue Four!"

Jacques broke away violently and his Spitfire flashed past a few yards under my nose, a white plume at each wing tip. To avoid a collision I waited for a fraction of a second and a Focke-Wulf—a real one this time—flashed past, firing with all four cannon. A shell ricocheted off my hood. As I went over on my back to get him in my sights, a second Focke-Wulf loomed up in my windshield, head-on, at less than a hundred yards. Its big yellow engine and its apparently slowly turning propeller seemed to fling themselves at me and its wings lit up with the firing of its guns. Bang! Stars appeared all over my splintering windshield which became an opaque wall before my eyes. Thunderstruck, I dared not move for fear of a collision. He passed just above me. A stream of oil began to spread all over my hood.

The sky was now alive with aircraft and full of flak bursts. I let fly at another Focke-Wulf and missed. Luckily! . . . it was a Typhoon. Robson was circling with a German fighter. I saw his shells explode in the black cross on the fuselage. The Focke-Wulf slowly turned over, showing its yellow belly, and dived, coughing smoke and flames.

"Good show, Robbie! You got him!"

My oil pressure was disquietingly down. The rain began again and within a few seconds my hood was covered with a soapy film. I slipped into the clouds and set course north on I.F., first warning Jacques and Yule over the radio.

I reached Tangmere as best I could, with my oil pressure at zero and my engine red hot and ready to explode. I had to jettison my hood to see to land.

In this business we had lost two pilots, as did 132. Seven Typhoons were destroyed, plus two which came down off Cherbourg and whose pilots were picked up by the launches.

As for the *Munsterland*, although seriously damaged and with part of her cargo on fire, she succeeded two nights later in sneaking as far as Dieppe. She finally got herself sunk off the coast of Holland by a strike of Beaufighters.

BALL-BEARINGS AND FLYING FORTRESSES

When the monthly "Met" forecasts had come in, the directors of planning on the American staff had decided in extremis to take advantage of the last fine days of the year to bomb Schweinfurt. There, south-east of Bremen, in the heart of Germany, sprawled the enormous ball-bearing factory, the biggest in western Europe. It was a high-priority target.

If the 8th Air Force did not attack on 13th October, at least four long winter months would elapse before as favourable weather conditions occurred again. And in four months that factory would supply ball-bearings for thousands of aero-engines for the Luftwaffe.

It was an extraordinary race against the clock. The whole operation had to be organized inside forty-eight hours. It was no small task to impose absolute secrecy on a hundred airfields, to mobilize nearly 1,300 British and American fighters, to bomb up hundreds of Flying Fortresses and to prepare 10-yard-long cartridge belts for each of their thousands of machine guns.

It was the first time, too, that Spitfires were going to fly over Germany. As the Forts would be over enemy territory for more than four hours, a formidable reaction on the part of the enemy fighters was anticipated. The Luftwaffe had about three thousand Messerschmitts and Focke-Wulfs at its disposal between Belgium and Denmark. The American Air Forces, foreseeing that the Thunderbolts and Mustangs would have too much to do and would get too short of ammunition and fuel to be able to cope by themselves, had asked the R.A.F. for reinforcements.

But Spitfires—fast interceptor fighters—were not designed for long-distance escort duties and had to have special auxiliary tanks to increase their radius of action as far as Germany.

In three days, not an hour over, a Watford factory undertook to manufacture 800 90-gallon tanks. Close on one thousand workmen worked day and night, and on the 13th October at dawn R.A.F. fitters were fixing them to the bellies of the Spitfires.

At the last minute, just as everyone was all keyed up, there was a counter-order: H-hour was put back to the next day at 12 o'clock.

*   *   *

14th October, 1943

From 8 a.m. heavily laden Fortresses and Liberators began to take off from 37 airfields. For an hour they circled Hull, forming into 4 impeccable boxes of 70 machines each, wing tip to wing tip.

At 1040 hours 19 squadrons of Thunderbolts (15 from the 9th A.F. and 4 from the 8th A.F.) set off to join the armada and take up their escort positions, while the Spits turned about.

At 1115 hours 20 squadrons of Lightnings and Mustangs left to protect the big four-engined machines on their final approach to the objective.

The Spitfires—rearmed and refuelled—were due to take off again at about 12 o'clock to cover the return of the whole force, the rendezvous being fixed for 1315 hours at the northern German-Dutch frontier.

*   *   *

The 10 Spitfire squadrons earmarked for the operation had massed on four airfields in Norfolk, the nearest point to our objective. The first take-off at 9 a.m. was awkward because the pilots were unaccustomed

to the extra weight of their machines. Two Spitfires
crashed. A number of others had tire bursts, some
had trouble with their tanks caused by air-locks.

Jacques and I were among the victims. Landing on
our flimsy tires, with 90 gallons of juice under the belly
and 150 more in the wings and fuselage was tricky—
like landing on eggs, as Jacques put it. Seething with
rage, we watched the swarm of Spitfires disappear towards Germany in the morning mist.

The fitters immediately set to work, emptying and
checking the tanks, while we slept under the wings, in
preparation for the second mission.

At 1145 hours the Spitfire Wings came back and
hordes of mechanics, perched on the bowsers, de-
scended upon them to refuel them in record time, while
the pilots, lurching on their stiffened legs, ate a sand-
wich and swallowed a cup of tea. They were surly and
not inclined to talk.

Everything had gone off well, quite a lot of flak, but
up to the time when they had left their charges—i.e.
1030 hours—not one German fighter had intervened.

A few minutes before 12 o'clock, just as we were
settling down in our cockpits, the loudspeakers started
blaring:

"Hullo, hullo, Station Commander calling all pilots.
The big boys over Germany are being very heavily
engaged by overwhelming enemy fighter forces. Squadrons are to take off immediately in order to relieve the
present escort. Everything possible is to be done to
bring the Fortress Boys home safe. They've been doing
a grand job to-day. Hurry up, and good luck to all!"

At 1204 hours, 132, 602, 411 and 453 Squadrons
took off from Bradwell Bay. Jacques and I flew as 3 and
4 respectively in Yellow Section, led by Sutherland.

1315 hours. "Attention, Clo-Clo, douze Boches
au-dessus, 5 o'clock!"

Jacques promptly got called to order by Maxie for
talking French:

"Shut up, bloody Frenchman!"

Everybody's nerves were on edge. We had been flying at 30,000 feet in arctic cold for nearly an hour and

a half now. All those instrument dials were dancing in confusion in front of my tired eyes—altimeter, artificial horizon, airspeed and "turn and bank" indicators, radiator, oil and cylinder-head temperature gauges, pressure gauges, warning lights—in a jumble of figures and needles.

I was obsessed by that tank weighing down my Spitfire. According to the clock I still had in theory about seven minutes' worth of juice before I could jettison it. My back hurt, my toes were frozen, my eyes were watering, my nose running—altogether I felt in rotten shape and everything struck me as being in a complete mess.

The weather, which had been so fine till midday, had deteriorated and big banks of cloud and mist rose vertically from the ground like ramparts. Going though one of these big cumulus Jacques and I had lost contact with the rest of the Squadron. Now we were lost in the inferno and we stuck frantically together, trying to get to the rendezvous.

But, in fact, we must be past that damned rendezvous, and how on earth could anyone recognize anything in this witches' sabbath of aircraft and clouds? It was quite impossible to pinpoint our position. Below on our left the last Frisian Islands were outlines—yellow and arid on the grey sea. Somewhere on the right below the mist must be Emden and the rich canal-bordered pastures of North Holland. Far behind us already, the Zuider Zee.

Up in the air it was a nightmare. I had never seen anything like it. Clusters of flak appeared from the void and silently hung on the flanks of the clouds. Space brought forth swarms of German fighters—a disquieting example of spontaneous generation.

We passed Lightnings and Mustangs hurrying home with empty magazines, their pilots worn out and dodging between the clouds to avoid combat.

* * *

At last the bombers!
A scene of frightful panic. It was the first time that

under the concerted efforts of the flak and the ava-
lanches of Junkers 88's and Messerschmitt 410's armed

Ju 88

with rockets, boxes of Fortresses had been broken up,
dislocated, reduced to shreds. The big bombers were
scattered all over the sky, vainly trying to bunch in
threes or fours to cross their fire. The Focke-Wulfs were
rushing in for the kill. And how many there were! They
appeared from everywhere and, down below, on Dutch
airfields, others were preparing to take off.

The Spitfires and the bombers were much too dispersed for an organized plan of defence to be possible.
It was a question of everyone for himself and the Devil
take the hindmost. The controller's voice in the radio
had become so distant that it was imperceptible; without it, without its support and advice, we felt cut off
from our world, all alone, naked, unarmed.

It was a miracle that we had not yet been brought
down! Twisting and turning, firing off our guns, we had
succeeded in gaining quite a lot of height over the
main scrap. I had exhausted half my ammunition. I
should have to find someone to go home with.

Suddenly Jacques spotted in the middle of the sky
dotted with parachutes and burning aircraft about 40
Focke-Wulfs pouncing on 4 Fortresses which were lagging behind trying to protect a Liberator, one of whose
engines was in flames.

What could we do?—it was impossible to call for help
in this infernal scrum. All the Spitfires, as far as the
eye could reach, were whirling about in dog-fights and

seemed to be banging into the clouds and bouncing off again like boxers against the ropes of the ring. A glance at my petrol gauge. Only two minutes' worth left. Never mind, it wouldn't be much loss.

"Hullo, Jack, dropping my baby!"

I stooped down and vigorously pulled on the release, while Jacques kept watch. Freed from the load, my Spitfire bounded forward.

"O.K., Jack, your turn!"

Jacques' tank fluttered down in a shower of petrol.

*   *   *

"Attacking!"

Sights switched on, finger on firing button, together we rolled on our backs and dived on the Focke-Wulfs milling round the bombers. As I dived I kept a look-out and tried to choose one. They were attacking from every side—front, side and rear. One of the Fortresses went into a spin, slowly. Another suddenly exploded like a gigantic flak shell, and the explosion tore a wing off the one to its right. A big dark mushroom spread out, incandescent debris dropping from it. The now asymmetrical outline of the Fortress grew smaller and fainter, falling like a dead leaf. Like shining new nails on a wall, one, two, four, six parachutes suddenly dotted the sky.

I passed a few yards from a disabled Focke-Wulf trailing a black veil—no point in wasting ammo, he'd had it.

I had the impression I was diving into an aquarium full of demented fish! Nothing but radial engines, yellow bellies, black crosses, and clipped wings beating the air like fins. The air was criss-crossed with multi-coloured tracer bullets, and instinctively I blinked.

Here we are! I tightened my stomach muscles, put my feet on the top pedal of the rudder bar to resist the centrifugal force, swallowed hard to get the bitter taste out of my mouth and pulled out violently. Before I had time to register, my finger had instinctively pressed the firing button. A burst at the Focke-Wulf, who for one second filled my windshield. Missed him! Sur-

prised, he stalled and fell away. Jacques fired on him
and missed him too—but a grey Messerschmitt, its
wings edged with fire, was after him. I yelled:

"Look out, Jacques! Break right!"

Quickly, I put all my weight on the controls, the
ground whipped round—but too late, the Messerschmitt
was out of range. I was drenched in sweat.

In front of me two Focke-Wulfs were converging to
attack a Fortress drifting like a wreck. A glance at the
mirror: Jacques was there. The red filaments of my
sight encircled a green and yellow Focke-Wulf—Jesus,
how close he was! The wings of my Spit shuddered from
the hammer-blows of my two cannon . . . three flashes,
a belch of flame and a grey tail unfurled in his wake!

Then I saw a sheet of flame on the flank of a cloud,
just where Jacques' aircraft was at that moment—my
heart missed a beat—but it was his triumphant voice
shouting in the radio:

"Did you see that, Pierre? I got him!"

Thank God, it was a Focke-Wulf, and out of the
corner of my eye I saw his Spit swaying 50 yards away.
What a relief.

Suddenly, a thunderclap, a burning slap in the face.
My eardrums were pierced by the shriek of air
through a hole just torn by a shell through my windshield. Bang! another . . . I broke frantically, the Hun
was so close that the flash of his guns made me shut my
eyes. But Jacques was there, and the Focke-Wulf broke
away.

                    *   *   *

For a time I lost all notion of what was going on. For
10 minutes I blindly followed Jacques' instruction
over the radio; when I picked up the thread again we
were in the middle of the North Sea. On my right was a
Fortress, holed like a sieve but flying all the same,
and on my left a red-nosed Mustang limped along.

England at last. Just inland I could make out four
crashed Fortresses in the fields.

We landed at Manston after the Fortress, exhausted,
drained. We parked by the Mustang. Introductions.

The pilot was the renowned Major Beeson, commander of the 7th Mustang Squadron. It was his last mission, for he was due to be repatriated to the States the week after.

"Jees," he said, roaring with laughter, "I hope I get sent on furlough, quick, against the Japs!"

*   *   *

The Schweinfurt factory had been razed to the ground, but out of the 280 Fortresses only about 50 were still airworthy. We had lost more than 100 crews; 197 German fighters had been shot down and 51 of ours.

DISCOVERY OF THE V-1

1st December, 1943

I had the impression that the R.A.F. had a flying-bomb complex. Some weeks previously the Germans—with Hitler in the lead—had launched their secret weapons campaign and the neutral press was full of horrific stories of gigantic rockets controlled by radio, capable of carrying 3 tons of explosives 150 miles, etc., etc.

We read the papers and shrugged our shoulders. One fine afternoon, however, all the pilots were called to the Intelligence Room. Willie Hickson, the senior I.O., gloomily unveiled a large-scale map of northern France studded with little numbered flags.

"Gentlemen, the situation is grave!" and he began a by no means reassuring speech in which he outlined the following facts:

Either on the one hand the Hun was trying to bluff us, or, on the other, he had really succeeded in producing these contrivances, and we might very well learn one morning that half London had been pulverized. We were choosing to suppose that it was a bluff. But Air Ministry was taking it seriously and talking of switching our bombing offensive against all these spots marked on the map.

"In two months, the Todt organization has begun the construction of nearly 200 sites. Not a single one must be allowed to be completed. The 18 you see there—marked by the red flags—where the work is most advanced, will be bombed tomorrow by 1,300 aircraft. We shall continue until they are all wiped out. Now, one last warning, the severest penalties will be imposed on the first one of you who mentions these facts to anyone at all. The public must not be given a chance to panic."

*   *   *

The No-balls—that was the cover name given to these sites—multiplied like mushrooms; the more we demolished the more cropped up again. If it really was a bluff the Germans must have been having a good laugh.

Gradually every type of aircraft was mobilized and thrown against the "rocket coast" as the coast from Boulogne to Cherbourg came to be called. 184 Squadron with its old Hurricanes was soon sent into the fray. With their four 60 lb. rockets the miserable machines dragged along at 200 m.p.h. Exceptional nerve was needed to go and try conclusions with the German flak at ground level and at that speed.

With childish levity and spite we poked fun at the pilots and their misgivings. These were all the more comprehensible as they were beginning to receive their new Typhoons and it was really a bit hard for them to get shot down just as their dreams were about to be realized.

We didn't laugh long at their expense, anyway. On the 4th December, 8 Hurricanes had just crossed the French coast when 10 Messerschmitt 109 G's attacked them. 184, Squadron Leader Rose at their head, defended themselves tooth and nail. Weighed down by their bombs and with only two 7.7 mm. against the

Germans three 20 mm. and two 13 mm. the Hurricanes hadn't much hope of coming through. Six were brought down and the other two crashed on landing, their pilots both seriously wounded by enemy bullets. And we laughed quite on the other side of our faces when it was decided that in future the Hurricanes would be escorted at ground level by Spitfires.

15th December, 1943

There was a mist and the damp clouds scraped the tree-tops. At least we would get some rest that day.

Sitting in front of bacon and eggs and several slices of toast done to a turn and dripping with butter, I was having breakfast in the mess, at the same time arranging the programme for the day. There would certainly be a "general release," I would have a hot bath, then, after lunch, Jacques and I would go—if his car had not fallen to pieces—to Maidstone. After a flick we would dine at the Star and, after a round of drinks, come back to bed.

"Hallo! hallo!" Damn! that blasted loudspeaker again. "Operations calling. Will the following pilots of 602 Squadron report to Intelligence immediately!" Seething, I heard my name among the eight called. I gulped down my cup of coffee, spread a double layer of marmalade on my last piece of toast and scrammed. At Intelligence I found I was the last to arrive. Everyone else was already there and seeing their long faces I soon caught on.

"Surely those G.C.C.*types can't expect us to fly on a day like this!"

I noticed that eight pilots from 184 were there. All was now clear. One of those escorts we had been hearing about. Delightful!

The I.O. explained our mission on the map. The eight Hurricanes were to attack No-ball No. 79, south-east of Hesdin, with rockets. As our Spits did 350 m.p.h. while they could just make 200 m.p.h., an escort as usually understood was out of the question. They were

*Group Central Control.

to cross the French coast at 1012 hours and make straight for their objective. Simultaneously four Spits each from "B" and "A" Flights were to patrol Hesdin and Abbeville, ready to intercept any German fighter reaction.

On paper it looked harmless enough—but in practice . . .

* * *

At 0940 hours the Spitfires took off and plunged into the mist towards Dungeness. In mid-Channel, as "Met" had predicted, visibility improved and the ceiling rose to 1,000 feet. The Channel was repugnant that morning. Its short foam-crested waves were cold, dirty and glaucous. As we were flying at sea-level we had to look out for gulls, which have a nasty habit of flying slap into radiators at full speed or of crashing into the windshield and covering you with blood and feathers.

"B" Flight left us, making for Point-au-Blanc, more to the north-east. Soon, slightly to the right, the cliffs of Tréport reared up their mass of whitish chalk. We opened up flat out and the four Spitfires seemed to slide from one wave crest to the next. Suddenly we were over the estuary of the Somme with its sandbanks and marshes. The beach swept past beneath my wings and I gently eased my Spit over the bumps in the ground, flying as low as possible. We followed the course of the Somme as far as Abbeville. All was quiet at first, no flak, everything seemed deserted and asleep.

Suddenly the ball began. From each bank light flak opened fire. The air filled all at once with long incandescent trails, red and green 20 mm. tracers crisscrossed, giving the disagreeable impression of being about to hit you between the eyes and then at the last moment curving off to one side.

Clusters of luminous balls came up from carefully camouflaged sites, crossed over our heads or ricocheted off the river in front of us. The 37 mm. soon joined in and the venomous black puffs began to appear all round. In spite of violent swerves between the trees and even making use of the hedges as cover, we were relentlessly followed by the light flak. Scarcely were we out of range of one emplacement than we came under fire from another.

We turned 90° left; to maintain our line-abreast formation we had to cross over at full speed. Suddenly I saw Ken coming straight for me and I pulled the stick to avoid him. For a moment, therefore, I was not protected by my closeness to the ground. Immediately three shells burst a few yards from me, one of them just over my wing; I could hear the shell fragments rattling on it like hail falling on a sheet of iron.

Right in front between two haystacks I made out some sandbags with the barrels of a multiple pom-pom emerging from them. All round vague grey shapes were rushing about frantically. A pressure on the button and my shells struck the flimsy parapet and my machine-gun bullets churned up the earth all round. One of the stacks caught fire, and I can still see with absolute clarity one of the loaders collapsing, mown down by the storm of bullets.

As I flew on, avoiding obstacles and watching out for high tension wires which stretch their deadly snare 30 feet above the ground, I kept an eye on Jacques flying 200 yards to my right.

He was clearly in form. Several times I saw him go slap between two trees instead of over them. Knowing him as I did, I knew he must be revelling in it—whereas I would rather have been in bed or, at a pinch, doing a fighter sweep at 20,000 feet.

The difficulty about low flying at 350 m.p.h. is that your field of vision is very limited. You just have time to evaluate an obstacle or a target, you have a fraction of a second to avoid the one and aim at the other, and they have flashed by beneath your wings.

Every light flak post must have been alerted, for streams of tracers were coming up on every side. After a few minutes you get used to it. . . . Suddenly the obstacle disappeared and flattened out before what I took at first to be a big meadow. It was an airfield!

I was flying along the perimeter and Jacques straight down the middle! He must have realized the danger at the same time as I. An absolute wall of flak rose up all round him. At any moment I expected to see him crash in flames. But he was too busy to take any notice of what he calls "those little details."

He had just caught a glimpse, in a corner, of three Messerschmitt 109's under camouflage nets. Desperately he tried to get them in his sights. Taking his life in his hands he throttled right back and tried to do a tight turn, his wing practically touching the ground. No good, he was going too fast. Without much hope he fired a burst but it merely bespattered a boundary wall. On the other hand his manoeuvre brought him slap in front of the airfield control tower, a two-storied wooden building with wide bay windows like a belvedere. The effect of his two cannon and his machine guns on such a target was terrifying. The windows flew into fragments and the bullets wrought havoc within. I caught sight of shapes diving out of the door and even the windows. With his finger on the button, Jacques let them have it and went on firing point blank, just dodging out of the way in the nick of time. The two Huns keeping watch on the roof, seeing the Spitfire coming straight for them, belching fire, did not hesitate; they simply jumped overboard. Everything happened in a flash, like a dream. I heard Jacques' triumphant voice over the radio:

"Hallo, Pierre, that shook 'em!"

For ten more long minutes we continued our patrol, and it was with relief that, unharmed—apart from a few gashes here and there in the Spits—we turned for home.

Drenched with sweat, swearing that we would never be caught at it again, we landed at Detling in pouring rain and a dense fog.

Home, sweet home.

"Douce France," infested with Huns, was less and less welcoming!

*   *   *

20th December, 1943

Out of the corner of my eye I watched the Hurricanes about to launch their attack. The target, carefully camouflaged against vertical photography, was visible in every detail at this angle: the high tension cables to the transformer, the concrete block of the control room with its curious aerials, from which the flying bomb is controlled. On either side, cleverly hidden in the undergrowth, the curious low ski-shaped construction, whose function still baffled the R.A.F. technicians and Intelligence Officers for all their cunning, and, lastly, the launching ramp, 45 yards long, pointing straight at the heart of England. On the rails, a sinister cylinder, about twenty feet long, with two embryonic wings.

Things seemed to be devilishly advanced! All round the No-balls stretched a 20-yard wide barbed wire barrier and light flak posts—15 in a radius of 800 metres, according to the interpretation of the latest photos taken by the P.R.U. Mustangs—all equipped with multiple pom-poms, and on the roof of the control block were two 37 mm.

The Hurricanes began their dive, slap into the machine-gun bullets. The tracer bullets formed a wall of steel and explosive round the target.

The inevitable happened. Powerless, I watched the tragedy. Flight Lieutenant Roughhead, just as he let go his salvo of rockets, was hit and killed instantly. His disabled Hurricane recovered with incredible violence and zoomed vertically upwards, its propeller stationary. At the top of the trajectory one wing wilted, the aircraft hung as on a thread suspended in space, motionless, then went into a spin.

As in a nightmare I saw Warrant Officer Pearce's Hurricane literally mown down by a burst of 37 mm. The tail came off, the machine crashed into a wood, scything down the trees, scattering jets of burning petrol.

The other two Hurricanes attacked simultaneously. Struck by a direct hit, Sergeant Clive's machine exploded and was soon nothing but an inchoate mass of flame, dragging a long trail of black smoke.

By a miracle, Bush the Australian was luckier; he succeeded not only in placing his eight rockets in the control room but even in extricating himself from the barrage of flak, in spite of an enormous gash in his fuselage, not to mention two bullets in the thigh and one in the side.

I sat there petrified, flying mechanically. Everything had happened in a fraction of a second.

Still out of range of the light flak we completed our round and I prepared to set course for home. I heard Ken detaching Jacques and Danny to escort Bush and shouting to me in the radio:

"Hallo, Beer Two, attacking the bloody thing!"

My blood froze in my veins. Ken must be absolute crackers. If he wanted to commit suicide, he ought to do it on his own. I wasn't feeling at all good when Ken, after a long feint in the neighbouring valleys, brought me back on the objective.

"Line abreast, go! Attack!"

We charged, skimming the ground at ten or twelve feet. Even before we were in position the flak had got our range. Their precision was diabolical. Five posts immediately caught me in their cross fire. With hammering heart I tried to put out their aim, kicking hard on the rudder bar to make my machine skid. No good. I got three direct hits which went slap through my main plane without exploding.

There was no question of attacking. All I could hope for was to save my own skin. Every flak post in the area was alerted by now. Dazzled by the showers of tracers, I crouched down and instinctively moved my head about, as if to avoid the bullets. I felt I was going to be hit any second and crash hopelessly, like the Hurricanes. Desperately I hurled my machine about. Taking my life in my hands I got right down on the deck, feinting violently to left and right. Too late I saw the obstacle—a row of poplars along a canal. I banked instinctively, putting on full left rudder. With a terrifying crash which reverberated through the fuselage and a jolt which nearly wrenched the stick out of my hands, my starboard wing caught the tree-tops. Only the momentum of the four tons of my aircraft, hurled at 340 m.p.h. prevented me from crashing into the raised towpath on the opposite bank.

Dazed by the shock, paralysed by fear, that fearful physical fear which twists your guts and fills your mouth with gall, I felt my muscles liquefy. . . . I avoided a high tension cable by a hair's breadth—passing like a flash under the gleaming steel wire.

My heart failed me then. Losing my head I pulled the stick back, seeking the refuge of the clouds rolling dark and grey about 2,500 feet above. I lost the protection of the ground and during the few seconds that my climb lasted I was hit five times—a shell exploding in my left aileron, three bullets in my elevator and another through one of the blades of my propeller. Never had the hollow damp shade of the rain-laden clouds been so welcome. It took me about a minute to go through the cloud layer, and I suddenly emerged in full sunlight, bathed in sweat as on awakening from a nightmare. The blue sky, the sun reflected in the sea of clouds passing beneath me—I was back at last in a glorious and reassuring world.

Timidly I tried the controls. My aileron had sprung its hinges and was held only by a thread of aluminum. The skin of the upper surface of my wings was crumpled like a piece of tissue paper and the shining metal showed through the cracks in the paint.

My jammed tail-trimmer was weighing on the stick.

*   *   *

Back at Detling I made a fairly sensational landing —two or three enormous bounces that I had to check violently. Ken had already landed a few minutes before me, writing off his aircraft in the process—his undercart, jammed by a bullet, had failed to come down, and he had had to land on his belly. Later, when we did a post-mortem on our aircraft, Ken discovered that an unexploded shell had smashed one of his magnetos to smithereens and gone through one of his exhaust pipes.

My old LO-D would be in dock for a week. In addition to the damage of the controls, the fuselage had been hit near the roundels by three shells. A bullet had ricocheted off one of my oxygen bottles. I had a fine retrospective fright at the idea that if the shell had hit that bottle fair and square the explosion of the gas under pressure would have turned me into heat and light.

RANGER OVER FRANCE

Half past six. The ringing of the alarm clock tore me out of bed. Christ, how cold it was! I peeped under the black-out curtain—low clouds, ceiling less than 2,000 feet, and what a wind! It screamed through the telegraph wires outside and every gust shook the twenty doors in our quarters.

I lit a cigarette and put the light on. Tom and Danny, my room-mates, had gone back to sleep. I hurriedly put on a couple of pullovers over my pyjamas, a leather waistcoat, my battle-dress, two pairs of long woollen stockings and my flying boots, into which I slipped my map.

The dark concrete bulk of the Ops. room loomed in the night. I could dimly hear the throb of the air-conditioning plant for the underground rooms. After the bitter cold outside, I felt as if I were plunging into a deliciously warm vapour bath as soon as I passed through the heavy metal doors. The room, lit by mercury vapour lamps, seemed like a scene from another world.

The Sergeant on duty was kept on the go answering a dozen continuously ringing phones. Without even looking up he handed me the "Met" report and the area controller's instructions. Ten-tenths cloud at 4,000 feet. Wind at sea-level 320 degrees, 35 m.p.h.; 50 m.p.h. at 5,000 feet. Visibility moderate, dropping to 500 yards in the showers. Twelve Typhoons were to carry out a sortie in the Chartres area from 0840 to 0850 hours at zero feet. A piece of cake, if it weren't for the wind.

I woke up the rest of the gang. Ken and Bruce were O.K. but Jacques proceeded to bind like hell. I shook him up. Five minutes later we were on our way over to Flight. On our way we checked the fixing of our big 45-gallon auxiliary tanks, slung like bombs between the Spitfires' two radiators. The mechanics lay on the ground, working away by the light of their storm lanterns.

"Take-off at 8 o'clock sharp," Ken shouted to them.

It was 7:25, just time to get outside a cup of coffee and a few biscuits. Time for breakfast proper when we got back—if we did get back.

Huddling round the miserable stove, Jacques, Dumbrell and I listened while Ken, map in hand, gave us the gen.

"We'll cross the French coast, either on I.F. or above the clouds, then we'll go as far as Amiens flying low. We'll turn left and patrol the area Saint-Quentin, Noyon, Beauvais, and we'll come back at 13,000 feet. Like that we'll stand a decent chance of intercepting a low-flying transport. Roughly line-abreast formation, 100 yards between aircraft, crossing over from left to right when we alter course. Every man for himself if it comes to a scrap. The first one who spots a target tells the rest and leads the attack."

0750 hours. Strapped in our Mae Wests, clustered up with our dinghy as well as the parachute, we climbed laboriously into our cockpits, helped by the mechanics. My breath immediately froze on the windshield. I switched on my radio, my camera, gun, the carburettor, pilot-head and gyro-intake heaters and the de-icing equipment. My fingers were numb under three layers of gloves—silk, wool and leather—and it was quite a business messing about with all those tiny buttons crowded together on the instrument panel.

0755 hours. I got them to see the mirror was properly adjusted. A glance at the sight. I set the safety-catch of the guns. All set. A glance towards Ken.

"All clear."

"Contact."

A whine from the starter. One cylinder fired, then two more. I pumped furiously and all at once the engine burst into life.

It was still very dark and the mauve flashes from the exhausts lit up the snow. It was two minutes past eight. Navigation lights on, wing tip to wing tip, we climbed through the black, threatening clouds.

We emerged at 13,000 feet above the thick layer of stratocumuli, over the Channel. At once we took up battle formation. Complete silence over the radio. In spite of icing we had switched over to our auxiliary tanks without anything going wrong. In the gathering dawn the clouds were edged with light.

The German spotters had probably picked us up. The usual irritating radar interference started up in our headphones, worse with each sweep of the beam. Suddenly Bruce Dumbrell waggled his wings and turned for home. The perfect ellipse of his wings was outlined against the pale sky for the space of an instant and I could make out a thin white stream flowing from his radiator. Glycol escaping. One aircraft less. In theory one of us ought to escort him over the sea but if we did that we should have to return to base without completing our job.

Ken said nothing and merely signalled to us to close up again for the dive through the cloud-layer. It was a tricky business. Ken had worked it out that if we didn't time it right there was a risk of coming out in the coastal flak belt. The "Met" forecast had to be right too as, if the cloud base was lower than expected, we wouldn't have enough margin to rectify any error in our I.F.

We plunged into the opaque mist. Ken had his eyes glued to his instruments, Jacques and I desperately clung to his wing tips. Suddenly we found ourselves in clear air again, at less than 1,500 feet, over a cluster of little wooded hillocks intersected by a narrow marshy valley. A fine rain was falling, shreds of mist dragged over the ground, the light was glaucous, like in an

aquarium. That awful curdling of the stomach muscles
as usual. We must watch out now.

"Hullo, Skittles, Red Leader calling. Combat formation, drop your babies."

Having got rid of our auxiliary tanks, we dived
to get up speed. Ken was skimming the river in the middle of the valley; Jacques beyond him was following
the road, keeping below the level of the telegraph wires.
I was half-way up a slope, bothered by constant clumps
of trees. I kept a cautious lookout for high-tension
wires. One hundred and seventy-five yards a second. In
that grisly visibility the fatal obstacle came on you in a
flash. On the ground, apart from a glimpse through my
hood of a couple of women sheltering under an umbrella, there wasn't a solitary cart, nothing. A few roofs
outlined against the horizon, a factory chimney or two.
White smoke from a small marshalling yard approached
rapidly. Doullens, probably. We veered towards the
south, to leave the French town clear on our left. We
had neither permission nor inclination to attack a train
—no point in risking flak unnecessarily.

The rain started to come down in sheets. I must
really watch out now. Amiens must be somewhere not
far away in the murk.

"Look out, flak!"

A shout from Jacques over the radio. Instinctively,
I turned, A fan-shaped cluster of white puffs spread in
front of my windshield. Tracers started whipping
through the trees. Then, under my wings, I saw roofs,
allotments. In a rift the towers of the cathedral loomed
up, too close. I roared over wet cobblestones, greasy
macadam, dirty slates, clusters of grey houses. It was
Amiens.

Skimming the chimney pots we veered to the left
and emerged level with a station. A glimpse of a few
railwaymen, rooted to the spot, caught between the
trucks of a goods train, then flashes from a loco park
as a battery of three automatic guns opened up, their
stuttering barrels wreathed in smoke.

Each of us on his own, weaving, full throttle, we
made off, pursued by orange tracers. It was only a

few miles from the town that we formed up again. I discreetly checked on the course Ken was setting and studied the map as best I could. No doubt about it, Ken had boobed as we came out of Amiens, at the Langean fork. We were heading for Noyon and Compiègne instead of Saint-Quentin. The Canal du nord passed beneath us, then the Oise. Sure enough, here was Compiègne forest, slashed by a bank of fog—apparently anchored to the trees.

Suddenly we heard the controller's voice, very distantly as we were flying low:

"Hullo, Skittles, look out for Huns and Tiffie boys around."

I wedged myself against the seat and tried to pierce the murk into which we plunged, six feet above the denuded branches. Suddenly all hell was let loose—we roared into a fearful madhouse of planes. Yellow cowlings marked with black crosses cut through the tracer trails. At least forty Focke-Wulfs, all apparently gone berserk. With my thumb I immediately released the safety catch of my guns. My earphones were screaming.

I just avoided colliding with a Focke-Wulf. Glued to the back of my seat by the centrifugal force I did a tight turn behind another and let fly with my machine guns as I passed. Then, my finger still on the button, I had to break away violently. I could see another hovering just behind in my mirror, his wings lit up by the flashes of his four cannon.

Having got rid of that one I drew a bead on another, who seemed to have lost his head and was waggling his wings. All of a sudden a Typhoon loomed up in my windshield, coming straight for me. I kicked the rudder bar desperately. I just about grazed him, and caught my wing tip a terrible crack in a branch. Sweating and holding my breath I righted my Spitfire, just as a Focke-Wulf in flames crashed in front of me, mowing down the trees in a fearful shower of sparks.

Stick right back I made vertically for the clouds, firing a burst of cannon on the way at a Focke-Wulf which was so close that the black crosses on his fuselage filled my gun-sight. With his tail-plane half torn off, he went into a spin and crashed into a clearing.

Once I got into the shelter of the clouds I breathed more easily. That bunch of pirates, 609 Typhoon Squadron, commanded by my Belgian friend Demoulin, must have dropped unexpectedly on a wing of Focke-Wulfs taking off from Compiègne airfield. We had landed in the middle of the party by mistake!

Nerves tensed, I came down into the scrap again. I saw three flaming masses on the ground and three thick columns of black smoke rose above the forest. Visibility was getting worse and worse. I caught a glimpse of a couple of Focke-Wulfs vanishing into the mist. No one left in sight. I could vaguely hear Ken and Jacques over the radio, excitedly chasing after a Focke-Wulf. They ended by shooting it down somewhere or other and then the wireless went dead for a bit.

I called Ken to tell him my juice was getting low and that I was going back to Detling. Half an hour's I.F. through cumulus with flanks heavy with snow and I found myself over the sandy spit of Dungeness, in a fog you could cut with a knife. I asked for a homing and was brought back slap over base by the controller. As I made my approach, skimming the tree-tops, I saw Ken and Jacques touching down, Ken doing a fearful ground loop. I taxied past him. He had caught a packet in his starboard wing from 20 mm., but he signalled that he had bagged a Jerry.

With the help of my mechanics I jumped down from my Spit, stiff and cold. Only to hear that immediately after breakfast I had to return to Dispersal on stand-by readiness.

ESCORTS

21st December, 1943

Briefing at 10:30.

Superb weather, a temperature fit for brass monkeys —not a trace of a cloud in the sky. The Spitfires' wings were streaming with water, for the hot-air de-icing trailer had just passed. The runway was covered with ice.

I had to take off my gloves to do up my straps, and so my hands froze, and I couldn't get them warm again. I opened up the oxygen, to put a bit of stuffing into myself.

The ice on the runway these last days had produced a crop of accidents, serious and otherwise—smashed undercarts, taxiing accidents, etc.—and now we only had 11 serviceable planes left.

Dumbrell, Jacques and I were Max section, with the C.O. With 132 we were to patrol the Gambrai area, where German fighters had been particularly active recently. We climbed to 22,000 feet, then, as the cold was intense, we came down to 17,000.

The winter sky was so clear, so dazzling, that after a mere 20 minutes over France we were continually blinking.

The controller told us there was a strong enemy fighter formation not far off, but it was impossible to spot anything in the dazzling light. To be on the safe side, as Grass Seed was getting urgent, we gained height again.

* * *

Suddenly, woooof! Thirty Focke-Wulfs were on top of us. Before we could move a muscle, the brutes

86

opened fire. A whirlwind of enormous radial engines, of short, slender wings edged with lightning, of tracer bullets whizzing in every direction, of black crosses all over the place. Panic. Everyone broke. In the space of one second the two flights' impeccable combat formation was disrupted, dislocated, scattered to the four winds. Too late! Old Jonah was on his way down in flames, and Morgan, the Scots Flight Sergeant, in a spin, one wing torn off by a hail of Mauser.

132 were no luckier. Three of their pilots were shot down. A fourth—as we learnt later—succeeded in bringing his badly damaged machine half-way back across the Channel, then baled out and was fished out an hour later.

Once the surprise had passed, we pulled ourselves together. Captain Aubertin, in command of Skittles, suddenly found himself isolated: his Nos. 2 and 4 had been shot down and his No. 3 had vanished into thin air—poor old Spence had got a 20 mm. shell 4 inches from his head which had smashed his radio to smithereens. Half knocked out, he had instinctively pulled the stick back and opened the throttle, and had woken up at 36,000 feet, absolutely alone in the sky.

A Focke-Wulf sneaked in behind the captain but missed him. The Hun overshot him. He was carried away by his speed and Aubertin settled his hash in no time at all; the biter bit. Unfortunately four other Focke-Wulfs engaged him and not only did he fail to see his victim crash but he himself only succeeded in getting away after an eventful 45-mile chase among the trees, round church steeples and through village streets. His Spitfire was hit seven times.

Meanwhile Jacques and I—contrary to our settled habits—followed on Sutherland's heels like faithful hounds and had the pleasure of seeing him liquidate another "190" at 600 yards range. The Hun disintegrated in the air, but the pilot escaped: a little later we saw a parachute open out below us.

Danny fired a sly burst at a "190" but missed.

If results were wanted, this sweep certainly produced them—out of 23 Spits, 6 were shot down, 8 others damaged, not counting Williams of 132, who was wounded and had to belly-land.

*   *   *

7th January, 1944

A long trip this time. We were going to Rheims to fetch home a strong formation of Flying Fortresses and Liberators coming back from Germany. 602 was to cover the first three groups—180 bombers in all—and 132 the three following.

We took off at 1210 hours after a rushed lunch, and we flogged our aircraft, weighed down by 45-gallon auxiliary tanks, up to 23,000 feet. After 30 minutes' flying we passed Paris on our right, sensed rather than seen below a cloak of mist and smoke. On the way German heavy batteries loosed some beautifully aimed salvoes which burst very close—we immediately scattered about the sky. The black puffs appeared on every side. Climbing at full throttle with Thommerson, we succeeded in getting out of range and re-forming, not without difficulty.

*   *   *

1050 hours. The Jerries seemed to be reacting and the Focke-Wulfs must be taking off all over the place because control was beginning to get agitated. Still nothing near us.

Soon a cluster of black dots appeared on the horizon, followed by others. Our bombers!

The Thunderbolts and Lightnings whom we were relieving returned to base, and we took up our positions —in patrols of four on either side of the formation.

*   *   *

A show of Fortresses certainly is an impressive sight! The phalanx of bombers in impeccable defensive formation—several massive boxes of a hundred or so 4-engined aircraft in banks at 27,000 feet, each box bristling with 1,440 heavy .5 machine guns—spread out over twenty odd miles.

On either side the Spitfire escort stretched as far as

the eye could see. The top cover of Spit VII's and IX's was only visible in the shape of fine white condensation trails.

The visibility that day was splendid. The sky was dark indigo blue, paler towards the horizon, passing from emerald green to milky white where it merged with the bands of mist over the North Sea.

Below, France unfolded like a magic carpet. The peaceful meandering Seine and its tributaries, the dark masses of the forests with their curious geometrical shapes, the multicoloured checker-board of the fields and meadows, the tiny toy-like villages, the towns sullying the translucent sky with patches of smoke clinging to the warm layers of air.

The sun burnt through the transparent cockpits, and yet I could feel ice forming in my oxygen tube, and the exhaust gases condensed in a myriad of microscopic crystals, marking the wake of my Spitfire in the sky.

Fatigue, stiffness, the painful cramp in my back, the cold searing my toes and fingers through the leather, the wool and the silk, all were forgotten.

*   *   *

Here and there in the Fortress formations there were gaps. From close to, you could see machines with one, sometimes two stationary engines and feathered propellers. Others had lacerated tail-planes, gaping holes in the fuselages, wings tarnished by fire or glistening with black oil oozing from gutted engines.

Behind the formation were the stragglers, making for the coast, for the haven of refuge of an advanced air base on the other side of the Channel, flying only by a sublime effort of the will. You could imagine the blood pouring over the heaps of empty cartridges, the pilot nursing his remaining engines and anxiously eyeing the long white trail of petrol escaping from his riddled tanks. These isolated Fortresses were the Focke-Wulf's favourite prey. Therefore the squadrons detached two or three pairs of Spitfires, charged with bringing each one back safe: an exhausting task as these damaged Fortresses often dragged along on a third of their total power, stretching the endurance of their escort to the limit.

On this occasion Ken sent Carpenter and me to escort a Liberator which was only in the air by a miracle. Its No. 3 engine had completely come out of its housing and hung on the leading edge, a mass of lifeless ironmongery. His No. 1 engine was on fire, the flames slowly eating into the wing and the smoke escaping through the aluminum plates of the upper surface, buckled by the heat. Through the tears in the fuselage the survivors were throwing overboard all their superfluous equipment—machine guns, ammunition belts, radio, armour plates—to lighten their machine, which was slowly losing height.

To crown all, there was a burst in the hydraulic system, freeing one of the wheels of the undercart which hung down and increased the drag still further.

At 1,800 revs., minus 2 boost and 200 m.p.h. we had to zigzag to keep level with him. We had been hunched up in our uncomfortable cockpits for two hours already, and we were still over France, 12 miles behind the main formation. Ten Focke-Wulfs began to prowl round us, at a respectful distance, as if suspecting a trap. Anxiously Carp and I kept an eye on them.

Suddenly they attacked, in pairs. Short of juice as we were, all we could do was to face each attack by a very tight 180° turn, fire a short burst in the approximate direction of the Hun, and immediately resume our position by another quick 180° turn. This performance was repeated a dozen times but we succeeded in making the Focke-Wulfs keep their distance. They eventually tired of it—or so we thought.

Over Dieppe the fighters gave way to the flak. We were flying at about 10,000 feet. The German light flak opened fire with unbelievable ferocity. An absolute pyramid of black puffs charged with lightning appeared in a fraction of a second. Violently shaken by several well-aimed shells, Carp and I separated and gained height as fast as we could with our meagre reserves of petrol. The poor Liberator, incapable of taking any sort of violent evasive action, was quickly bracketed.

Just as, after a few agonizing seconds, we thought it was out of range there was an explosion and the big bomber, cut in half, suddenly disappeared in a sheet of flame. Only three parachutes opened out. The blazing aluminum coffin crashed a few hundred yards from the cliffs in a shower of spray, dragging down the remaining members of the crew.

With heavy hearts we landed at Lympne, our tanks empty.

Luckily we were often more fortunate than this and succeeded in bringing our charges back to our airfield at Detling, where their arrival always caused the greatest agitation—ambulances, fire service, curious onlookers. We felt fully repaid by the gratitude in the eyes of the poor exhausted fellows. In many cases it was only the moral support of the presence of a pair of Spits that gave them the courage to hold out to the end, to resist the temptation of baling out and waiting for the end of the war in some Oflag or other.

DEPARTURE FOR THE ORKNEYS

17th January, 1944

We were about to leave for the Orkneys. There was a regular pea-souper and the Harrows would be prevented from coming to fetch us.

Alea jacta est—we would go by rail. Just the job, something like twenty-eight hours of more or less comfortable travel.

We piled our luggage into the lorries and went and had lunch at the "Star" in Maidstone, where we found Jimmy Rankin and Yule. A few last rounds of drinks, promises. . . .

As usual I was cluttered up with a mass of belongings—mandoline, Irvine jacket, etc. Luckily Jacques was there to help.

On the way through London we dropped in in a body—24 pilots—at the "C——," a very swanky and exclusive club in Soho. After half an hour the manager, fearing for his interior decoration and seeing the alarm of his immaculately dressed clientele, came and asked us to move on. A few well-chosen arguments, including the transfer of his magnificent white carnation to Ken's button-hole and a threat of public debagging, were enough to calm him down.

From 6 to 9:30 (our train was at 10:20) we drank hard—whisky, beer, whisky. By 9:30 we were bottled, and singing our squadron ditties. "I belong to Glasgow!" followed "Pistol-packing Momma" and "Gentille Alouette," and gradually we embarked on the more lurid items of our repertoire. Our fellow-guests began to feel embarrassed, to blush, and some of them even discreetly made themselves scarce.

Robson climbed up on a table, upset a few bottles, and we began to intone in chorus 602's war cry:

"Is it one, two, three?"

"No!"

"Is it one, two, three, four, five, six?"

"Siiiiiiiix!"

"Oh?"

"Oooooooh!"

"One, two?"

"Twoooo!"

"One, two, three, four, five."

"Six, hooooo! Twooooooo!"

At that point the captain very nicely reminded us that we had a train to catch. It was just as well he did, for as we were getting up, the proprietor burst in escorted by two policemen and half a dozen M.P.'s. After a few minutes of confused explanations we succeeded in getting rid of them, and surged down the Piccadilly Circus underground. A civilian permitted himself an out-of-place remark about "those good-for-nothing R.A.F. blokes." Robson and Bob Courly inserted an umbrella into the moving staircase, which jammed with a terrifying din. We took a compartment by storm, the passengers regarding us with a mixture of incredulity and horror, and finally we found ourselves at King's Cross.

We piled our luggage on the electric trolleys. Carpenter took over the controls and embarked on an epic dash along the platforms crowded with travellers, warning bell going full blast. It was such a riot that the stationmaster took a hand in person, followed by an imposing escort of Military Police. An unwise move on his part, for within a minute or two his beautiful cap covered with gold braid had mysteriously found its way into Tommy's suitcase. This cap now figures among the Flight's most valued trophies, together with a London policeman's helmet, a Canadian general's beret and a Panzer Grenadier colonel's forage cap, brought back from Dieppe by Bill Loud.

The platforms were swarming with people and, what with the blackout, it was hard to find our way about. However, we did eventually succeed in finding our reserved compartment, at the door of which an M.P. and a railway official were mounting guard.

Our Pullman was divided into two, with a communicating door. The other half was occupied by 129 Squadron from Hornchurch, also going "on rest." We soon made friends. A terrific racket again, everyone singing, bottles flying. Round about 2 a.m. we organized a Rugger match, but it fizzled out, for lack of players.

By 3 o'clock everyone was asleep, on the seats, under the tables, on the carpet in the gangway, even in the luggage racks.

* * *

18th January, 1944

It was a pitiful squadron which emerged from the train at Aberdeen at about 5 o'clock in the morning. Dishevelled, unshaven, covered with soot, our mouths like the bottom of a parrot's cage, we first had to unload our luggage and manhandle it over to the lorries and buses taking us to Peterhead.

There we embarked in two gigantic Harrow transports, piling our baggage in the fuselages. I noticed that each one of us unobtrusively sat down on his parachute bag. Some clot began repeating the story of how a Harrow had been shot down on this trip by a Junkers 88 a few weeks earlier.

During the take-off, we all clenched our teeth, but when we were airborne we heaved a sigh of relief and began to crack a few jokes. Not for long! The air was far from calm and the machine began to pitch and toss, shaken by air pockets.

The laughs soon gave way to a general mood of profound gloom. This pathological state was not unconnected with the state of our stomachs, which had not yet recovered from the corrosive mixture of beer and whisky.

Every pilot held his head in his hands, his elbows on his knees, and nobody thought of admiring the superb snow-covered country over which we were passing.

We reeled out of the Harrow at our destination with dry throats and asleep on our feet. We wished the Station Commander would go to hell as he did his utmost to make us welcome in a charming little speech, which we had to listen to standing in the open under the piercing blasts of the wind.

Skeabrae in winter might just as well be the North Pole. God knows what maniac at Air Ministry had the bright idea of setting up a fighter base in those god-forsaken islands. A few hours' daylight in the twenty-four; occasionally a gleam of sun pierces the wan clouds, disperses the arctic mist and reveals a desolate countryside, wind-swept rocks emerging from the thick snow.

A few miles away, sheltered by a group of islands similar to ours, was the great naval base of Scapa Flow where the Home Fleet lay, protected by mine barrages and anti-submarine nets.

602's role was to foil any attempts at bombing or aerial reconnaissance on the part of the Luftwaffe.

We found our aircraft sheltering against the ice-laden hurricanes in hangars scattered all around the airfield. Seven or eight Spitfire V's, "clipped, clapped, cropped," and in particular four magnificent Strato-Spit VII's, comprised our equipment.

Those Spit VII's were special machines. Their wing span had been increased and thanks to their Rolls-Royce Merlin engines with 2-stage superchargers, and their pressurized cockpits, they could go up to practically 50,000 feet. Only a dozen aircraft of this type had been built, and distributed to strategic points in Great Britain.

Our fitters quickly adopted them and furbished them with loving care. We removed the two machine guns in the wings to lighten them, keeping only the two 20 mm. cannon.

From time to time the Germans hazarded a Junkers 88, which came over at sea-level to try and observe the movements of the Fleet and, just recently, an aircraft of unknown type had succeeded in photographing Scapa from 47,000 feet. We therefore always kept a couple of Spit V's and two of our Strato-Spits at immediate readiness.

*   *   *

A most monotonous week passed. An over-daring Junkers 88 stupidly got itself shot down by a Bofors battery, under the nose of Carpenter and Ken Charney, who came back seething with rage.

To cap all, "B" Flight was detached to the Shetlands, about sixty miles still farther north. They took some fitters and four Spit V's with them. We commiserated with them hypocritically—sooner them than us.

*   *   *

Jacques and I organized an egg-round. Using the little Tiger Moth attached to the Station, we raided the archipelago twice a week, landing near the farms and snaffling all the eggs. At the end of a fortnight of eggs for breakfast, lunch, tea *and* dinner, the very sight of an egg made our gorges rise. Ken even made out that feathers were growing down his back.

*   *   *

Snow fell, the wind blew, snow fell again for a change. We spent our days roasting our fronts and backs in turn round those little R.A.F. stoves. Our poor fitters had the hell of a time with engines freezing and spent hours and hours keeping the wings and the four aircraft in readiness free of ice.

TUSSLE IN THE STRATOSPHERE

21st February, 1944

In a Victorian novel this chapter would be sub-titled, "Or the unexpected consequences of a game of chess."

Jacques and Kelly were on "readiness" from 1030 hours to 1400 hours. Superb weather, but bitterly cold. Not having anything much to do, Ian Blair and I were playing a game of chess. At 12 o'clock everybody went off to lunch, but we decided to finish our game. Kelly enviously watched the others going—this cold sharpened the appetite, and, as usual, he was famished. We ended up by taking pity on him and offered to take their place. They accepted joyfully, for it must be admitted that this high-altitude readiness business was rather a bind.

They went. We slipped on our Mae Wests, put our parachutes and helmets ready in the two Strato-Spit VII's. Ian had not flown one yet and wanted the new one with the pointed tail fin. I gave way, after calling him every name under the sun, and we resumed our game of chess.

*   *   *

1222 hours. "Your queen's had it," said Ian. My queen certainly was cornered, but just as he stretched out his hand to take it, the air-raid siren went.

In the ensuing turmoil, queens, pawns, rooks, everything went for six. The fitters rushed into the corridor with a clatter of nailed boots. I dived for the door, shouting "scramble, scramble!" Ian leapt out of the window.

In less than 50 seconds I was installed, strapped in, oxygen switched on, engine ticking over, while the fitters were screwing down the air-tight hood over me. Three white rockets from control, showing that the runway was clear. The ground was frozen so hard that we could safely cut across the grass to get on the runway.

At 1223 hours 35 seconds exactly, we took off at full throttle, and already control was giving us our first instructions.

"Hallo, Dalmat Red One, Pandor calling, bandit approaching B for Baker, at angels Z for Zebra, climb flat out on vector zero, nine, five. Out!"

I fumbled inside my boot for my code card, which had got mixed up with my maps. I was so clumsy about it that I had to ask Pandor to repeat.

O.K. a Jerry was approaching Scapa Flow, at altitude Z—I looked it up on the card. Phew! Z meant 40,000 feet. I set my course, still climbing at full boost. Ian's Spit hovered a few yards away and I could feel his amused eyes on me under the sun goggles.

It was a wonderful winter's day—not a trace of a cloud in the sky—and the arctic sun pierced my eyeballs. I switched on the heating and set the pressure in my cabin.

"Hallo, Dalmat Red One. Pandor calling, bandit now over B for Baker. Hurry up!"

"Hallo, Pandor, Dalmat answering, am climbing flat out on vector 095, am angels R for Roberts."

What did the controller take us for—rockets? In five minutes we had got to 23,000 feet; not bad going.

In the meantime I had been thinking: this Jerry must be a reconnaissance aircraft. In this weather he must be able to get perfect photos. The Fleet's ack-ack couldn't shoot because of us, naturally, and the Navy must be cursing. At all costs we had to get that Hun. If we didn't, the admirals would get us!

* * *

We passed Scapa and continued on course 095°. I glanced back and saw a white "contrail" describing a wide circle over the naval base, about 10,000 feet above us. That must be him.

I wondered what kind of machine it could be—one of the new Junkers 86 P's? Anyway, he wasn't worrying in the slightest and calmly went on taking his photos.

"Hullo, Pierre, Red Two here, smoke trail at 6 o'clock above!"

We were now at 33,000 feet, between the German and Norway. If we could climb another 7,000 feet without being seen, we would have cut off his retreat.

I opened up flat out, easily followed by Ian, whose Spitfire was superior to mine. The Jerry, still showing no sign of alarm—he probably thought he was perfectly safe at that height—started a second run. The heavy ack-ack opened up, but the black puffs were well below the white trail.

Forty-one thousand feet! The cold was really getting frightful and I turned the oxygen full on. Thanks to the pressurized cockpit the pain was bearable. From now on our exhaust gases left a heavy white trail which stretched out and widened behind us like the wake of a ship. We had the sun behind us.

The Jerry was now coming towards us. Either he had seen us and was trying to get by before we were in a position to intercept him, or else he had simply completed his task.

Our special engines were pulling beautifully and our lengthened wings supported us well in the rarefied air. Ian was parallel to me, about 900 yards away, and we had gained about another 2,000 feet, which brought us roughly 1,000 feet higher than our quarry, who was about 2 miles away and approaching rapidly.

He must be as blind as a bat.

"Tally-Ho, Ian, ready to attack?"

"O.K."

* * *

He had seen us, but too late. We converged on him. To our surprise it was a Messerschmitt 109G equipped with two fat auxiliary tanks under the wings. He shone like a newly minted penny and he was camouflaged pale grey above and sky-blue underneath. He had no nationality marks.

First he turned left, but Ian was there, veering towards him. He reversed his turn, saw me, and, with a graceful continuous movement, banked more steeply, rolled gently over on his back, diving vertically in the hope of leaving us standing.

Without hesitating we followed him. He dived straight towards the grey sea which looked congealed, without a wrinkle. He was half a mile ahead of us, with his tanks still fixed to his wings. The speed increased dizzily. At these heights you have to be careful because you soon reach the speed of sound and then, look out! There is a strong risk of finding yourself hanging on a parachute, in your underpants, in less time than it takes to describe it.

The Hun made full use of his GM-1 booster and kept his lead. At 27,000 feet my A.S. indicator showed 440 m.p.h., i.e. a true speed of 600 m.p.h.! I had both hands on the stick and I leant on the controls with all my strength to keep the aircraft in a straight line. The slightest swerve would have crumpled up the wings. I felt my Spitfire jumping all the same, and I could see the paint cracking on the wings, while the engine was beginning to race.

The controls were jammed. We still went on down —15,000 feet: Ian passed me; 10,000 feet: Ian was 200 yards ahead and 600 from the Hun. He opened fire—just a short burst.

The Me 109G suddenly tore in half like tissue paper, and exploded like a grenade. One wing flew off to one side, the engine and half the fuselage went on falling like a torpedo, while debris fluttered in every direction. One of the tanks went spiralling down leaving behind a trail of burning petrol vapour.

*   *   *

Eight thousand feet. I must straighten out. I pulled on the stick, gently but firmly. In the denser atmosphere the elevators reacted, and I saw the horizon beginning to slide under the nose of my aircraft—but the sea was already there! It was no longer the solid block I saw at 40,000 feet—but a moving greenish mass, fringed with foam, rushing towards me.

I pulled the stick again—no good, I felt I wasn't going to straighten out in time. Then, taking a chance, I gave the trimmer a full turn back. Immediately a veil of blood spread over my eyes, I felt my back and my bones twisting, my guts tearing, my cheeks pulling at my eye sockets, fingers tearing my eyes out. Everything went black. The whole aircraft creaked and groaned.

When I opened my eyes again the headlong momentum had carried me up to 13,000 feet. There was a warm trickle from my nostrils, dripping on to my silk gloves—blood. My head was swimming. I could vaguely hear the controller's voice in the headphones, but the centrifugal force had damaged the valves in my radio and I couldn't make out what he was saying.

I was alone in the sky, I couldn't see Ian anywhere. Down below, a large iridescent patch of oil and petrol and a puff of smoke wafted away by the wind showed the grave of the Messerschmitt.

I set course for the islands I could see on the horizon and soon I could make out the big Scapa Flow barrage with its balloons shining like a rope of pearls. Waves of sickness swept over me and I flew by instinct. Only the thought of our reception when we landed revived me a little. Just as I touched down, I thought I heard Ian over the radio. He was therefore O.K. thank God. I landed with the wind and taxied mechanically up to Dispersal. I hadn't even the strength to help the fitters unscrew my cockpit. Sutherland, warned by control, was there with the intelligence officer. They told me straightaway that Ian was safe and sound. He had made a belly landing in a field on Stronsay, his aircraft damaged by the debris from the Hun. So everything was all right and this success got copiously celebrated in the mess.

The next day the London papers were full of it. You would have thought that we had saved the entire British Navy. We received telegrams of congratulation—from the A.O.C. 12 Group, from Admiral Ramsay, the C. in C.

Ian was brought back from his island in a motor-boat, frozen to the marrow but as happy as a sandboy.

EVENTFUL LANDINGS

7th March, 1944

What a day for the flight! At 6:30 a.m. Oliver and Danny Morgan took off for the dawn patrol over the naval base. At 6:40 Oliver succeeded, with his oil-pressure at zero, in getting back to the airfield and landing without an incident. He immediately changed aircraft and took off again. At 7:20 Ops. rang up in a flap to tell us that Oliver had made a forced landing on the tiny island of Shapinsay.

I was Joe'd for this job, as usual. I was detailed to go and collect him. I took an armourer with me in the Tiger Moth and succeeded in landing without mishap in the only possible field. It was covered with eight inches of snow and mud, and there was a cross-wind. Ollie had pancaked on to it, undercart up.

I brought Ollie back, leaving the armourer to unload the cannon and machine guns and dismantle the secret equipment.

*   *   *

At 7:45 p.m. Jacques and I took off for the night patrol. The sky was cloudless, the moon was in the first quarter, but a very dense mist hugged the ground. For a quarter of an hour, at 7,000 feet, we circled the naval anchorage surrounded by a barrage of balloons.

"Look out, Dalmat Red One, bandit approaching H for Harry from East, 30 miles out, angels O for Orange."

"Roger Novar, Red One out!"

Oh hell! Another game of hide and seek. We switched off our navigation lights. I could only place Jacques' aircraft by the slight glimmer from his exhausts.

By the dim light of a red bulb fixed in the side of the cockpit, I decoded the message with the help of the key for the day. From what we had just been told, the Jerry must be approaching the Fair Isle radar station at a height of less than 1,000 feet.

"Hullo, Dalmat One, steer zero, six, zero—open up if you can, bandit very fast."

We opened the throttle full out and, as soon as we passed the hills on the mainland, we came down to sea level, as in bad visibility it is easier to distinguish an aircraft from below upwards than vice versa—especially over water.

The controller didn't seem in form this evening and, after giving us a dozen contradictory courses amongst the little islands in pursuit of an elusive Junkers 88, he ordered us home. It was 8:30.

The visibility had got worse and worse and Jacques was obliged to follow me in close formation so as not to lose me. I concentrated on my instruments and called my radio station at regular intervals to get a fix. We ended up by finding ourselves over the base, sensed rather than seen, thanks to the regulation red lights indicating obstructions on the ground.

"Hallo, Control, Dalmat Red One calling, over base, about to pancake."

The flarepath was immediately lit up. Its carefully screened flares twinkling in the mist—indistinct, but comforting.

The fog was getting thicker, but as long as I had those flares I wouldn't get lost. Cheered by this thought, I decided to add a quarter of an hour to my night-flying time and let Jacques land first. Ten minutes later I began my approach, opened my cockpit and a moist salt-laden mist swept in. I started on my last 90° turn, which brought me in line with the flarepath and I pushed down the undercart lever. I throttled back and immediately the alarm buzzer went off in my ears! Instinctively, keeping my eye on the runway coming towards me, I felt for the lever and pushed it right down. It gave and I immediately realized the position —the pneumatic system must have packed up and the wheels were not locked in the landing position.

This kind of accident is fairly rare and disagreeable enough in daylight. At night it assumes considerably graver proportions.

I immediately informed flying control of the position and, opening the throttle full out, gained height again, which would enable me to try and get my wheels down by some violent manoeuvre.

Commotion on the ground. Loudspeakers warned my C.O., the station C.O., the ambulance, the M.O., the fire tender, etc. In spite of my efforts nothing happened and, as a last resort, I tried the bottle of compressed carbonic acid gas, but with no result. Clearly not my lucky evening.

A glance at the gauges showed the radiator temperature going up alarmingly and my oil pressure beginning to drop: 110, 115 degrees—80, 70, 60 lbs.

Christ! Spitfire V's have only one radiator, set asymmetrically under the right wing, and the leg of my half-down undercart was masking the radiator air intake; 120° F. being the maximum temperature permissible, I had to make a quick decision.

"Hallo, Belltop Control, Dalmat Red One calling, will you put the floodlight on the patch of grass in front of the watch office—out."

"Roger Red One."

As I had to resign myself to landing wheels-up before the engine exploded, I couldn't do it on the con-

crete runway. With the sparks and the heat produced
by the friction of four tons of metal going at 100
m.p.h., my machine would catch fire immediately.

The 30,000 candle power floodlight lit up a big triangle of grass in front of control and I was going to
try to land my Spit on its belly. Sweat began to
trickle down my back and my vest stuck to my skin
like a cold wet towel. I did my best to prepare myself
for the formidable deceleration—from 100 m.p.h. to
dead stop in the space of 30 yards and half a second.
I tightened the straps of my harness, firmly fixing myself to the seat. I lowered the seat to protect my head,
in case I turned turtle, and I slid back the hood and
locked it tight; at least there was no risk now of being
imprisoned in a burning box. I released my parachute,
undid my oxygen tube and, before pulling out my
headphones, I called control:

"Hallo, Belltop, Dalmat Red One calling. Coming in
now. Switching off to you now. Off!"

It was high time. A continuous stream of sparks was
escaping from my radiator and noxious glycol fumes
were beginning to invade the cockpit. I took in a big
gulp of air and with a slightly shaking hand reduced
throttle, set the propeller to fine pitch, lowered the flaps
and began my approach.

The lamps marking the edge of the airfield shot past
below me and the brightly lit triangle rushed towards
me. I levelled out at about twelve feet, still in shadow.
Suddenly my aircraft flew into the blinding flood of
blue light. Fumbling, I switched off the engine and the
petrol. A cloud of smoke belched forth to left and
right of the cowling.

I held my breath, my eyes fixed on the grass passing
beneath my wings. I could sense the ambulance following me at full speed, followed by the fire tender.
Gently, I eased the stick back, still more, still more,
reducing my speed to the minimum—90 m.p.h.—my
propeller must be just about touching the ground, the
aircraft began to tremble, and I pulled the stick hard,
right back.

No longer held up by anything, the machine crashed

to the ground with an appalling din. Bits of propeller blade flew about, my engine churned the ground, raising mounds of earth and grass. The port cannon twisted like a wisp of straw, tearing the wing.

The shock hurled me forward with incredible violence and the safety straps cut into my flesh, ripped my shoulders. The thought flashed through me that if they didn't hold, my face would be smashed against the sight. I felt a searing pain in my right knee, heard the slapping of the stick against my leg, when the aileron wires broke. Carried forward by its terrific momentum the aircraft stood up on its nose, rose up on one wind and, for one agonizing fraction of a second, I was suspended in space, clinging desperately to the windshield, with one foot on the instrument panel, the ground standing up in front of my eyes like a wall. Would it land on its back? With a crash like thunder, which reverberated in the stretched aluminum box of the fuselage, the aircraft fell back on its belly. A last jerk, then silence . . . which pierced the eardrums. A drop of sweat trickled down my cheek. Then suddenly the hissing sound of glycol and petrol vaporizing against the white-hot metal of the engine. Thick smoke began to emerge through every chink in the cowling. The ambulance bell brought me back to my senses. I pushed open the door with my elbow, threw my helmet outside, jumped on the earth-covered wing, tore out my parachute and, forgetting the excruciating pain in my knee, I removed myself as fast as I could from the neighbourhood of the aircraft. I covered a few yards, staggered and collapsed in Jacques' arms. He had run all the way from our Dispersal 500 yards away and was completely winded. Good old Jacques! Leaning on his shoulder I limped to safety, to where the spectators were outlined in the glare of the floodlights, at a respectful distance. The fire crew were already dousing the aircraft with carbonic foam. I sat down on the grass. Somebody offered me a lighted cigarette and the doctor and his orderlies fussed over me. A screech of brakes and my Squadron Leader emerged dishevelled from his car—he had dashed out of the cinema when the loudspeaker announced that an aircraft was in difficulties.

"Hallo, Closter, old boy! Are you O.K.?" I was bundled into the ambulance in spite of my protests and taken to the Sick Quarters where a cup of hot, sweet tea, generously laced with rum, was waiting for me. My knee was already all swollen and blue, but the M.O. said it was nothing. He then examined my shoulders where the straps had raised two painful purple weals.

By and large I had had a lucky escape.

8th March, 1944

Immediately after breakfast I went and examined the traces of my eventful landing. The aircraft lay at the end of a deep furrow ploughed in the rich earth by the cowling. The oil and glycol radiators had been torn off on the way. The plastic propeller blades had snapped off flush with the spinner, scattering in a thousand fragments.

Afterwards I had to fill in a dozen "crash reports" and, as usual, the technical officer tried to prove to me by A plus B that it was my fault. A heated argument followed until, disconnecting the hydraulic pump, he saw that its spindle was broken. As I really couldn't have broken it with my teeth he had to agree that I had done what I could. Sutherland and Oliver on their side fished out the "pilot's notes" from the bottom of their drawers, to prove that I had acted correctly in the circumstances, and defended me energetically. After a lively interview with the Station Commander, whom I treated to a long technical dissertation (of which he didn't understand one word), I retired to the mess absolutely vindicated.

DIVE-BOMBING

The No-balls question was still giving the R.A.F. a considerable headache, and on our return from the Orkneys it was decided to equip some Spitfires with 500-lb. bombs and make them dive-bomb the flying-bomb sites. 602 and 132 Squadrons were to be the guinea-pigs in this experiment.

On the 13th March we left with our Spitfire IX's, which we had recovered, for Llanbedr, on the North Wales coast, for the first trials.

Dive-bombing with Spitfires is a technique on its own, as the bomb is fixed under the belly of the machine, in the place of the auxiliary tank. If you bomb vertically the propeller is torn off by the bomb. If you bomb at 45°, aiming is very difficult. After various attempts Maxie evolved the following method:

The twelve aircraft ot the squadron made for the objective at 12,000 feet in close reversed echelon formation. As soon as the leader saw the target appear under the trailing edge of his wings he dived, followed by the remainder, at 75°. Each pilot took the objective individually in his sights and everyone came down to 3,000 feet at full throttle. At that point you began to straighten out, counted three and let go your bomb. It was rather rudimentary, but after a fortnight the squadron was landing its bombs inside a 150-yard circle.

During the three weeks we spent at Llanbedr we were the object of visits from every V.I.P. from Inter-Allied G.H.Q., each time we staged a demonstration. They had their money's worth. At the first visit Dumbrell's bomb landed plumb on Fox at 450 m.p.h. and

the poor blighter had to bale out *in extremis*. At the
second visit one bomb, McConachie's, hung up. He decided to land with it and made a run over the airfield
to warn them. As he passed the bomb came free at
last and exploded bang in the middle of the airfield,
covering the dismayed visitors with earth and mud.

Really, apart from Max and Remlinger, who were
always eager beavers and dreamt of nothing but blood
and thunder, nobody was very keen on this brand of
sport. We preferred to await the first results against an
objective well defended by flak before making up our
minds.

In the meantime we had constant lectures on No-
balls. After the first bombardments, in the course of
which 16,432 tons of high explosive had been dropped
on the launching sites in four months, the Germans
had evolved a new type of much simplified installation.
They were erecting more than fifty a month, very well
camouflaged and hard to detect. The total German
layout consisted of nine sectors, four directed against
London and the other five against Southampton,
Portsmouth, Plymouth, Brighton and the harbours of
Dover and Newhaven respectively.

According to the latest information the Flying
Bomb, or V-1, was a jet-propelled device capable of
carrying about a ton of explosive a distance of 250
miles at roughly 425 m.p.h., and highly accurate, i.e.
to within 1,000 yards.

*   *   *

We returned to Detling on the 8th April and waited
without exaggerated impatience for our first dive-
bombing trip.

13th April, 1944

The day before, for the first time, Spitfires had dive-
bombed the Continent. 602 and 132 had attacked the
flying-bomb installation at Bouillancourt, 12 miles
south of Le Tréport.

Although our objective was in an area crammed
with flak, the Germans had been so surprised at the

sight of 24 Spitfires, each carrying a 500-lb. bomb, that they had opened fire only after we were out of range.

16th April, 1944

We were going to repeat the prank on a big scale. We were to bomb Ligercourt, by the forest of Crécy. It was much less funny this time as in a radius of 2,000 yards round the target there were 9 88 mm. guns and 24 20 and 37 mm.—not to mention the fact that we should be within range of Abbeville's formidable defences.

We took off at 1225 hours. We were to attack first, followed by an Australian squadron (453), while 132 covered us against possible enemy fighter reaction. We passed the French coast at 10,000 feet and Sutherland put us into our attacking positions:

"Max aircraft, echelon port, go!"

I was the tenth of the twelve and didn't feel at all happy.

"Max aircraft, target 2 o'clock below."

I could see Ligercourt woods just under my wing and I recognized the target—another flying-bomb site cleverly camouflaged among the trees—from the photos we had been shown at briefing.

We were now immediately above it. With a turn of the hand I depressed the switch that fused the bomb and removed the safety-catch of the release mechanism.

"Max, going down."

Like a fan spreading out, all the Spitfires turned on their backs one after the other and dived straight down. This time the flak opened fire straightaway. Clusters of tracer began to come up towards us. Shells burst to left and right, and just above our heads a ring of fine white puffs from the 20 mm. guns began to form, scarcely visible against the streaky cirrus clouds. Our acceleration, with those heavy bombs, was terrific: in a few seconds we were doing well over 400. I had only just begun to get the target in my sights when the first bombs were already exploding on the ground—a quick flash followed by a cloud of dust and fragments.

Max and Skittles Flights were already climbing again, vertically, jinking hard, stubbornly followed by the flak.

My altimeter showed 3,000 feet and I concentrated on my aim. I pulled the stick gently back to let the target slip under my Spitfire's nose, following our technique—a tough job at that height. I counted aloud—one, two, three—and pressed the release button.

For the next few seconds, as a result of the effect of the violent centrifugal force, I was only dimly aware of what was going on. I recovered to find myself hanging on the propeller, at full throttle, at 8,000 feet. The flak seemed to have given us up. A turn left soon showed me why. 453 were beginning their dive. The aircraft went over like a waterfall and were soon only tiny indistinct patches against the ground.

The flak redoubled. Suddenly there was a flash and a Spitfire turned over, leaving a trail of burning glycol, and crashed into the middle of the target. A horrifying sight, which I couldn't get out of my mind.

*   *   *

A bitter blow, one of the dead pilot's friends told me back at the airfield. It was Bob Yarra, brother of the famous "Slim" of Malta, also brought down by flak the year before. Bob had got a direct hit from a 37 mm. between the radiators as he was diving at well over 400 m.p.h. The two wings of his Spitfire had immediately folded up and come off, tearing off the tail-plane on the way and spattering with debris the aircraft behind, which had to take violent avoiding action. Three seconds later the plane crashed into the ground and exploded. Not the ghost of a chance of baling out.

Those No-balls were certainly beginning to cost us dear.

THE NORMANDY LANDING

The great moment approached. 4th May. 125 Wing left Detling for its new base at Ford, near Brighton.

The transfer of the aircraft took place in very bad weather and our patrol of eight, under Ken Charney, had to land on an American field near Dungeness in pouring rain and visibility zero. This field was occupied by Thunderbolt squadrons which had arrived from the United States the week before. It was the first time these Americans had seen Spitfires from close to. They were flabbergasted to see that people flew in weather like this (what did they expect?—England isn't California) and the manoeuvrability of our machines, our sideslips and S approaches gave them something to think about.

Towards evening the weather cleared and we gave them a demonstration of steep climbing take-offs. With our Spit IX's we were airborne in 50 yards while a laden Thunderbolt needs 600. Immediately after retracting my undercart I did a slow roll that cut the daisies.

At Ford there were already twelve fighter squadrons, and general congestion on the runways and in the billets. We decided to camp out in tents near our aircraft, rather than go and live in a big requisitioned building 6 miles from the airfield, near Arundel.

We were kept pretty busy. On 8th May two dive-bombing trips. On 9th May two dive-bombing trips, including an attack against the famous viaduct at Mirville. There we got a very hot reception from automatic flak and the following official report was published in the press: "Squadrons of Spitfires dived through a wall of flak to attack the big viaduct at Mirville on the railway line between Paris and Le Havre. The viaduct has 39 arches. The Spitfires hit it in the middle and at the northern end."

For those who know the restraint of R.A.F. communiqués the term "wall of flak" was no exaggeration. In fact the bombardment was rather pathetic and I don't know who were the heroes of 132 or 602 who scored hits. I know that my bomb at least fell over 200 yards from the viaduct. Gerald and Canuck were reported missing as a result of this affair.

On 10th May in the morning we carried out a sweep—Marauder escort—which lasted 2 hours 20 minutes. We met some very clever Germans in a mixed formation of Me 109's and Fw 190's. Maxie Sutherland got one, Jacques and Yule probably another each. As for me, my shooting was beneath contempt. In the afternoon of the same day another dive-bombing trip against No-ball 38.

On the 11th, dive-bombing of No-ball 27 (Ailly-le-Vieux-Clocher). On the 12th ditto of a railway junction at Steenbecque. On the 13th two dive-bombing trips, including one against No-ball 86 defended by a formidable array of flak. The constant-speed mechanism in my propeller packed up, which gave me a considerable fright at the time.

At this tempo we were quickly reduced to wrecks. Dive-bombing tests the body severely and we had some bad cases of internal lesions—hæmorrhage in the pleura, abdominal ruptures and other disagreeable complications.

As for me, I was completely creased. Luckily, on the 15th May, Group Captain Rankin was summoned to Allied Expeditionary Air Forces G.H.Q. at Uxbridge. He took me with him. My French uniform provided a bit of local colour, as he put it.

The concrete underground vaults at Uxbridge, which had sheltered British Fighter G.C.C. during the crucial days of the Battle of Britain, had become the Allied air forces centre for the Normandy landing.

It was an absolute Tower of Babel, thronged with

pink and olive-green American uniforms and the blue-grey of the R.A.F. I never in my life saw so many stars and so much braid—up to the elbows. The most insignificant little man you met was at least an Air Commodore. Air Marshals were thick on the ground.

There were Leigh Mallory of the R.A.F., who was C. in C., Quesada; the big noise in American fighter circles, General Arnold, C. in C. U.S. Army Air Forces; Doolittle, of Tokyo raid fame, etc.

Being in the secrets of the great is no joke. I had pocketfuls of passes and all day long I was challenged by hordes of M.P.'s cluttering up the entrances and the underground corridors lit by mercury vapour lamps.

It was difficult to get a general view of what was being hatched, but the invasion date seemed to have been fixed for the first few days in June and the zone too, the strip from Le Havre to Cherbourg. Things did not seem to be going too smoothly. There was a lot of friction between the R.A.F. and the American 8th Air Force.

In particular there were discussions where an attempt was made to decide the number of German fighters available. The production of fighters for the Luftwaffe, from the very accurate reports of the Intelligence Service, had been, from 1st November, 1943, to 1st April, 1944, 7,065 fighters; 150 jet-propelled, about 4,500 Messerschmitt 109 G's and K's, and the rest Focke-Wulf 190's, with a few twin-engined Messerschmitt 410's.

From 15th November to 15th April on the other hand, German fighter losses were estimated as follows: 878 destroyed, 102 probables and 347 damaged by R.A.F. fighters; 73 destroyed, 5 probables and 22 damaged by ack-ack.

The American 8th Air Force, however, claimed that its bombers (Fortresses and Liberators) had obtained the following results during the same period: 2,223 destroyed, 696 probables and 1,818 damaged; plus 1,835 destroyed by their fighter escorts.

The British regarded these figures as ridiculous.

They admitted the right of the American press communiqués to produce such results to sugar the pill for
the American public, which was finding the enormous
Air Force daylight losses hard to swallow. But the
R.A.F. categorically refused to base its plan of campaign on fancy propaganda figures.

The argument soon got heated. The British maintained that it was better to underestimate the number of successes, as they did, by means of a very strict
method of confirmation by cinefilm, than to base them
on individual verbal accounts which were hard to
check. Naturally, when in a box of 72 Flying Fortresses you had 300 or 400 machine gunners blazing
away at 20 Focke-Wulfs, and 5 were in fact brought
down, there were in the nature of things bound to be
several dozen gunners who swore black and blue and
in perfect good faith that they had brought one down.

In addition it seemed very odd that, in a raid like
the one on Augsburg, 900 British and American escort
fighters declared they had brought down 118 German
aircraft while 500 Forts claimed 350 successes, i.e.
almost a third of the German fighters in the air that
day.

In a similar mixed show, for instance, on the same
objective, after a very severe dog-fight, an R.A.F.
squadron (i.e. 12 Spits of the latest type) applied for
the confirmation of 7 successes, while one single American fighter pilot claimed 6 successes, in circumstances
which would have led to his being credited with scarcely one by R.A.F. standards.

It was finally decided to take as a working basis one
third of the American figures for bombers and one half
their fighter pilot claims, which still gave the fairly
impressive figure of 800 successes for the Forts and
900 for the fighters, giving a grand total for the allied
forces of 2,700 Me 109's and Focke-Wulfs out of
action.

Taking into account inevitable wastage, losses in
training and so on, that left the Luftwaffe about
4,000 first-line fighters, out of which a maximum of
2,500 could be operating on the western front.

Against these the Allied Expeditionary Air Forces could pit exactly 2,371 first-line fighters, of which 1,764 were R.A.F.

Next we were kept busy planning the preliminary fighter operations for the second fortnight in May. On the 21st a general offensive was laid on against railway locomotives in the whole of northern France and Belgium; 504 Thunderbolts, 433 Spitfires, 16 Typhoons and 10 Tempests took part in this simultaneous

Tempest Mk V

operation and, in the "Nord" French railway system alone, 67 locomotives were destroyed and 91 seriously damaged.

From 19th May to 1st June, 1944, there were 3,400 fighter sorties against locomotives in France, Belgium, Holland and Germany: 257 were destroyed and 183 seriously damaged. These unimpressive results were due to the pilots' lack of experience against this type of target.

At the same time the fighter bombers had to carry out a very heavy programme of attacks against road and railway bridges; 24 bridges were put out of action over the Seine, 3 at Liège and others at Hasselt, Hérenthals, Namur, Conflans (Pointe Eiffel), Valenciennes, Hirson, Tours and Saumur.

I had the opportunity of seeing the aerial photographs taken after the heavy bombing raid by the R.A.F. on Trappes on the night of 6th-7th March. This important marshalling yard had been completely destroyed. At least 240 one-ton bombs had hit the target. Two-thirds of the loco sheds had been razed to the ground; all the tracks destroyed, including the electrified Paris-Chartres track.

All the marshalling yards from Paris to Brussels were attacked and razed in the period from April to May. The plan to isolate the chosen zone was beginning to bear fruit.

We next had to prepare detailed plans for the aircover of the landing proper which had by then been fixed for 5th June.

The task of the fighters was to destroy on the afternoon of 4th June the three chief German radar stations at Jobourg, Caudecote and Cap d'Antifer. On the 5th, the day of the landing, it was to furnish a permanent protection of 15 fighter squadrons for the convoys and the beaches. It was decided that on days D plus 1, D plus 2 and D plus 3 even the strategic reserve would be used, which would bring the number of fighters and fighter-bombers to 3,483, the R.A.F. providing 2,172 of them.

The programme of advanced bases for our fighters in Normandy was elaborated according to "Shaef" estimates. Favourable sites had been worked out after careful study of P.R.U. photos and on day D plus 10 —i.e. 15th June—we would theoretically have at our disposal:

Three E.L.S. (Emergency Landing Strips), strips of more or less flat ground, 600 by 30 yards, with an ambulance and a fire pump capable of receiving aircraft in distress that had to do belly-landings.

Four R. and R. (Refuelling and Rearming), strips of well-rolled, well-levelled ground, 1,300 by 60 yards, with two dispersal areas well out of the way, each 100 by 50 yards. These runways were to enable fighters to land to refuel and rearm. Special "R.A.F. commando" personnel were earmarked for these, with sufficient technical training to undertake these jobs.

Eight A.L.G. (Advanced Landing Grounds), provided with wire-mesh runways 1,300 by 60 yards with space prepared for the dispersal and protection of 48 fighters permanently based there. Arrangements were made for fixed ack-ack and also for the billeting of the ground and flying personnel. They were to be occupied by 8 fighter wings.

Special engineer units entitled Airfield Construction Units were to leave on D-day with their complete equipment of bulldozers, steam-rollers, tents, steel-mesh, etc., to carry this programme out.

The following spots were chosen: Bazenville, Sainte-Croix-sur-Mer, Camilly, Coulombs, Martagny, Sommervieu, Lantheuil, Plumetot, Longues, Saint-Pierre-du-Mont, Criqueville, Cardonville, Deux-Jumeaux, Azeville et Carentan, Chapelle, Picauville, Le Molay et Cretteville.

*   *   *

After a fortnight spent at Uxbridge in this way, I was not sorry to join my comrades at Ford again. As I had had to sign an undertaking not to breathe a word to a soul of what I might have seen or heard, I could not answer any of the thousand questions they plagued me with. I had also had to undertake not to fly over enemy-held territory until D-day plus 10 hours. It is easy enough to see why. I might be shot down, and if ever my interrogators should suspect what I knew—in particular the place and the date of the landing—the Germans would stop at nothing to make me talk. To avoid any possible weakening the British, who wished to run no risks and had few illusions as to the ability of the human systems to resist certain arguments, allowed no one who knew even a small part of "Neptune" and "Overlord" to cross the Channel and risk being taken prisoner.

*   *   *

As a result of atmospheric conditions D-day was put
back to 6th June. Bound by my oath, I had to wait
until 5 p.m. before flying. That meant I was able to
watch the formidable procession of gliders and para-
troop-carrying aircraft which started at dawn and
lasted for hours.

Everybody was worn out. 602 carried out a sortie at
0355 hours, another at 9 o'clock, one at 12 o'clock,
one at 1730 hours and finally one at 2035 hours. I
took part in the last two.

It is difficult to give a general impression of the
landing as we saw it from the air. The Channel was
congested with an inextricable jumble of warships,
merchant vessels of every tonnage, tankers, tank landing craft, minesweepers, all dragging their little silvery
barrage balloons at the end of a string. We passed
half a dozen tugs sweating and puffing away, dragging
a kind of enormous concrete tower sitting on a frame
as big as a floating dock—one of the sections of the
"Mulberry" prefabricated harbour.

The weather was not very good. The Channel was
angry and choppy and the smaller craft seemed to be
making heavy weather of it. The low cloud made us
come lower than altitude Z at which we should have
been flying, and leave the safety corridors. As a result
we flew slightly too close to a 10,000-ton cruiser,
Southampton class, escorted by 4 big MTB's. The
cruiser immediately started tacking desperately and signalling by Aldis lamp all sorts of violent things that
nobody could understand. Personally I have never been
able to assimilate Morse, still less visual Morse. To
avoid unpleasantness from her ack-ack we turned our
backs on her as far as we could.

We flew along the Cotentin peninsula. There were
fires all along the coast and a destroyer surrounded by
small boats was sinking near a little island. Our patrol
zone was the area between Montebourg and Carentan.
Its cover name was "Utah Beach." We were covering
101st and 82nd American Airborne Divisions while
the 4th Division which had just landed marched on

Sainte-Mére l'Eglise. We couldn't see much. A few houses were in flames. A few jeeps on the roads. On the German side, to all intents and purposes nothing. Two cruisers were bombarding coastal batteries near the fort of L'Ilette.

The sky was full of American fighters, in pairs. They were wandering about rather haphazard, and showed a tendency to come and sniff at us from very close to. When they seemed too aggressive we showed our teeth and faced them. One Mustang coming out of a cloud actually fired a burst at Graham. Graham, whose shooting was as good as his temper was bad, opened fire on him, but luckily for the Mustang, he missed.

Astonishing absence of reaction on the part of the Luftwaffe. According to the latest Intelligence gen they had in France 385 long-range bombers, 50 assault aircraft, 745 fighters, 450 twin-engined night-fighters, plus reconnaissance aircraft—in all 1,750 first-line aircraft. This force would certainly soon be reinforced if the airfields were not bombed too much.

My second patrol was a desk patrol over "Omaha Beach." It was a nightmare. The night was dark, with low cloud. In the gloom hundreds of aircraft were stooging about without being able to see each other, blinded by the fires raging from Vierville to Isigny. The battle seemed to be bitter in that sector. On the beaches high sea swept charred remnants of landing craft, lit up by salvoes from the batteries planted on the sands.

All the pilots concentrated on I.F. and tried in particular to avoid colliding. About 20 Junkers 88's—the first appearance in force of the Luftwaffe—took advantage of the situation to dive-bomb, rather at random, the concentrations of troops and material compressed on the narrow strip of the beachhead. I heard over the radio 3 pilots from 611 chasing 6 of these Ju 88's and I recognized Marquis' voice shouting:

"I got one of the bastards!"

Sure enough over there to the left a ball of fire fell down from the clouds.

The return to Ford in the inky darkness, and with

the fog beginning to rise, was tricky. Four squadrons of Spitfires arrived in the circuit together. There was a confused medley of green and red navigation lights flashing past in every direction, swearing over the radio and general panic. Almost all the aircraft were short of juice and piled invective on the poor controller to get landing priority. As Jacques and I had carefully saved up our petrol with just this situation in mind, we left the far too crowded and dangerous neighbourhood of the airfield and climbed to 10,000 feet above the scrum. We landed after everyone else without any fuss and bother.

WE SHOOT UP SAINT-ANDRÉ

The first few days of the Normandy landing had not brought the expected swarms of German fighters in our gun-sights. Jacques and I decided to carry out a little scheme that we had been hatching since the previous December.

At that time at Detling we had carefully prepared a shoot-up of the airfield of Evreux/Fauville. A P.R.U. Mustang had sown the seed. It had brought back a remarkable oblique photo showing the German base in minutest detail, including a row of Focke-Wulfs being serviced by a swarm of mechanics which had particularly arrested our attention. In theory it was pure madness—airfield flak almost always got you. In practice, with a bit of luck and a carefully managed element of surprise, we might easily get away with it.

The problem now was not quite the same as in December, as Evreux/Fauville was too close to the battle zone to be in permanent use. Failing Evreux-Fauville our choice fell on Saint-André-de-l'Eure and

Dreux, further inland. We would let circumstances decide which to go for.

It was now a question of convincing Sutherland,
who had been impossible to move the previous time
over the Evreux business. We tackled him at breakfast, not too directly. We suggested he should let us go
on a sort of free-lance sweep. We might take off as a
kind of reserve for the morning's first beachhead patrol, and then, with his consent, break formation and
take a turn round Caen at high altitude. Maxie was
not very keen, but for the sake of peace and quiet he
ended up by giving in.

We took off at 0950 hours behind the 12 Spits of
the squadron. Half-way over we quietly gave them the
slip and we at once gained height. We veered towards
the south-east and the estuary of the Seine. Jacques
was 400 yards to my right and slightly above. Like
that we were mutually covered against any surprise.
The weather was possible—four-tenths cloud at 7,000
feet. Naturally I would have preferred a layer of cloud
farther down which would have given us better protection against flak.

At 1020 hours we were immediately over Lisieux,
its church tower standing out against the surrounding
green. From 15,000 feet we could see the great German airfields at Fauville, Conches, Beaumont-le-Roger
and Saint-André, with Dreux in the distance in a patch
of mist. We circled for a quarter of an hour, scanning
the sky. No one else in the air.

We listened in on the wavelengths of all the different
controls. No information which might interest us.

O.K. then, let's go.

Conches was the nearest airfield. We gave it the
once-over; at first sight everything seemed deserted.

Then Saint-André. Some sort of activity had continued there, according to the Intelligence reports. We
must examine it from closer to. We went down in a
wide spiral. The clouds intermittently hid the airfield,
but on the other hand they prevented us from being
observed by the watchful flak spotters.

Saint-André seemed to have had a terrible pasting

—sticks of bombs criss-crossed over the runway, the hangers were in ruins. On the other hand, all around were trim villages and barns in clumps of trees, connected by little roads.

Mm! Those roads seemed very straight. We came down to 10,000 feet. Just so! Those roads were taxi-ing strips and the barns were hangars, perfectly camouflaged. We must look into this! Yes, sure enough, in front of what looked just like a farm a ray of sun projected the sharply defined shadow of two Heinkel 111's covered with nets.

"Look out, Jacques, two Heinkels down below!"

"O.K. Pierre, they're lovely!"

I opened the throttle and made another circuit, to get into position for the dive, sun behind us. I jettisoned my auxilary tank. In the meantime those blasted clouds had made me lose the two Heinkels. I was almost in position for an attack but however much I stared and stared, it was no good. Only that ray of sun, throwing that revealing shadow, had given the game away. I simply couldn't dive down without a definite objective and risk getting shot up by the flak wandering about in the middle of the airfield at ground level, looking for something to shoot at.

I waggled my wings to warn Jacques of my indecision. He had come in close and we made signs at each other. It was really too silly. I looked at the airfield again. We were going to have to make our minds up quickly—everyone would be on the qui-vive if we went stooging around for hours.

"Look, Pierre, a Hun!"

Jacques and I saw him simultaneously—a small brilliant cross, skimming along the main runway, probably a fighter.

"Going down!"

"Look out, Jacques, your baby is still on!"

"I know!"

I had warned him, and now I had to work fast, before the flak got going. At full throttle, I dived down —450 m.p.h.—quickly, because it would soon be getting unhealthy round here.

The details began to show up more clearly. Between the destroyed hangars there were others, of a different type, half-buried and covered with turf. Bomb craters, most of them filled in. The large main runway was carefully repaired and the craters which pitted it (as we thought, from 13,000 feet) were dummy ones, artistically painted to give the impression of an unserviceable runway. I caught a brief glimpse of men working and of lorries.

I levelled out two or three miles from the airfield and kept right down on the deck, to keep the flak off, roaring over the hedges. At the far end of the airfield I could now see the German in silhouette—it was a Messerschmitt 109. I skimmed along the edge of the field, registering what I could see. In the shade of a clump of trees about 20 brand-new emerald green Focke-Wulfs were warming up. . . . A pilot leapt off a wing on to his face in the grass. . . . More Focke-Wulfs along a hedge. . . . Some Messerschmitts in an orchard . . . some bowsers, covered by branches. . . . Variegated tents scattered about among the bushes. This airfield, which at 13,000 feet had seemed deserted, was simply swarming with aircraft and personnel.

My "109" was getting close—he turned left—I made for the centre of the field to cut him off—I climbed to 150 feet—the flak began, a clumsy cluster of tracers far away to the left. . . . I suddenly found myself nose to nose with another Messerschmitt which, intent on the other one, I hadn't seen. Too late to shoot. His undercart was down, perhaps even his flaps. His fuselage was grey, spotted with green and brown and he had big black crosses on a level with the cockpit.

I passed a few yards from him. He was probably landing, doing about 150 m.p.h.—I was doing 420. The pilot must have had a heart attack!

I was gaining on the other at amazing speed. The flak let fly with all it had, without bothering about him. He must have wondered what on earth was going on. I got him in my sights—only 500 yards—I pressed the button—cannon and machine guns—200 yards, I went on firing—50 yards. Before breaking I had time to see three of my shells burst: one between the engine and the pilot, another on the tail-plane, and the third smashed one of the oléo legs of his undercart. I just avoided him in time, and as I cleared him I saw him turn over on his back and go into a spin.

The flak—and what flak!—was coming up in a sort of wavy curtain, shedding deadly little black puffs everywhere. I turned right and climbed desperately towards the clouds, 10,000 feet a minute, with full boost. It seemed to take ages.

Even when with a sigh I reached the haven of the clouds, the long red trails of tracers kept on stabbing the damp gloom around my aircraft.

What had happened to Jacques? Although he had failed to get rid of his tank he had followed me into the dive, but had lost me as we went through the cloud layer. He had found himself in the middle of the airfield at ground level a few seconds after me, and naturally he got the benefit of all the flak. Hampered by his tank he missed the second Messerschmitt, which landed under his nose. Keeping straight on through the bursting shells he spotted a row of mine-laying Heinkels which he machine-gunned. One of them collapsed in flames with a colossal explosion and another got a burst of 200 mm. and incendiary bullets at point-blank range.

Hard pressed by the flak but, by a miracle, unscathed, he succeeded in joining me above the clouds. We once again passed over the airfield, now covered by an umbrella of black and white puffs, at 10,000 feet. The light flak persisted, in spite of our being out of range, and a salvo of 88 mm. burst far behind us.

My Messerschmitt 109 had crashed in a field at the southern tip of the main runway and the remains were still blazing away near a white ambulance. Trucks were tearing to the scene of the disaster in a cloud of dust. A column of thick black smoke rose from the direction of Jacques' Heinkels.

We came back via Evreux, turning right towards Le Havre, where we caught a glimpse of the concrete

U-Boat pens half wiped out in the recent Lancaster raid. Along the estuary were the oil refineries bombed by the Marauders—a large devastated stretch of land where only the round foundations of the storage tanks were visible. One or two still stood intact, like silver coins.

We climbed to 20,000 feet to avoid the flak, and to take a quick look at a nimbo-stratus layer where, a few hours previously, Johnson's Wing, 126, had shot down three Dorniers.

Going into a shallow dive we set course for Ford, where we landed at 1133 hours. As we taxied towards Dispersal we passed in front of the Intelligence Room. By the door was a deck chair with James Rankin in it, sunning himself. When he saw the black trails on our guns and wings he shot up and came running towards us. He climbed up on my wing and helped me to get unstrapped.

"Any luck, Clostermann?"

I was not too proud of our exploit, which constituted after all a serious breach of control discipline, but I told him what we had been up to. Jacques joined us, bubbling over with joy. Rankin, for appearances' sake, greeted my account rather coldly, but he was not too displeased at bottom. Like a fool I mentioned the flak to Maxie, who landed a few minutes later with the squadron. He hated losing any of his chaps through flak and consequently tore me off a hell of a strip.

The Intelligence Officers were lukewarm, but when we described the rows of camouflaged German fighters they brightened up. G.C.C. was very interested by our report and shut its eyes to the escapade, and called us in after lunch for further information. We were asked to indicate on large-scale plans of Saint-André* the approximate layout of the camouflaged dispersals and we were questioned as to the types of aircraft, etc.

The P.R.U. Mustangs would bless us for they would

---

*N.B.—The author learned after the war at Air Ministry that the airfield he had strafed was Dreux, not Saint-André.

certainly get sent in the late afternoon to take low-level obliques and, after that morning's show, they would get a pleasant reception.

* * *

The next day we had the satisfaction of seeing our report confirmed by the daily Air Ministry secret bulletin, which added that the Luftwaffe had in fact reinforced that sector by withdrawing six wings from the Russian front.

FIRST NIGHT IN FRANCE

11th June, 1944

We were on "readiness" after tea when suddenly we were informed that we were going to spend the night in France.

The "Met" forecasted fog over the south coast for the next morning, which would immobilize the fighters. On the other hand the weather over France would be reasonable and, clearly, if the Spits did not patrol the beachhead the Luftwaffe would come out in strength over Normandy and make a nuisance of itself.

To avoid this, half a dozen squadrons were to take off that very evening, land as best they could on half-finished emergency fields, spend the night there and be ready at dawn for any eventuality. Each pilot must take two blankets and a box of K rations.

Jacques and I were distinctly excited at the idea of being the first French pilots to land in France. We decided to don our full regalia and Jacques took his flask of brandy to celebrate the occasion suitably.

A dash for the billets on our motor-cycles. We took

off at 1830 hours and, after a normal patrol—nothing out of the ordinary to report—we met over Bazenville.

"Hallo, Yellow Three and Four; hallo, Blue Three, you pancake first. Good luck!"

Sutherland was telling us, the Captain, Jacques and me, to land first. Very decent of him.

Jacques and I, in close formation, landed just behind the Captain in an impenetrable cloud of dust. Christ, what dust! It was white and as fine as flour. Stirred up by the slipstream of the propellers it infiltrated everywhere, darkened the sky, suffocated us, found its way into our eyes and ears. We sank in up to our ankles. For 500 yards round the landing strip all traces of green had disappeared—every growing thing was covered by a thick layer, stirred by the slightest breeze.

Two commandos whose eyes only were visible under a crust of dust and sweat, with Tommy-guns slung on their backs, helped me to jump down from my plane and laughed when they recognized my uniform.

"Well, Frenchie, you're welcome to your blasted country!"

Jacques emerged out of a cloud, a handkerchief over his face, and we shook hands—a moving moment all the same. We were treading French soil after four years' absence.

If the truth must be told, instead of the deep emotion I was expecting, what I felt most was profound regret at having brought my smart new "best blue" uniform to such a dump. Already I looked much more like a powdered circus clown than an officer of the Armée de l'Air!

A Captain from the Canadian division stopped in his jeep on his way past to warn us:

"No straying from the airfield. No crossing from one side of the track to the other. Don't touch anything. Avoid areas marked by cloth strips, they are still mined. The Huns have left mines everywhere and only half an hour ago a man was killed and two others wounded by a German sniper hiding in a wood half a mile away who has got telescopic sights."

We all met again behind a hedge where a mobile canteen gave us tea, biscuits and marmalade (all liberally sprinkled with that blasted dust).

Our strip was absolutely stiff with ack-ack—at least a dozen Bofors on the alert with the crews in position.

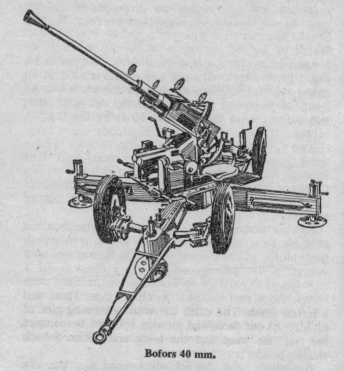

Bofors 40 mm.

When we expressed astonishment at the enormous quantity of empties round the guns a sergeant told us thât if we waited until 11 o'clock that night, we would soon understand.

We spent the next two hours dispersing our planes and refuelling them with two-gallon cans; we puffed, we sweated, we coughed. I spent my time bemoaning

my uniform's fate. When night began to fall we opened
our rations, had a slice of ham and a few biscuits, then
set off in search of a hole to spend the night in. Cautiously ferreting round in the orchard next door
Jacques and I discovered a tent full of chairs, tables,
coco-nut matting and large boards covered with maps.
After a bit of rearranging we succeeded in dossing
down with our blankets in reasonable comfort.

*   *   *

2230 hours. It was now quite dark. Jacques and I
went off to have a smoke and a chat with two Canadian
officers. A few stars were shining. To the south-east we
could see the glow of Caen burning. All was quiet.
Suddenly we heard the hum of an aircraft in the sky.

"Hallo," I said, "that's odd. It sounds like a twin-
engine, but it certainly isn't a Mosquito."

We looked up, trying to locate the sound. It seemed
almost immediately above us.

"Don't worry, Pierre," said Jacques after a moment's
thought, "if it was a Hun the ack-ack would already
have opened fire."

He had scarcely finished when a characteristic
swishing sound disclosed the fact that a large bomb
was coming straight down on us. In a fraction of a
second the two officers evaporated. I dived under a
lorry and Jacques, trying to follow me, tripped over
an apple-tree root and fell flat on his face. There was
a terrific crash. The earth quivered, a burning gust of
air slapped our faces and glowing splinters bespattered
the tent, the trees and the lorry and bounced back
sizzling on the dew-covered grass.

At that moment the ack-ack opened fire. The sky
above us turned into a moving mass of 40 mm. tracer
shells rising in thick snaky clusters. It was as light as
day. Our heads buzzed from the continuous roar.
Shell fragments fell as thick as hail, bringing down
branches and leaves from the trees, riddling the tents
and clanging on the lorries and empty drums. Somewhere on the field a Spit caught fire and the flames
brought the Junkers 88's clustering round like moths.

The bombs began to fall thick and fast. You could tell them apart by the sound—the big thousand-pounders went "Frrrooommm" as they fell, while the medium ones whistled, phweephweephweeeeee—Bang! One fell so close that the impact threw me in the air and I gave myself a large bump against the lorry's differential. A Bofors, less than ten yards away, was blazing away all the time in bursts of five shells. The barking noise pierced our ear-drums. Deafened, battered, we crouched under our lorry, shivering with funk.

Round about 1 a.m. there seemed to be a lull. I sprinted across to our tent to fetch our blankets. I managed to find them under a pile of big boxes and boards, which had collapsed when the first bomb had gone off. If we had been there, we should have had all that down on our heads.

When I got back Jacques had crawled out and was dusting himself and swearing.

Suddenly a pyramid of tracers rose from Arromanches, where the convoys were concentrated, and, like a gas ring with jets lighting up in succession, the whole sky again flared up. The searchlights leaped out of the shadows and started probing the clouds.

Within a radius of twelve miles from our strip there must have been a good three thousand ack-ack guns. As the radar equipment was primitive and control non-existent, all those guns—Bofors, 3½-inch, 7-inch, etc. —fired away more or less haphazard, all at once. The ammunition seemed inexhaustible and the crews just kept their feet on the pedal.

The Junkers 88's and Dornier 217's came over in groups of about a dozen every five minutes or so and stooged around in the middle of this inferno, letting go their bombs more or less anywhere. It didn't really matter where, as the beachhead was so full of troops, ammunition dumps, convoys of lorries, concentrations of tanks and planes that they could scarcely fail to score a bull practically every time.

The nightmare went on until 3 a.m. Worn out, petrified with cold, we ended up by going to sleep, only to be awakened an hour later by the stand-to siren. We emerged from our lorry haggard, grimy, dusty, hirsute, with rings round our eyes and coated tongues and . . . we nearly passed out from the shock —we had spent the night under a lorry-load of 20 mm. shells!

Scarcely able to breathe, we staggered off to join our comrades (who were in no better shape) round the field kitchen where we queued up for a drop of tea. It took a long time as there were only five mugs, the tea was scalding and there were twenty-four of us. Our two Canadian friends from the evening before were there—we thought they had been pulverized by the explosion.

"Oh, you know," said one of them modestly, "we are now pretty hot at sprinting. We've been here a week and we're unbeatable!"

Just at that moment we heard the noise of several engines approaching. Everyone climbed the bank round the perimeter to get a better view. Bang! bang! bang! bang! Three Focke-Wulfs jumped the hedge at the other end of the field and opened fire.

I remember hearing a few bullets whistling past, a few shells exploding in front of us on the field, raising spurts of dust, and suddenly we found ourselves in the shelter, a good length ahead of the Canadians, in an avalanche of pilots, mugs, tea, biscuits and flying boots. After all that we didn't even have our cup of tea!

We went back to Ford in time for lunch—minus four aircraft destroyed or damaged during the bombing. We spent two hours sitting under a nice hot shower.

* * *

The A.L.G. programme had been considerably delayed in our sector by the unexpected resistance of the Germans in Caen, which, according to the plan, ought to have been taken in the afternoon of D-day.

In fact the three first landing-strips built were to all intents and purposes under the fire of heavy 88 mm.

flak batteries. Bazenville, where we had landed four days before and which was to be our real A.L.G., had had to be abandoned.

In the end B11 at Longues was to be our field. Our ground staff, with our mobile echelon, our tents and our lorries, was embarking that evening to prepare our base and we were to settle definitely in France on the evening of 18th June and operate from there thenceforward.

Exactly four years to the day after General de Gaulle had said over the B.B.C.: "Rien n'est perdu parce que cette guerre est une guerre mondiale. Les mêmes moyens qui nous ont vaincus peuvent faire venir un jour la victoire." We were coming back weapon in hand.

*   *   *

17th June, 1944

This time we were finally leaving for France. We were to leave at 8:30 a.m. Two minutes before, cheering news: three-quarters of our matériel had gone to the bottom when the TLC carrying our advance personnel had been sunk by a torpedo. Squadron Leader Grant, the senior M.O., was reported missing, together with two "H.Q." officers.

Hell of a flap. I tore round on Jacques' motor-bike to collect my kit. Naturally, I had too many things to take, as usual; my mechanics kept on screwing and unscrewing all the panels of my Spitfire, trying to stow away the maximum amount of gear in the minimum of space. I scarcely had room to sit down. I hoped to God there wouldn't be a fight on the way over as I could only just move the controls. A clumsy mechanic smashed my superb thermos. I could have murdered him! I sincerely hoped my parachute bag, somewhat insecurely hitched to the wireless set, wouldn't come adrift; it would jam the controls for certain. The rear armour plate had been removed to make room for my sleeping bag and three extra blankets. My camera and my steel helmet were both slung over the hand pump. I had with me two enormous bolonies, a gift of the

Ford cook, my revolver and ammunition and my Mae West stuffed with oranges.

Once I was inside and swaddled up in my cockpit, they went and bunged in a dozen fresh loaves of bread for the mobile echelon which had been existing on biscuits for a week.

We still didn't know where we were going to land. B5 had been intended for our airfield but it had been recaptured by the Germans. All night long work had gone on to make the biggest possible number of planes serviceable. As a result we had 18, 132 had 20 and 453 had 17. As best they could, all these Spitfires crowded in disorder on to the runway. Miraculously there were no collisions.

Everybody took off without mishap and we succeeded in forming up in groups of four. I partnered the captain but after a few minutes he had to return to Ford with engine trouble.

The trip was uneventful. Only a few minutes after we had landed at B9—Bazenville—and had jumped into a trench to shelter from the usual cloud of dust, a dozen Messerschmitts came over the landing strips to cover two Focke-Wulfs which were shooting up B7. A flight of Norwegian Spitfires joined the party and a "109" was brought down a few hundred yards from us. The Jerry baled out.

We spent all day at B9—stifling heat, sand, dust in our eyes; our noses, our teeth. Nothing to eat, nothing to drink. We soon ran out of cigarettes. How I regretted the loss of my thermos full of delicious sugary tea! During "readiness" I had a chat with a few peasants who had come to have a look at our aircraft. Really they gave the impression they couldn't care less about what we were up to. Their chief worry seemed to be our landing strip encroaching on their fields.

In the afternoon we carried out a few patrols, four planes at a time, and dropped our bombs over a variety of objectives. I got rid of mine over the little bridge at Mézons.

At 5 we had a meal in a farmyard. We were famished. Some crafty fellow had unearthed a few highly

welcome cartons of 200 Canadian cigarettes. The farm
was on the edge of a small wood; everything seemed so
calm, the war so distant. The boom of the artillery
hammering Caen reached us in snatches like thunder
on a summer's evening.

However in front of us in a fine, sloping golden
cornfield were three charred Sherman tanks. Quite
close in the shade of a flowering dog-rose hedge there
was a freshly dug grave, covered with flowers, with a
simple board nailed to the wooden cross:

"Ici reposent les restes de neuf soldats et officiers
    du Xᵉ bataillon du Royal Armoured Corps.
        Ils sont morts pour la France.
                Priez pour eux.
                13 juin 1944."

A bit further on behind the hedge, enormous and as
horrible as the corpse of a prehistoric monster, was a
Tiger tank, the one which had destroyed the three
Shermans. It had been hit by a rocket-Typhoon and at
first sight it seemed intact. From closer to, however,
you could see three small holes—two above one of the
tracks and the other plumb in the middle of the black
cross painted on the turret, under the long barrel of
the 88 mm. gun. Impelled by curiosity Jacques and I
went and examined the inside. A shapeless stinking
black mass like molten rubber had flowed over the
driver's seat and the ammunition boxes and covered
the floor. I poked with a stick and a wave of nausea
came over me when a shin bone came to light with
a few shreds still adhering to it.

                *   *   *

Towards dusk we received instructions to land at
B11, i.e. at Longues near Arromanches, where our
airfield was ready for us. Eight aircraft had to carry
out the evening patrol in two sections. Ken led one, I
led the other. The remaining planes left straight for
Longues. Jacques undertook to get our tent in shape.

After an uneventful patrol, we landed at Longues
and were very glad to see our ground crews again.

They had been working for three days to get the base ready and were as hairy as savages.

Second night in France—four German raids during the night—naturally we didn't sleep a wink. Out of curiosity we got up to see the firework display put up by the ack-ack boys.

AN UNNECESSARY DISASTER

You have to be careful of those bloody Huns—you never know whom you are up against.

1730 hours. We were attacking a lorry convoy near Bény-Bocage, led by our new Wing Commander. With these low clouds and the flak I took a pretty dim view of the new system of flying in two sections—one of two planes and one of four. I was flying that day with an excellent section; Jimmy as No. 2, Bruce Dumbrell as No. 3, and Mouse Manson as No. 4. No need of long explanations over the radio with them. Just a waggle of the wings and they went into line abreast—pursuit and battle formation.

"Hallo, Pierre. Two aircraft at 11 o'clock!" came Jimmy's voice.

They were far ahead to the left, flying at tree-top level. At two miles range I could identify them as Focke-Wulfs. I warned the Wing Commander who didn't answer. My section dropped its auxiliary tanks and increased speed. We easily gained on the Jerries. They must be escorting something on the road, probably big priority convoys of petrol bowsers for the panzers hemmed in near Bény-Bocage. A thousand yards from them I left the shelter of the ground and went into a steep climb to put the section in battle formation. The Huns saw us and immediately climbed towards us.

At that precise moment the Wing Commander and his No. 2 cut slap into us and passed through us just as if we weren't there. To avoid a collision I had to break, but the formation of my section was shattered. The two Huns boldly attacked vertically from below. They were pretty hot stuff, those two. Their daring manoeuvre took me completely by surprise. I had meant to cut them off from the clouds, but I hadn't expected to see them on top of us so fast. The new Wing Commander's boob had made me lose my initial advantage. Before I had time to take the slightest avoiding action an enormous radial engine appeared in my windshield and a stream of tracers came straight for me. Instinctively I pushed the stick forward and felt his slipstream on my tail-fin. I just avoided a tree. I turned desperately, stick right back, in time to see a terrific flash on the ground near a farm and a big black cloud. A Spitfire wing bounded up into the air, torn off at the root.

The Wing Commander and his No. 2 had disappeared.

The second Focke-Wulf was chasing a completely panic-stricken Spit which succeeded in reaching the clouds but not without collecting three or four shells on the way. I engaged the Hun, who turned so tight that I almost touched him, without being able to get a sufficient correction to shoot him. A chap who knew the ropes.

"Hallo Max Red Section, Red Two here, please help me; I have had it."

It was Jimmy calling for help.

The Focke-Wulf came back in a vicious side-slip and I had to break so violently that I stalled and only righted myself by a distinctly risky half-roll just above the tree-tops. My heart was in my mouth. I now fired on the Focke-Wulf in my turn but the bastard cleverly skidded out of the way on his short wings and I missed him.

I gained height by an Immelmann. The flak began again—the usual tangle of red and green arrows. I climbed towards the clouds at full throttle. The Focke-Wulfs had disappeared; the engagement had lasted perhaps sixty seconds.

At that moment, in front of me, I saw a Spitfire coming down in a glide, its propeller scarcely turning. A long cloud of burning glycol trailed from its punctured radiators, I read the squadron letters and felt a punch in the stomach which knocked all the breath out of me—LO-S, that was Jimmy. I passed quite close to see—I called:

"Hallo, Jimmy, are you O.K.?"

No answer.

I wanted to do something, to help him, not just sit by horrified and impotent and watch the end of a good friend. In the cockpit I could only make out a vague crumpled shape collapsed over the stick and just behind, in the fuselage, a series of gaping holes regularly spaced.

"Bale out, try, please, for Christ's sake, Jimmy!"

Slowly the Spitfire went into a steeper and steeper dive as if it was trying to do an outside loop. I closed my eyes, feeling sick.

Nothing left but a blazing mass by a roadside.

*　　*　　*

Coming back I felt tears streaming down my nose. What was Max going to say?

I hoped to God Dumbrell had got back. To get shot to pieces in such conditions, four against two—what a disgrace! O God, grant that Bruce got back, I just couldn't explain it away on my own.

Bayeux. . . . Longues at last. There was a busy group round a Spit that had crashed on the edge of the runway. I flew over it to have a look. The pilot thanks be to God, was waving his arms; it was Bruce, safe and sound.

When I landed I found Sutherland completely shattered. He had just heard that he had been posted, and the death of Jimmy and Mouse Manson, his two best friends, had finished him off. When he heard the circumstances he went into one of his berserk rages and we and the captain had to restrain him forcibly, to prevent him from doing something desperate.

Ken Charney took over the temporary command of the squadron until Max should be replaced, and Jonssen, a Norwegian, took over "B" Flight.

FIGHT IN THE FOG

29th June, 1944

It was pouring with rain and on the rounded perspex of my cockpit flowed a thousand rivulets that seemed to appear from nowhere. Under the pressure of the air the water infiltrated through the cracks and collected in small streams which ran on either side of the sight and landed on my knees. A damp patch gradually spread on each of my trouser legs.

I came down lower still amongst the trees, which in the murk I could sense rather than see. Scraps of cloud hung on the hilltops. Half-unconsciously I kept on repeating to myself: I am going to hit a high-tension cable. . . . I am going to hit a high-tension cable. . . .

Suddenly the fog receded and emerging from the rain-cloud I found myself in a gloomy cavern with greenish reflections like an aquarium, bounded by pillars of rain. A funereal light succeeded in penetrating through chinks in the clouds, producing tiers of rainbows hanging from the lowering cloud ceiling like spider's webs.

Then once again I plunged into a thick vapour which blurred the landscape and hid its dangers. Rivulets once again began to course over my cockpit. Each time I turned to avoid a shower I got more lost. My compass, shaken up by my violent manoeuvres, turned

slowly and erratically like a diseased top, stopped for a
second, then almost regretfully started off the other
way. I no longer had the foggiest idea where the north
was. My restricted horizon merely showed a row of
unknown hills bathed in twilight; anonymous roads and
cross-roads succeeded one another, villages drowned
in the mist all looked the same. Through an open door
I caught a momentary glimpse of warm firelight.

Impossible to get my bearings. I daren't ask for a
course by radio. I expected to emerge into a flak zone
at any moment or over an airfield or a strongly defended
marshalling yard. I began to feel the terror of being
alone in a hostile world. I began to expect a deadly
stream of tracer bullets from every hedge, every cross-
road, every wood.

Lost . . . lost . . . lost.

Oh well, to hell with it. I began to climb through
the treacle. My artificial horizon was still all of a dither
but I had to risk climbing on I.F.

The cockpit was now quite steamed over. I climbed
straight up, my eyes on my instruments. My aircraft
was swallowed up. I couldn't even see my wing tips,
though I could feel them shaken by invisible eddies of
warm air. I came out at 10,000 feet into a maze of
clouds. Enormous towering cumuli rose up in the blue
sky to vertiginous heights, forming canyons, gigantic
corridors walled in dazzling white. The shadow of my
Spitfire, projected by the sun, looked like some frolic-
some porpoise. It jumped from cloud to cloud, hugging
the contours, came near, receded, disappeared in
the crevasses, scaled the white ramparts.

Setting course on north and out of range of the flak
I made for the coast, where it would be easier for me
to pinpoint my position. All the same I felt very alone,
and the feeling of independence which you get when
operating on your own gave way to a vague feeling of
anxiety. The Huns had reacted strongly recently in
this neighbourhood and, for once, I would have been
glad of company.

I began to keep a close watch on the sun and the

blue of the sky. To anyone above me my Spitfire must be visible miles off against this cloud background. A glance at the petrol—still about 50 gallons.

The minutes ticked by. I must now be fairly close to the coast, and on the whole I would rather come out under the clouds over France than risk coming out in the middle of the Channel above some trigger-happy naval convoy. I hadn't fired one shell yet and I might perhaps keep my hand in on a German lorry.

As I turned round a cloud I suddenly discovered a dozen black spots coming towards me at full speed—at such speed that they were on top of me before I could make the slightest move. They passed on my right. Jesus! Focke-Wulfs!

They had spotted me too, and broke up in perfect formation, two by two, to cut off my retreat. I was just cruising along, they were doing about 350 m.p.h.—no hope of getting away by climbing; in any case two of them were already immediately above me, waggling their wings. My only hope was to reach the clouds and throw them off by I.F. For one fraction of a second I found myself spiralling down with one pair of Focke-Wulfs above, another turning into me from in front, another one below me and a last one preparing to cut off my retreat. The bomb rack hanging between my two radiators was an unnecessary drag and reduced my speed. I must get rid of it. I pulled desperately on the emergency handle but it wouldn't shift—probably iced up. Sweating, I braced myself and tugged desperately —the handle came away in my hand with part of the cable. I avoided a lateral attack by a quick skid and before another section had time to attack, putting my whole weight on the stick I reversed my turn. Damn! My safety-catch was still on, so although I instinctively pressed the button the Focke-Wulf in my sights slipped by ten yards away. Christ! What about all those other Huns? I couldn't see more than four. Indistinctly I remembered the vital rule. Look out for the Hun you don't see; that's the one that will shoot you down!

I pulled so hard on the stick that I partially blacked out. I couldn't even turn my head, but I felt that those who had disappeared were up there, just waiting for the moment to pounce.

I just avoided a stream of tracers by breaking sharply upwards—unfortunately this manoeuvre put me back just as far from my cloud as I had been at the start. I was in a lather. A nervous tremor in my left leg made it useless. I crouched down in my cockpit with my elbows into my side and keeping my head down so as to be better protected by my back plate. My oxygen mask, pulled down by the g, had slipped over my nose, and I couldn't get it up again, as I had both hands on the controls. I tried breathing through my mouth and felt a trickle of saliva running down my chin into my scarf.

It was now only a question of time. They had me taped; their attacks, perfectly co-ordinated—one from the right followed by one from the left—were going to catch me flat-footed at any moment.. My limbs stiffened, the muscles in my neck contracted, I felt the arteries thumping in my temples, in my wrists, under my knees. . . .

The dust, the earth accumulated under my seat, loosened by the violence of my manoeuvres, flew about in the cockpit. A drop of dirty oil went slap into my eye.

Suddenly a stream of tracers shot past, pretty close. I looked at the rear mirror and nearly passed out; a Focke-Wulf 190 followed by three others was less than 50 yards behind me, its wings lit up by the fire of its four cannon. I vaguely remember being paralysed for a second, frozen to the marrow of my bones and then suddenly feeling a hot flush. The instinct of self-preservation had returned in a flash; a big kick on the rudder bar, stick right back, then sideways, in one continuous movement. The violence of the manoeuvre took me by surprise too. A black veil passed in front of my eyes. I felt something tearing into the fuselage and then an explosion. Luckily my back plate stopped the fragments.

I found myself on my back and saw my four assailants, surprised at my unexpected movement, pass by beneath me. Now or never. I pulled the stick and straightening out on the ailerons hurled myself vertically towards the clouds.

Saved! I stabilized my plane as best I could—none too easy: my instruments were completely haywire. I heaved a sigh of relief. I tried the controls. Everything seemed to answer. Normal engine temperature—nothing vital seemed to have been hit, at least not seriously.

I flew around for 3 or 4 minutes, changing course every 30 seconds. They must have been thrown off the scent by now; however, better come out under the clouds than above, where they must be waiting for me.

I was now rather worse lost than before and I only had 30 gallons of juice left. No possibility of pinpointing my position as my map didn't cover the area I was over. I set course north-east, thinking I had drifted westwards during the fight. I crossed a broad river which could only be the Seine; but that didn't help much. The Seine meanders and the visibility was practically nil. I daren't risk following it down to Le Havre

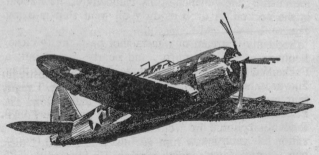

P-47 Thunderbolt

as the Germans had put up strong flak all along its banks, to protect the bridges against the constant attacks from Thunderbolts and Typhoons.

I had to make up my mind: the petrol was getting low. I reduced boost to the minimum and set my propeller to coarse. I had a vague idea I was about 30 miles south-east of Rouen. I flew just below the clouds so that I could nip back into them if any flak started firing at me, and followed a railway line which ought to get me to Rouen without too much trouble. I might even, if a suitable opportunity arose, take a potshot at a locomotive.

* * *

I was mulling over this prospect when, 1,000 yards ahead, an aircraft hove into sight, also following the railway line. I waggled my wings to have a better look at my find. It was a German plane, a Focke-Wulf 190.

I was sure he hadn't seen me. It was certainly one of the bastards who had put me through the hoop—he must have lost contact with the others in the fog.

A discreet glance round me to make sure I was alone. Cautiously, "on tip-toe," I prepared to take my revenge. I daren't open up too much to catch him up, as I was short of juice. But I could turn my 1,300-foot altitude into speed by going into a shallow dive.

I got right behind him, 300 yards away, in the blind area behind his tail-plane. The pilot, unaware of what was going on, was having a fine time, jumping over telegraph poles and hedges along the track and jinking to right and left, incidentally presenting me with a difficult target.

I pulled the stick slightly to get out of his slipstream and got him plumb in the middle of my sight. I really felt like a murderer when I pressed the button. The first burst—the only one—was a bull and the Focke-Wulf disappeared in a cloud of fragments. When the smoke cleared, I saw him go into a left-handed turn, one leg half-down, engine blazing. He mowed down a row of trees along a road by a level-crossing and crashed into the next field, where he exploded.

A couple of runs over the burning remains to photograph them—for confirmation—and then I made for home.

* * *

The return flight was a nightmare, as I only had just enough juice. Wing Commander Yule encouraged me over the radio and gave me a direct course, adding that, if I'd rather, he could direct me towards a convoy where I could bale out.

I decided I preferred trying to get back. On the way I recognized the viaduct at Mirville, which we had dive-bombed a few weeks before. The Germans had begun to repair the two arches we had destroyed. As I passed I let fly at the scaffolding with a few shells.

I landed at B11 with just under a gallon of juice in my tanks and had a large strip torn off me for wandering off so far by myself without letting anybody know.

A SUCCESS AND THE END

2nd July, 1944

"Scramble, south-east of Caen, as many aircraft as possible!"

Frank's shout tore us out of our lethargy. Great commotion! Where were the pilots? Were the aircraft ready?

Most of the pilots were having lunch and, as the squadron had just returned from a show, only a few of the aircraft were refuelled. I unhooked my helmet as I passed, looked for my gloves for a moment, then gave it up; as I hurriedly strapped on my Mae West I asked what wavelength was being used.

"Channel B! Hurry up, for Christ's sake!" shouted Ken who was already racing like a madman towards his plane. Luckily my old LO-D was ready, and my mechanics, who had heard the scramble siren, were already on the wing, holding out my parachute half done up. I put it on like a jacket while Woody started up my engine. I strapped myself in in a hurry. Three aircraft from Flight B were already taking off in a cloud of dust and Ken was waiting for me, with his engine ticking over, at the edge of the track. I took up my position and we took off.

* * *

Queer sort of weather, eight-tenths cloud at 3,000 feet, five-tenths at 7,000 and a great bank of stratus covering the whole of our sector as far as the Orne canal. At 12,000 feet, there was a ten-tenths layer of nimbo-stratus. Ken and I managed to catch up with Frank, the Captain, and Jonssen the Norwegian over Caen at 6,000 feet. Control gave us vague courses to patrol, and told us to keep our eyes open for two unidentified aircraft moving about in the clouds near us. We climbed to 7,000 feet, just on a level with the second cloud layer. In the distance, out of range, a few suspicious black dots were moving among the cumuli. Suddenly Frank's voice sounded in the earphones:

"Look out, chaps, prepare to break port." I went into a slight left-handed turn and looked up. A solid mass of 40 German fighters was emerging from the clouds, 3,000 feet above us. We couldn't identify them yet—Messerschmitts or Focke-Wulfs—but one thing was certain, they were Jerries. The way they flew was unmistakable. The nervous waggling of the wings, their, at first sight, untidy formation. A heady feeling of elation swept over me and my hand trembled so much that I only succeeded in taking off the safety catch at the third attempt. I felt on top of my form. Instinct schooled by long training functioned smoothly; I tightened my safety straps, huddled down on my seat and shifted my feet up the rudder bar. Excitement keyed my muscles to their highest pitch of efficiency, all fear vanished. My fingers were in harmony with the controls, the wings of my plane were extensions of myself, the engine vibrated in my bones.

I began to climb in a spiral. Now! The first 15 Huns

released their auxiliary tanks, fanned out, and dived towards us.

"Break port! Climbing!" Full throttle, 3,000 revs. a minute, we faced the avalanche.

They were Focke-Wulf Ta 152's.* My Spitfire was climbing at 45, hanging on the propeller. I intercepted the first group, which was diving in line ahead on Frank's section. Frank made the mistake of diving for the clouds, presumably to gain speed but forgetting the vital principle: "Never turn your back on the enemy." As we crossed I managed to get in a burst on the front Hun whose wing lit up with the explosions. Three or four puffs of white smoke appeared in his slipstream. Two "long-nose" Focke-Wulfs did a tight turn bringing them head-on to me, and the tracers from their 20 mm. Mauser 151's formed long glittering tentacles snaking towards me and curling down just under my fuselage. The sky began to be a whirling kaleidoscope of black crosses.

In a dog-fight at over 450 m.p.h. you sense rather than see the presence of aircraft circling round, until suddenly your eyes fix on one of them.

I fixed one of them now! A Focke-Wulf. He was circling, his black crosses edged with yellow and his cockpit glittering in the sun. He was waggling his wings looking for an opponent too. Now I had him framed in my sights. Ought I to fire? Not yet. Patience . . . still out of range. But he had seen me, fell off to starboard and went into a tight turn. Two white "contrails" appeared at his wing tips. He then began a vertical climb, straight up like a rocket. Suddenly he turned on his back with such violence that in spite of his change of attitude, his momentum continued to project his glittering belly towards the sun. Within range at last! I jammed my thumb down on the button and my wings shuddered with the recoil of the cannon. With one motion of the stick I made the luminous spot of my gunsight travel along the Hun, through his propeller

---

*A redesigned version of the Fw 190, with a lengthened nose accommodating a DB 603 L engine.

slowly churning through the air like some pathetic windmill. I was now so close to him that every detail was clear. It was one of the latest "long noses" with a Daimler-Benz in-line engine. I could already see the little blue flames of the exhausts, the oxide trail left by the burning gases along his fuselage, his emerald green back and his pale belly like the pike I used to fish for in the old days in the Mayenne. Suddenly the sharp clear picture shook, disintegrated. The gleaming cockpit burst into fragments. My 20 mm. shells tore into him, advancing towards the engine in a series of explosions and sparks that danced on the aluminum. Then a spurt of flame, thick black smoke mingled with flaming particles. I must get out of the way. I put all my weight on the controls and as my Spitfire flicked off I had a last vision of the Focke-Wulf, disappearing down below like a comet towards the shroud of clouds covering the Orne canal.

The whole thing had hardly lasted a few seconds. Never before had I felt to the same extent the sudden panic that grips your throat after you have destroyed an enemy aircraft. All your pent-up energy is suddenly relaxed and the only feeling left is one of lassitude. Your confidence in yourself vanishes. The whole exhausting process of building up your energy again, of sharpening your concentration, of bracing your battered muscles, has to be started all over again. You would be glad to escape, you hurl your aircraft into the wildest manoeuvres, as if all the German fighters in the entire Luftwaffe were banding together, and concentrating their threat exclusively on you. Then the spark strikes again, the partnership of flesh and metal reforms.

To my right a Spitfire broke off and dived behind a Focke-Wulf. I caught a glimpse of the markings—LO-B; it was Ken. I must cover him and, avoiding several determined attacks by Huns, I went into a tight spiral dive—they were moving too fast to follow me.

Ken fired; his wings disgorged long trails of brown smoke and a rain of empties. Intent on watching him I was paying no attention to anything else. A shadow

formed, covering my cockpit. I looked up. Thirty feet
above, a Focke-Wulf's enormous oil-bespattered belly
passed me. He had missed me and opened fire on Ken.

Instinctively I throttled right down, pulled gently
on the stick, aligned him in my sights and, at point-
blank range, opened fire. The stream of steel belched
forth by four machine guns and two cannon smacked
into him at 150 yards range just where the starboard
wing joined the fuselage. The Focke-Wulf, shaken in
its course, skidded violently to the left, and the right
wing folded up in a shower of sparks, parted company
with the fuselage, smashed the tail-plane and whizzed
past me in a hail of fragments.

I had scarcely recovered from my surprise when six
other Focke-Wulfs attacked me. Turmoil ensued and I
defended myself like one possessed. Sweat poured off
me and my bare hand slipped on the stick.

Three thousand feet above, Frank's section was trying to hold its own in a whirling mass of Focke-Wulfs.

The only thing to do was keep constantly turning, while the "152's" stuck to their usual tactics—diving attacks, followed by vertical climbs. We had one
factor on our side; we were fighting 15 miles from our
base, while the Huns were 150 from theirs. They would
be the first to pack up.

All the same, I got a bit fed up with this rigmarole.
I succeeded in nabbing one who was slow in
straightening out from his climb: shells exploded under
his belly. The usual spin, the usual tail of thick black
smoke. It would have been hazardous to go down after
him—I should immediately have had half a dozen
others on top of me. Oh well, he wouldn't be a "certain" but I should be satisfied to have him put down
as a "probable."

No time for repining, anyway. Other things to think
about. My port cannon jammed. I pumped my remaining twenty or so starboard shells into a Focke-Wulf
whom I caught doing an impeccable roll. What an extraordinary idea to do a roll in the middle of a scrap!
As the British say, there is a time and place for everything!

The Focke-Wulfs seemed to have had enough and showed signs of weakening. Apart from three or four who continued to attack, they set course south. I took the opportunity of sidling discreetly off to the clouds. I was exultant, for, in 40 minutes, I had scored three successes, two of which would be confirmed, and I had damaged two other planes. I indulged in the luxury of five victory rolls over Longues, to the joy of the country folk.

*   *   *

I had just returned with Jacques from a shooting-up trip in the Saint-Lô region. We had been greeted by dense flak along a sunken lane crammed with Jerry lorries. One run had been enough to put me off. A 20 mm. shell had exploded under the plate below my seat. I had prudently climbed to 3,000 feet and, in spite of my urgent calls, Jacques had made three attacks through a barrage of tracers. His plane was riddled with holes.

We were having a pint at the mess before getting outside our ration of corned beef and tinned carrots. Lapsley, who had been watching us in an embarrassed way for several minutes, eventually joined us. He ordered a beer from the barman and then hurriedly, like someone taking the bull by the horns, blurted out that I had been recalled from Ops., by superior orders.

I had been half-expecting this for a fortnight, and dreading it. The wing M.O. had found me out and had been surreptitiously doubling my dose of benzedrine, so that my nerves should hold out a bit longer. The bastard must have sent in a report.

After all, that was his job, and I was certainly in pretty poor shape. Jacques himself had several times pointed out that I had a nervous tic like a decrepit drug-addict. And I had certainly lost seventeen pounds in a fortnight. *Sic transit.*

I hated leaving the Flight, particularly at that moment. I had reached that stage of nervous depression when you are afraid of nothing, when you are just not aware of danger. It is also the stage when your reflexes disappear, when you fly mechanically in a sort of artificial complacency produced by benzedrine and fatigue.

A few hours later a strongly escorted Dakota landed at B2. It carried Sir Archibald Sinclair, Minister for Air, accompanied by Air Marshal Sir Arthur Coningham, A.O.C. in C. 2nd Tactical Air Force, and Air Vice Marshal H. J. Broadhurst, A.O.C. 83 Group. It was the classic morale-raising inspection.

The Minister inspected us just as we were, dirty, bearded, covered with dust, dropping with fatigue. The contrast between him in his impeccable striped trousers and morning coat and us with our bedraggled uniforms and our grimy scarves was absurd. The Minister showed true British phlegm, particularly when a Focke-Wulf flew low over the airfield in the middle of his speech. The ack-ack opened up, bits of shell fell like rain and there was a general uproar, but he went on without even raising his head. Jacques whispered that perhaps he was very deaf and very shortsighted.

He took particular notice of the three French pilots in the party—Jacques, Aubertin and I— and congratulated us on our successes. Then taking a small box from his pocket, he discreetly handed me the D.F.C.

Later on I sat on my camp bed gloomily sewing the ribbon on my uniform, surrounded by my untidy possessions, which I was going to have to pack for the nth time.

Exasperating days passed waiting for a boat. There I was, sitting on the grass, while fight followed fight and my LO-D, now piloted by Jacques, took off in a cloud of golden dust, and bursts of 20 mm. ripped the air. It was then that I really understood what friendship meant. I saw an old pal, a comrade in arms, going off on ops. and had to wait for him to come back with my nerves all on edge and a feeling of dread in the pit of my stomach. When we flew together it was quite different.

Jonssen got himself shot down, then Carpenter, then Connolly, one of the new arrivals. Jacques continued his dazzling series of flights.

Finally on 7th July in the evening, Frank Woolley and I left—he had just got his return ticket too—for Arromanches, our kit piled into a jeep. At 2130 hours we embarked on L.C.T. 322

The Second Officer gave me his cabin. I was just about to turn in when a German raid of incredible violence began. I rushed on deck. The scene was lit up by the flashes from the angry Bofors guns. Columns of water thrown up by the bombs raised ghost-like shapes amongst the anchored vessels. A muffled explosion, like a heavy door closing in a cellar, a vast glow, flames rising to the moon, a monstrous pyramid of smoke. It was a tanker blowing up.

Then the hum of the Dorniers faded in the distance, the ack-ack was silent. I remained leaning on the rails, my eyes fixed on the Arromanches cliffs showing through the network of masts and funnels. Over there, from Longues, the clear note of a Spitfire engine rose in the starry night. The battle for Caen was in full swing, yet how calm everything seemed, how peaceful, how distant the sounds. Spasmodically the southern horizon lit up with flashes accompanied by a muffled growling. The town was enduring its martyrdom.

From time to time a cluster of tracers rose up in the sky and then vanished, like a handful of shooting stars. Round me the only sound was the lapping of the rising tide. The air was heavy with the smell of oil and brine. The black waters mirrored the red glow of the burning tanker.

It was all over. I felt in my bones that the liberation of France was now but the question of a few weeks and that by the irony of fate, I would only watch the liberation of Paris from afar.

The tide was up. The Diesel engines began to vibrate in the bowels of the L.C.T. and a big flower of white foam blossomed at the prow. The propellers began to beat their slow and monotonous rhythm, in tune with my heart, heavy with memories, friendship and mourning.

PART THREE

COMMANDS IN THE R.A.F.

THE TYPHOON

After mature reflection, I decided at the beginning of December to return to active operations. I didn't really breathe freely in that H.Q. atmosphere and the three months I spent there, in spite of the many charming people I met, were painful. I did a hop to Paris and the atmosphere there was, to say the least, unpleasant.

Through Jacques, who was now a Squadron Leader at "Tactics," Fighter Command H.Q., Bentley Priory, I kept in touch with the latest phase of the war in the air. When I visited Pete Wyckham, the man most responsible for postings in Fighter Command, he promised to do what he could to help me quickly get into 122 Wing, which was due to return to the Continent equipped with Tempest V's.

A few days later H.Q. French Air Forces in Great Britain received a courteous note from the Air Ministry roughly to the effect that, in view of my experience and record, etc., etc., the R.A.F. would like to have me back, on operational service. The Ministère de l'Air in Paris bluntly replied that there was nothing doing.

A few days later I met General Vallin and, as we strolled about, I put the question of my possible return to the R.A.F. to him. He very decently gave his consent in principle, observing, however, that I was on the list of pilots whom General de Gaulle wanted to retain and prevent from returning to operations. He promised to put in a word at the Ministère.

But time was pressing, and 122 Wing was making preparations to leave.

Then Colonel Coustey, O.C. French Air Forces in Great Britain, came to my rescue. When he saw the state I was reduced to, like a good commanding officer he took it upon himself to authorize my return to the R.A.F. At the same time, with that humour which characterized him, he begged me not to get myself killed, else he would get into trouble.

Quickly, to forestall a possible counter-order from Paris, I said good-bye to Monsieur and Madame Hermann—a French couple who had been living in London for over forty years, and who had looked after me and spoilt me with inconceivable kindness.

That same afternoon I reached Aston Down, where I was to do a quick conversion course on Typhoons and Tempests. Wing Commander Shaw, the Station Commander, when he saw my service flying log-book, decided to skip the formalities and to spare me the theory part of the course.

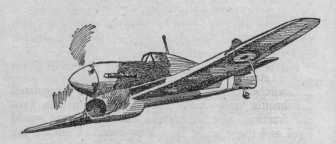

Hawker Typhoon

"All right, old boy, do a few circuits and bumps, and off you go to 83 Group Support Unit. If the weather's good, you can be in Holland within a week."

That evening in the mess I plunged happily back into the clean, frank, open atmosphere of the R.A.F.

* * *

At last a ray of sunshine. In the afternoon I would therefore be able to have my first crack at a Typhoon.

I arrived at my flight with all my kit, and reported to my instructor, MacFar, an Australian, called "Immaculate Mac" because of his scruffy appearance.

With my parachute on my back it took three people to help me up to the Typhoon's cockpit, which is nine feet off the ground. As the plane is very streamlined there is nothing to hang on to. You have to get your fingers in hollows which are covered by metal plates on spring hinges. They close up again when you remove your hand or your foot, just like a rat trap. In the end they hoisted me up, settled me in, slapped me on the back, shouted "good luck," and I found myself all alone inside the bowels of the monster.

I rapidly called back to mind all the gen. my instructors had given me. As the exhaust gases had a high carbon dioxide content, and seeped into the cockpit, you had to breathe oxygen all the time. I therefore hurriedly put on my mask and opened the intake valve. On take-off Typhoons swing hard right and I therefore adjusted the rudder trim very carefully. I opened the radiator wide. I checked the locking of the undercart—the lever looked uncomfortably like the one for the flaps. I lowered the flaps control to open up the pneumatic circuit in order to avoid ram effect just as I started up.

I switched on the instrument panel light. I regulated the throttle lever—open five-eighths of an inch (not one fraction more, otherwise the carburettor would flood and there might be a blow-back). I pushed the pitch-control lever right forward, and then back an inch or so, to avoid run-away in the constant speed unit.

I verified that my tanks were full and selected the centre fuselage tanks for the take-off (gravity feed in case the pump packed up). I unscrewed the Wobble pumps; one sent a mixture of alcohol and ether into the carburettor, the other a mixture of petrol and oil to the cylinders.

I inserted a cartridge into the starter. (The Koffman system, which uses the violent expansion of explosive gases to get the engine turning. If the engine doesn't start first time it will almost certainly catch fire, being bung-full of juice.) With one finger on the coil booster and another on the starter button, I fired the cartridge. The mechanic, hanging on to the wing, helped to "catch" the engine and it started up with a deafening roar. The amount of noise is about five times as great as in a Spitfire. After missing a few times, the engine settled down to a reasonably steady rhythm, though not without exuding oil at every pore. The sound of the engine and the way it vibrated struck me as suspicious. My nerves were very much on edge and I didn't feel at all easy in my mind. What on earth had ever induced me to return on ops.?

These reflections probably lasted some little time because, when I looked up, there were the mechanics looking slightly surprised and waiting for a sign from me to remove the chocks.

I began to taxi—a bit too fast. I must be careful not to overwork the brakes. They over-heated very quickly, and hot brakes don't function.

That engine! You moved forward quite blindly, picking out the way like a crab, with a bit of rudder now left, now right, so as to be able to see in front. Once I was on the edge of the runway, before venturing further I cleared the plugs, as per instructions, by opening up to 3,000 revs., and a film of oil immediately spread over my windshield.

Two Typhoons who were in the circuit landed clumsily, but the controller seemed disinclined to give me the green light. I stuck my head out to make a sign, even though I would probably get a dollop of boiling oil in the eye. Still a red light. Christ, I must have forgotten something—and my confounded engine was beginning to heat. My radiator had already got to 95°. A glance round—my flaps were at 15° all right, my radiator was open.... Hell, the radio! I quickly switched it on and called:

"Hullo, Skydoor, Skydoor, Tiffie 28 calling. May I scramble?"

The controller replied by at last giving me a green light. Here goes! I tightened my straps, released the brakes, carefully aligned myself on the white line down the middle of the concrete and slowly opened the throttle, with my left foot hard down on the rudder bar.

I had been warned that Typhoons swung, but surely not as much as this! And the brute gathered speed like a rocket! I corrected as much as I could with the brakes, but even then I found myself drifting dangerously to the right.

Half-way down the runway my right wheel was practically on the grass. If I came off the concrete I would gracefully flip on my back!

To hell with it! I tore her off the ground.

This plane just had no lateral stability at all. I still went on drifting to starboard and, with those miserable ailerons that only "bit" at speeds higher than 100 m.p.h. I daren't lower my port wing too much.

Luckily they had hauled F hangar down, after a series of accidents all due to the same cause, but even then I passed uncomfortably close to E hangar.

I retracted my undercart but forgot to put the brakes on. A terrific vibration which shook the whole plane from stem to stern reminded me that my wheels had gone into the cavities in the wings still revolving at full speed. I only hoped the tyres hadn't been ruined.

Really, it had been very pleasant behind that office desk. . . .

In the end I got my hand in a bit and felt better. There was a tendency to skid in the turns, but it wasn't too bad.

Just a wee dive to see what happened. Phew! With its seven tons, the thing's acceleration downhill was simply fantastic. I realized with satisfaction that as far as speed was concerned this was much better than a Spitfire. What would it be like in a Tempest!

Half an hour quickly passed and I began to summon up courage for the landing. First a circuit at full throttle at 420 m.p.h., to clear those bloody plugs all over again. But after that I couldn't seem to reduce

speed enough to lower my undercart with safety, even
though I throttled back, swish-tailed violently, and lowered my radiator. One circuit, engine ticking over, at
300 m.p.h. Another circuit, at 250. In desperation I
did a vertical climb, without the engine. This took me
up about 3,000 feet but it reduced my speed to about
200 m.p.h. At this low speed the machine was horribly unstable, and letting down the undercart had an
unexpected effect on the centre of gravity. Once again,
though I had been warned, I was taken by surprise, this
time by terrific swings, more like incipient spins than
anything else.

I asked for permission to land. Cautiously, nice
and straight, and with a good reserve of speed, I made
my approach, lowered the flaps, and everything went
off fine until I tried to level out—those thick wings
seemed to have plenty of "lift," but they were treach-
erous. I had just begun to ease the stick back when
the whole contraption stalled and dropped like a stone.
Then it bounced back a good 30 feet with its nose
in the air, amidst an appalling din.

I opened up like mad to break the fall, wrestling at
the same time with the ailerons so as not to land on
my back.

Eventually, after bucking two or three times like a
mustang, my Typhoon finally calmed down and rolled
drunkenly down the runway, which now looked distinctly short. However, I managed to stop before ram-
ming the scenery, in a cloud of smoke and oil. A
strong smell of burnt rubber rose from my poor tires,
which had stood up valiantly to seven tons landing on
them at 120 m.p.h.

Luckily my poor landing didn't seem to have at-
tracted much attention—there had been such rotten
ones that afternoon, including two involving serious
damage, that, as long as the kite was still in one
piece, it was considered as a good "arrival." My face
was moist, but my morale was better.

A NEW PHASE OF
THE WAR IN THE AIR

The Hawker Tempest V, with its formidable Napier Sabre engine of 24 cylinders arranged in H-form, was the most modern fighter not only of the R.A.F. but of all the Allied Air Forces.

Sydney Camm, the chief designer in the firm of Hawker—he had already designed the famous Hurricane—had taken his latest creation, the Typhoon, which was an assault plane, heavy, massive, thick-winged, capable of carrying a good load, and after 6 months' work had transformed it into the Tempest.

The fuselage was two feet longer, enabling it to house 80 extra gallons of petrol. The undercart was lengthened, to allow for the use of an enormous four-bladed propeller nearly 12 feet in diameter. The spread of the undercart was increased to 16 feet, to increase stability on the ground. Special ultra-thin tires—they had to fit into the wings themselves—were evolved by Dunlop's. Indeed the Tempest's elliptical wings were so thin that special cannon (Hispano type V) had to be designed for them.

The cockpit was moved further aft, to improve downward visibility, and reduced in size to the strict minimum, until it was only a transparent plastic blister on the perfect streamlining of the fuselage. The area of the tail-fin had been doubled to ensure perfect stability at very high speeds, and flaps had been fitted along practically the whole of the trailing edge of the wings to give the maximum safety in landing. All the same, the landing speed was nearly 110 m.p.h.

Nothing was left undone to give the Tempest a

maximum performance at medium and low altitudes. Special auxiliary tanks were designed even, with perspex connecting pipes, to fit under the wings. Quite extraordinary attention was paid to the riveting, the joints and the surface polish. The result was a superb combat machine.

It had a thoroughbred look and, in spite of the big radiator which gave it an angry and wilful appearance, it was astonishingly slender. It was very heavy, all of seven tons. Thanks to its 2,400 h.p. engine it had a considerable margin of excess power and its acceleration was phenomenal. It was pretty tricky to fly, but its performance more than made up for it: at 3,000 feet, at economical cruising speed on one third power (950 h.p.) with two 45-gallon auxiliary tanks, 310 m.p.h. on the clock, i.e. a true air speed of 320 m.p.h.; at fast cruising speed, at half power (1,425 h.p.) without auxiliary tanks, 350 m.p.h. on the clock, i.e. a true air speed of nearly 400 m.p.h.; maximum speed straight and level with +13 boost and 3,850 revs.: 430 m.p.h. on the clock, i.e. a true air speed of 440 m.p.h.

In emergencies you could over-boost it up to nearly 3,000 h.p. and 4,000 revs., and the speed went up to 460 m.p.h. In a dive the Tempest was the only aircraft to reach, without interfering with its handling qualities to any marked extent, sub-sonic speeds, i.e. 550–600 m.p.h.

With its operational radius of 500 miles, its four 20 mm. cannon fed by 800 shells (almost 20 seconds of firing time) and 360 gallons in its tanks, the Tempest was the ideal fighter, a worthy companion to the nocturnal Mosquito.

The two first R.A.F. Tempest units (3 and 56 Squadrons) had been hurriedly equipped and hurled into the battle in June 1944, against the V-1's which were threatening London. Nearly 900 V-1's were exploded by these aircraft over the sea. American Mustangs and P-47 Thunderbolts and R.A.F. Spitfires could only catch these diabolical contrivances by diving on them, which reduced their chances of success.

The Tempests, on the other hand, could stooge about on half-power, then, when they spotted a V-1, they opened up, got into firing position and fired in their own time, thanks to their overwhelming speed.

However, this hasty rushing into action had not been without its disadvantages. The Sabre engine found a diet of 150-grade fuel uncongenial. There were some serious accidents. Snags arose over the induction system (the Sabre was a sleeve-valve engine), over the lubricating system—the oil pressure sometimes suddenly dropped to zero—carbon dioxide found its way into the cockpit, etc.

The worst was the accumulation of petrol and oil fumes in the carburettor air intake, which led, we were told if ever the engine back-fired, to the plane bursting into flames, and sometimes exploding in the air in a matter of seconds.

As soon as the V-1 menace had gone, the Tempests were withdrawn from service. While the organization of a Wing of four squadrons was put in hand, the technical experts from Hawker's and Napier's put their heads together to eliminate these faults. In the meantime, with the winter of 1944, the war had entered a static phase. The allied troops were reforming and consolidating their positions on the left bank of the Rhine.

What was the Luftwaffe up to? For the general public, naturally, Germany had no aircraft and no pilots left. This belief was carefully fostered by the Allied information services for a variety of reasons.

In the first place, the large-scale bomber offensive against the Reich's aircraft factories, in spite of the complete destruction of Warnemünde, Marienburg (Focke-Wulf factories), Wiener-Neustadt and Regensburg (Messerschmitt factories), didn't seem to have produced any visible reduction in the first-line strength of the Luftwaffe.

This created an awkward situation, especially as the Americans published figures of German fighters shot down in the two or three hundreds after every raid over Germany. As these results were gained at the cost of colossal losses (187 Fortresses out of 250 engaged in the raid on Schweinfurt on 14th October, 1943) which made the American public blench, a discreet veil had to be drawn over the activity of the Luftwaffe.

For us who were in daily contact with it and from whom it was obviously impossible to hide the real state of affairs, the optimism of American O.W.I. was not without a certain piquancy. The more Hun fighters the Americans shot down, the more there were!

One fact was certain: the offensive against the assembling factories and the repair workshops of German military aviation, although terribly efficient, had not prevented the production of fighters from going up substantially from July 1943 to March 1945. The Germans succeeded in maintaining a monthly production of 1,200 to 1,700 machines (2,325 in November 1944). It must naturally be added that, had it not been for this bombing, the Germans would have reached the expected production of about 3,000 machines a month in 1944 and 4,500 at the beginning of 1945.

This extraordinary vitality was due to two things: firstly the speed of reconstruction and rehabilitation of bombed factories; secondly the increasing number of invulnerable underground factories.

The Wiener-Neustadt factory for instance, 6 weeks after what seemed to have been total destruction, was turning out 2 Messerschmitt 109's a day. Two weeks later it was 9 and less than 3 months after the raid it was turning out its 15 Messerschmitt 109's per diem. It was a real tour de force, and another costly raid by Fortresses had to be laid on (about 100 never came back). The Germans couldn't keep this up indefinitely. Although the Fortresses' bombs were not heavy enough to destroy the machine tools, the buildings themselves became unusable in spite of makeshift repairs.

It was at that stage that the Germans began to bury their factories. Dr. Kalmmler, in close touch with Goering and through Sonderstab H and Dr. Treiber, took over the direction of the operation. It was an extraordinary feat. As early as January 1944, the Germans had taken a census of all quarries, caves and other suitable sites. They even went to the extent of diverting railways for dozens of miles so as to use the tunnels. The Berlin Underground itself sheltered some assembly lines. As early as April 1944 the R.A.F. and the British Information Services had conclusive proof that the Germans were producing in their underground factories at least 300 complete aircraft and a large number of engines a month.

It was only later, when Germany was occupied, that the full extent of this troglodyte activity could be assessed. In the middle of a large forest near Alt Ruppin the Russians discovered a clearing where nearly 100 Heinkel 162's and Fw 190's were lined up under the

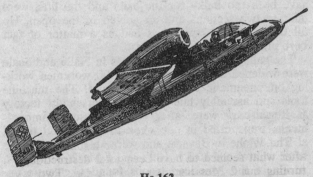

He 162

trees, carefully camouflaged. A little farther on, following a railway line that seemed to lose itself in a clump of trees, they found the entrance to a subterranean factory, 6 acres in extent and with a production capacity of 4 fighters a day. The aircraft were transported in lorries as far as the Berlin-Hamburg autobahn, still under construction, a few miles away. One of the completed sections, 60 yards wide and 2½ miles long and perfectly straight, was used as a runway. The aircraft were then parked in, and sometimes even went on operational flights from, shelters spaced out along this magnificent improvised airfield.

In the Trier region several thousand workmen from Opel and Russelsheim worked in two of the tunnels on the Koblenz-Trier line, producing accessories, undercarriages for the Rochlitz firm, superchargers and turbines for jet aircraft for the Munsfeldwerke of Breslau.

In the great quarries of Halberstadt, near the airfield, wings and fuselages for Focke-Wulf Ta 152's were assembled and taken by lorry to the assembling plants.

In the Berlin underground, between Bergstrasse and Grenzallee stations, the Henschel factory had set up a construction belt for fuselages and tail-planes for Junkers 188's. The completed fuselages, which would have been too bulky for the exits and the lifts, were built in two sections and assembled in the open. Up till the Liberation the joints had as a matter of fact been produced by a firm in Paris.

The galleries in the potash mines in Halle and Saale were widened and each sheltered 800 workmen working on pneumatic and electrical parts. The machine tools and assembly line of the Messerschmitt factory at Regensburg were, after two successive bombardments, transported in one week to a big road tunnel at Eschenlohe in Bavaria and were able, three months later, to turn out 10 Me 109's and 5 Me 262's a week. At Egeln the American troops found a gigantic underground factory which in December 1944 turned out 6 "long-nose" Fw's a day, and in March 1945 10 He 162's a day!

One could quote dozens of similar cases. The Germans were therefore able, contrary to all the estimates, to maintain a very high level of production, in spite of the bombing attacks, of the order of 2,000 aircraft a month.

*   *   *

What were these aircraft and what were they worth? The Germans were mass-producing:

(1) Two types of orthodox single-seater single-engined fighters—the Messerschmitt 109 series K and the Focke-Wulf Ta 152 series C.

(2) Two types of single-seater jet fighters, the Messerschmitt 262 and the Heinkel 162 "Volksjäeger."

(3) A bomber with a crew of three, the Junkers 188.

(4) A bomber-reconnaissance single-seater jet aircraft, the Arado 234.

The Focke-Wulf Ta 152 C was a variant of the standard Fw 190, equipped with a 12-cylinder in-line DB 603 engine of 1,675 h.p. using MW 50 power-boost, instead of the normal radial engine.

This remarkable machine formed the equipment of about half the Jagdgeschwaders in January 1945. It was very fast (440–480 m.p.h.), very manoeuvrable, armed with a 30 mm. cannon mounted in the engine, two 20 mm. Mauser cannon in the wing roots. This Ta 152 was a formidable opponent. Its general performance put it in the same category as the Tempest and gave it a very distinct edge over the American Mustang, Lightning and Thunderbolt, as well as the Spitfire XIV. The Messerschmitt 109 K, equipped with Daimler-Benz 605 of 1,700 h.p. was a lighter equivalent of the Mustang and, in capable hands, could hold its own with the Tempest.

The Messerschmitt 262 jet, with its two Jumo 004-B1 and its four automatic 30 mm. cannon MK 108, was the most sensational fighter aircraft produced up till then. It was the first jet aircraft effectively used in combat. It was mass-produced, and used on a large scale from November 1944. It might have been the greatest fighter of all. Its speed was phenomenal, about 550 m.p.h., and it had a formidable armament with a useful range and 100 shells per cannon, and a very finely designed 89 mm. thick plating. This machine might have revolutionized aerial warfare, but unfortunately (or rather, fortunately), once more Hitler's intuition came into action. He intervened in person, after being present at a demonstration of the machine in April 1943, and forced the designer to modify it in order to turn it into an aircraft for reprisals against England. After a year of alterations, discussions, orders and counter-orders, and in face of the growing Allied counter-offensive, O.K.W. ended up by convincing Hitler. The Messerschmitt 262 was restored to its original rôle of "Kampfzerstoerer" ("destroyer of bombers").

The Messerschmitt 262 was very tricky to fly with a wing loading of 44 lbs. per square foot, a landing speed of just under 200 m.p.h. and a difficult take-off. The turbines also gave trouble and there were certainly high losses through accidents—JG-52, for instance, losing 23 pilots in three months. Nevertheless, the Luftwaffe had *in the line,* as early as January 1945, at least 200 Me 262's of which a third were based on the famous airfield at Rheine-Hopsten, where a concrete runway 3,000 yards long and 70 yards wide was built specially.

The "Volksjäeger"—People's Fighter—Heinkel 162 was also a fascinating machine. It was specially designed for mass production, very easy both to build and to fly and equipped with the minimum armament necessary (two 30 mm. cannon and an endurance of 45 minutes). The "Volksjäegers" were churned out like sausages from 85 factories scattered all over Reich territory.

The Junkers 188 was a fast long-range twin-engined bomber. Although more than 800 of them were built, indeed mass-produced, it was doubtless sacrificed in the last months of the war, since it could only operate with difficulty from improvised airfields, and the last stocks of C3 petrol (96 octane) needed for its BMW 803 and Jumo 213 engines were reserved for the fighters, and the last suitable airfields were turned over to the Me 262's.

The Arado 234 was a jet single-seater and built specially for reconnaissance and bombing. It was not so fast as the Me 262 (530 m.p.h.) but it carried, however, in addition to its two 20 mm. cannon, either

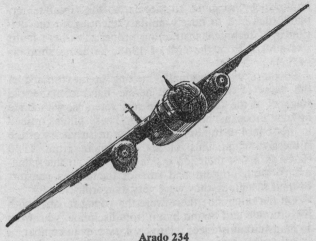

Arado 234

4,400 lbs. of bombs or several automatic cameras. At least three Aufklrungsgruppen (recce. squadrons) were equipped with them by the end of 1944.

*   *   *

The Germans therefore had the machines, and good machines. What about their pilots? Were they up to the crushing task which was imposed on them? Generalizations on this point are more tricky. However, the question can be answered.

In the Luftwaffe there seems to have been no "middle," and German pilots could be divided into two quite distinct categories:

The "aces," 15 to 20 per cent. of the whole—pilots who were really superior to the average of Allied pilots. And the remainder—not up to much. Very brave but incapable of getting the best out of their aircraft.

This hiatus was above all due to the hasty way in which new flying personnel—following on the heavy losses in the Battle of Britain and the Russian Campaign—were hurled into the fray. Their training was over-rapid and not very well balanced; an inordinate importance was given to morale, to the Greater Germany idea and to purely military theories, to the detriment of technical instruction proper. To these faults was added, from the end of 1943, an acute shortage of fuel.

So there was—gradually melting in the furnace of the skies of Europe—the heroic band of "the old stagers" of the Luftwaffe, the real veterans, with three or four thousand hours of flying. These pilots, trained in the school of the Spanish Civil War, survivors of the successive campaigns of the Luftwaffe from 1940 onwards, knew their job inside out, with all the refinements. Both prudent and sure of themselves, masters of their machines, they were very dangerous.

On the other side there were the young fanatics with high morale and bound by an iron discipline, who were in many circumstances relatively easy prey in combat.

All in all the average standard of German fighter pilots was much higher at the turn of the year 1944–5 than at any other time since 1940. This can only be explained—apart from possible considerations of morale, such as the defence of the Fatherland—by the fact that the crack fighter units had absolute priority in everything, including personnel and also the handing out of fuel and lubricants. We were therefore very likely to meet in combat nothing but very experienced pilots, while in 1942, 1943 and early 1944 there had been a rotation of pilots between the Western and Russian fronts which often brought us in contact with units of very middling worth. These were later concentrated exclusively on the Eastern front. In principle the Russian front was a rest cure for the Luftwaffe, quantity mattering more than quality, and the best units were kept in reserve to face the R.A.F. and protect German towns against American daylight bombing. Such, *grosso modo,* was the situation of the Luftwaffe at the end of 1944.

*   *   *

Allied superiority in numbers was effective only as far as reserves were concerned, as there was not a sufficient number of airfields within a reasonable distance of the northern front to cater for the thousand or more aircraft comprising 83 and 84 Groups of the Second Tactical Air Force. The Luftwaffe on the other hand, skilfully scattered over a hundred small airfields grouped round the large major bases of the Arnhem-Osnabrück-Koblenz triangle, could operate in strength.

The Messerschmitt 262's could indulge in tactical reconnaissance over the entire Allied front with impunity, and once again we saw large German formations, sometimes 100 aircraft, machine-gunning and dive-bombing our troops and convoys in daylight.

The Allied reconnaissance aircraft and our fighter bombers had a hard time. Typhoon formations frequently lost 6 or 7 machines out of 12 in encounters with Fw 190's and Me 109's. The Spitfires were powerless. There was only one Wing of 3 Spitfire XIV squadrons and the rest were equipped with Spitfire IX's or Spit XVI's (Spit IX's with Rolls-Royce engines built by Packard in the U.S.A.). In any case all the Spit IX squadrons operated most of the time as fighter-bombers. The Huns, knowing the Spit's quality in a dog-fight, carefully avoided taking them on, and the poor Spits had neither the speed nor the range necessary to force the new German fighters to fight.

The Allied Staff was beginning to get seriously worried by this state of affairs. The situation was similar in the American sector round Luxemburg, but less acute, as the Germans knew that the final attack would come from north of the Ruhr, and they were concentrating on Holland.

The Rundstedt offensive had come as a surprise, and our staffs for once were finding themselves less well-informed than the enemy. The Messerschmitt 262's had given the German General Staff a clear picture of the situation of our troops, while our reconnaissance aircraft were neutralized by the German fighters.

*   *   *

It was to remedy this state of affairs that 122 Wing of the R.A.F. was sent to Holland equipped with Tempests. It was a crack unit and on it depended the entire offensive and tactical system of the British front. Only pilots with at least one complete operational tour or who could prove they had had adequate experience were taken. The Wing comprised Squadrons Nos. 486 (New Zealand), 80, 56 and 274, and in addition No. 41, equipped with Spitfire XIV's.

The Tempests' performance being so sensational, a crushing task was assigned to them:

(1) Neutralization of the German fighters, especially the jets.

(2) Paralysing of the Reich's railway system from the Rhine to Berlin by a systematic daylight onslaught on the locomotives.

With its morale sky-high, feeling it was the apple of the eye of the R.A.F., the Tempest Wing settled down at Volkel in Holland and was hurled into the fray.

It was pretty tough. Flying in twelves and twenty-fours the Tempests went and ferreted out the Focke-Wulfs even on their airfields. Sections of four flew at ground level as far as Berlin several times a day, leaving on their way there the railway lines blocked by locos holed like sieves, and on their way back pitilessly ambushing the Luftwaffe. Pairs of Tempests were kept in a state of immediate readiness, pilots sitting strapped and harnessed in their cockpits, their finger on the starter, ready to take off as soon as an Me 262 crossed our lines.

In a month 52 German fighters were brought down, including 3 Me 262's, and 89 locomotives destroyed. We lost 21 Tempests.

Then came 1st January, 1945, which was to treble Wing 122's task and its responsibility.

THE LUFTWAFFE'S LAST EFFORT

1st January, 1945

When this day dawned the situation of the German armed forces was not exactly rosy. When the Rundstedt offensive petered out, the Nazis, hemmed against the Rhine and hard pressed by the Russian troops in Poland and Czecho-Slovakia, were reduced to the defensive.

However, at about 0745 hours strong formations of Focke-Wulf 190's and Messerschmitt 109's took off from twenty or more snow-covered airfields. At 0805 hours a tiny Taylorcraft "Auster" artillery-spotting aircraft sent over the air a frenzied message: "Have just passed formation of at least 200 Messerschmitts flying low on course 320°."

At 0830 hours on twenty-seven Allied bases stretching from Brussels to Eindhoven, dozens of British and American aircraft were nothing but smouldering heaps. Everywhere tall columns of black smoke rose as straight as cathedral pillars in the still air, where the small grey and white clouds marking the bursts of thousands of ack-ack shells still floated.

General Sperrle had just risked a bold stroke which had no precedent in the entire war. On the airfields of Twente, Appeldoorn, Aldhorn, Hagelo, Münster, Lippstadt, Rheine, Neuenkirchen, Metelen, Harskamp, Teuge, and all their satellites he had massed ten élite Jagdgeschwaders. It was possible later to identify them as JG-2, JG-3, JG-4, JG-5, JG-26, JG-27, JG-52, JG-53 and a few others, in all about 650 Focke-Wulf 190's and 450 Messerschmitt 109 K's.

The evening before, the German pilots did not know

the aim of the operation. At twilight they had taken off from their usual bases and had concentrated on airfields. At 2100 hours lights out—no staying up, no drinking, just a light but substantial meal for all the flying personnel.

At 5 a.m. on the 1st of January they were woken up and Sperrle's masterly plan was unfolded amid general enthusiasm. Goering himself did a lightning tour round the units to encourage them. Every pilot received a large-scale map on which all the Allied airfields and bases were clearly marked (the results of reconnaissance by Me 262's), together with return course, landmarks and detailed routing instructions. At H-hour they took off, concentrated into three massive formations of 300 or 400 machines each, and these three forces, led by three Junkers 188's who were responsible for navigation, set course for the Allied lines.

One of them came down over the Zuider Zee, skimming the waters and the beaches, and came up as far as Brussels. Another came at ground level through Arnhem down as far as Eindhoven, and the third, passing through Venlo, debouched on the American lines. The surprise was complete. For almost half an hour the Messerschmitts and Focke-Wulfs machine-gunned the Allied aircraft massed on the ice-covered perimeter tracks. A few isolated Spitfires succeeded in taking off while the shoot-up was actually in progress.

By an extraordinary twist of fortune 122 Wing was doing a sweep over Germany in force and, when they were called back, most of the Tempests were short of ammunition. By a miracle Volkel was one of the three airfields which were untouched. Everywhere else it was a catastrophe. At Brussels/Evère alone 123 transport aircraft, Flying Fortresses, Typhoons and Spitfires were wiped out. At Eindhoven a Canadian Typhoon Wing, 124, and a Polish Spitfire Wing were nearly destroyed. In all nearly 300 Allied aircraft had been put out of action in a few minutes.

The few Tempests and Spitfires which managed to intervene shot down 36 Huns from the shoals while British and American ack-ack accounted for 57 more, i.e. about 93 German aircraft, whose remains were found after a week of search in our lines.

This operation had been brilliantly worked out and superbly executed. Allied public opinion would have been dealt a staggering blow if it had known of it. The American censorship and the press services, in a flat spin, tried to present this attack as a great Allied victory, by publishing peculiar figures. We pilots were still laughing about them three months later.

The Luftwaffe's success, won at the cost of 100 or so machines, succeeded in nearly paralysing the tactical air force for more than a week. It was only thanks to Air Marshal Broadhurst's energetic action that within twenty-four hours it was possible to reorganize a few fighter squadrons to hold the front. He was in command of 83 Group (the most hit in the affair) and he immediately mobilised in a central pool all the aircraft which had escaped. In addition he rapidly called up reserves from England. I arrived at this juncture.

In the week following, 122 Wing in effect alone kept the aerial offensive going, from dawn to dusk, and in 16 days lost 18 pilots and 23 aircraft.

A DISAPPOINTING RETURN

My training, such as it was, in Typhoons and Tempests being completed, I set off for Holland. I spent my few remaining hours with Jacques, before climbing into the duty Anson with all my paraphernalia.

The usual monotonous and uncomfortable journey on board the old crate. The duty Anson transported everything—pilots posted to units of 83 Group, the post, the newspapers, a bottle of whisky or two, laundry for a mess, somebody's uniform back from the cleaners, sometimes a dog or a mascot. All that piled up in a cabin ten feet by five. Everything vibrated, icy draughts materialized from nowhere and, worst of all, you inevitably felt air-sick within a quarter of an hour.

As I sat on my parachute bag, frozen to the marrow in spite of my Irvine jacket, I went over my conversation with Jacques again, full of a curious mixture of bitterness, fear, and haste to reach my journey's end. How hard this return to active operations was, compared with our arrival at Biggin Hill or 602 Squadron, two years ago. I was in a hurry to get back to the healthy, open atmosphere of a squadron, after four depressing months of offices and liberated France. But I also recognized again the old sinking feeling, the fear in the pit of your stomach before you take off for a flight.

Would I be able to take it?

After 300 operational flights, I was returning with neither the zest of the young pilot newly hatched from O.T.U. nor with the calm self-confidence which comes of long experience. I knew I had been pushed off in a hurry, as soon as permission had been obtained from the French, because flight commanders for Tempests were scarce. Pete Wyckham at Air Ministry had at least been frank with me—122 Wing had lost on an average during the last two months one squadron commander and three flight commanders a fortnight.

"Good luck, Closter old boy. Bags of promotion over in 122 Wing!"

After being comfortably chair-borne for four months, going back on ops. on a type of plane I didn't know, after an hour and a half in a Typhoon and three brief trips in a Tempest, seemed not only risky but practically mad.

I saw myself back in Warmwell, not daring to do a barrel roll in a Tempest, not even a simple loop! How was I going to react to flak, which, according to Jacques, had gotten simply appalling? It had been tough enough in Normandy.

Oh well! At least now they would leave me alone! I wouldn't have to worry about the Ministère de l'Air in Paris, with its incoherence, its senile colonels, its "mem-

bers of the Resistance," its counter-orders, and all those
fishy characters in their shady uniforms who had come
to the surface over there, like the scum on boiling
jam.

We of the Free French Air Force, to whom the
Armée de l'Air owed everything, especially honour, we
who rushed into the holocaust one after the other, as
happy as kids all the same—we, who were proud to
start all over again, to mock the odds against us, wan-
gling extra hours of ops., fagged out, dead beat, nerves
in tatters, lungs burnt out with oxygen—we always got
the thick end of the stick.

The rare survivors of this four-year-long effort had
wanted more than anything else to go home, to tread
French soil again, to see their loved ones again, to live
again the life of the Paris streets, or of their peaceful
native town. But they had quickly come back, bemused,
uncomprehending, though as yet unembittered. They
had been overwhelmed with Resistance stories, with
tales of heroic deeds; the same words had been dinned
into their ears a hundred times over:

"How lucky you were to be in London. Here, we
suffered. If you only knew what risks we ran! In spite
of all that, we kicked the Huns out."

"You can't understand, you don't know what it was
like. So-and-so was shot, so-and-so was tortured, de-
ported."

"What! You're a pilot sous-lieutenant? It's easy to see
decorations weren't hard to come by in London!"

Pilots didn't understand all this. They had done their
best. They didn't want flowers and jollifications. They
expected no reward, except to see their homes again,
even if they were in ruins. They preferred to keep quiet,
but deep down there was a feeling of profound injustice.
What had they gone through? They had only risked
being roasted alive, trapped under the blazing remains
of a Spitfire, or seeing the earth surge up before them,
when, imprisoned in the narrow metal coffin of a cockpit with its hood jammed, you count the four, three,
two seconds left to you to live. Three times a day, for
months on end, they had hurled their poor shrinking

bodies into the flak, missing death by a hair's breadth each time, until the last. . . .

War, for us, was not the desperate bayonet charge of a thousand human beings, sweating with fear, supporting and sustaining each other in a helpless, anonymous massacre. For us, it was a deliberate, individual act, a conscious, scientific sacrifice. Unaided, alone, each one of us had every day to conquer the stab of fear in our breast, to preserve, reform, our ebbing store of will power.

We had to do all that ten times, a hundred times, a thousand times, and then after each mission, take up again a normal healthy life—an appalling strain. The moment we stepped down from our plane, we found other human beings like us, the same flesh and blood, but who walked about, made love, went to the pictures, listened to the wireless as they smoked their pipes and read a book—and who knew they would be alive the next day!

What merely human nerves could go on standing up to this? L——, as brave as a lion for two years, had become a pitiful shadow of his former self. Gouby had crashed into the lorry he was machine-gunning, betrayed by his worn-out reflexes. Mouchotte, lungs burnt out by daily flights at 35,000 feet, had collapsed in his Spitfire in the midst of the fight and disappeared.

There was no relief. It was always the same ones who flew to retain France's stake in the sky. While the others. . . .

After the liberation of France, we went on, to get away from the rank atmosphere of lust and hatred, of servility and haggling, and to preserve our remaining illusions.

For four hours I brooded. The Anson was now over Belgium. The pilot carefully kept to the safety lanes between the ack-ack zones, set up to protect Antwerp against the V-1 offensive.

After that, the south of Holland, monotonously flat, with its canals carving up regular squares of snow. Military convoys congested the roads. Suddenly, an enormous airfield, pitted with craters, with two great brick runways. Wrecked hangars, gutted buildings, here and there what looked like gypsy encampments—piles of empty petrol tins, camouflaged tents. Round each encampment, twenty or so Spitfires or Tempests in impeccable alignment. A snow-plough, surrounded by a cloud of powdered snow, was clearing one of the runways.

"Volkel," said our pilot simply. A green rocket from the control tower and the Anson made its approach. The controller arrived in his jeep just as I was getting out.

"I'm Desmond. You're Clostermann, aren't you? We've heard about you from Lapsley. Yes, he's Kenway's Wing-Co. Ops. I'll take you to Wing H.Q. straightaway. Your kit will be taken to the mess."

122 Wing was commanded by Wing Commander Brooker, D.S.O., D.F.C. He received me standing at the door of his command-post trailer. I was introduced to him and handed him my posting order and my flying log. As he examined them in silence, I had a chance to have a good look at him. He seemed very tired. He looked about thirty and, although his features still looked young enough, his eyes were bloodshot.

"Well, Pierre, I'm glad to have you here. As you know, we are having a pretty busy time. You'll be posted to 274 Squadron and command "A" Flight. You've come at just the right moment, as Fairbanks, who's C.O., was wounded by flak this morning, and Hibbert, the senior flight commander, left yesterday on ten-days' leave; so you'll be in charge until he comes back."

As I climbed into the jeep, he added:

"Don't take too much notice of what the other pilots tell you. Their morale's a bit low, these last few days, because of losses and bad weather. Here are the ops. reports. Have a good look through them and give them back to me tomorrow morning. Get your stuff unpacked—we'll meet in the mess for dinner and I'll introduce your pilots to you."

NORTH SEA

DENMARK

Copenhagen
Kastrup

N

Flensburg
Schleswig
Rendsburg
Fehmarn I.
Plöner Lakes
Lübeck Bay
1 2 3 4
Schwerin
Warnemünde

54°   54°

Bremerhaven

Frisian Islands

Elmshorn
Hamburg
Schwartzebeck
Elbe R.

HOLLAND
Amsterdam
Zuider Zee
Emden
Bremen
Hoya
Steinhuder
Langenhagen
Hanover
Wunsdorf
Egeln

Appeldoorn
1 2 6 8
Arnhem
4 3 5
Osnabrück
Bielefeld
Halberstadt
Halle
Nijmegen
Mettingen
Münster
Uden
Bocholt
Ringenberg
Altenbecken
8
Goch
Wesel 7
Dortmund
Venlo
Ruhr R.
Arnsberg
Herenthals
Cologne
Marienburg

Hassett

Liege
BELGIUM
Remagen
Koblenz
Namur
Rhine R.
GERMANY
Saale

Schweinfurt

Meuse R.
Trier

LÜBECK SITES
1. Neumünster
2. Bad Segenberg
3. Lübeck
4. Ratzeburg
5. Eutin
6. Heiligenhafen
7. Grossenbrode

Augsburg
Lechfeld

DUTCH SITES
1. Harskamp
2. Teuge
3. Twente Canal
4. Hengelo
5. Eindhoven
6. Volkel
7. Gennep

RHINELAND AIRFIELDS
1. Nordhorn
2. Plantlünne
3. Metelen
4. Neuenkirchen
5. Rheine-Hopsten
6. Bramsche
7. Lünen
8. Lippstadt

VOLKEL

Uden was a typical small Dutch town of 2,000 inhabitants, with clean, trim, brick houses, a church every 50 yards and 2 schools. We came back to the mess by jeep, jolting along through the snow and the mud, over the slippery cobblestones, past an interminable convoy which filled the street with its roaring and clanking.

That convoy had become an obsession. When we left in the morning it was already on its way past, engines revving away and back-firing. When we came back in the evening it was still on its way past, a dangerous black mass punctuated by the glimmer of an occasional lamp. From time to time we passed a squadron of tanks, thundering to the front, with smiling crews hanging on to their monstrous steeds.

In the school courtyard were the electricity generators, their Diesel engines corrupting the air. Innumerable wires connected them to the dark building. The engineer officer watched over his dynamos with tender care, especially at night. That didn't prevent him, every time we had a breakdown or atmospherics in our radio receivers, from being abused by us all. Over the door of his trailer he had put up a notice:

"Don't shoot the electrician, he is doing his best."

The officers' mess of 122 Wing was reached down a big school corridor with rows of coat pegs along the walls. On the right were the kitchens, the dining-room and the bar, on the left a ping-pong room and a library. The classrooms had been turned into dormitories. An appalling disorder reigned everywhere: camp beds at all angles, suitcases bulging with dirty clothes, period armchairs, oriental rugs, dirty crockery, cigarette ends, buckets of soapy water, dried mud, revolvers and ammunition, empty bottles, newspapers. On the first floor it was the same again, except in one room, 80 feet by 30 feet, divided up by wooden partitions like dormitories in public schools. A more or less decent order prevailed there.

The Unit Commanders and the old pilots lived there and the batmen had the situation more or less in hand.

The floor above was still inhabited by its rightful occupants and we sometimes passed them on the stairs on their way to the services in the church nearby, silent, lost in a spiritual world which ignored our war and soared above its ills. Yesterday they shared the building with gunners from a German flak battalion, to-day it was an R.A.F. Wing, and tomorrow? Only God knew.

Like was very quiet at Volkel. Perhaps the atmosphere of the seminary had something to do with it. On Sunday evenings a curious scent pervaded the corridors—fried bacon, beer and incense!

After a frugal dinner the flight commanders put up on the big blackboard in the dining-room the list of pilots on dawn "readiness" for the next day, who would have to be awakened.

The pilots off duty after tea had to dress up and shave for the evening. They queued up from 4:30 p.m., bucket in hand, in front of the only hot water tap. This was supplied by an oil furnace that was fed with 150-octane petrol. It couldn't take it and blew up every third day.

The others appeared at nightfall, returning from an alert or a trip, muddy, dead beat. They ate their dinner in silence, drank down a glass of beer by the corner of the bar and hurried off to turn in. For a mess bar ours was very quiet—too quiet. The bar is always a gauge of pilots' morale; here it was positively mournful. Yet it was very well stocked, thanks to what we had found in Jerry cellars, thanks to the lorry which the stores types took every fortnight to Naafi headquarters in Paris, thanks also to the arrangements which the more resourceful had made with breweries in Brussels. Never once did cigarettes, liqueurs, whisky, gin, champagne or beer give out.

However, on our Roll of Honour board, on top of an already long list of 123 pilots lost since the Normandy landing, there were now the names of 47 pilots killed or reported missing in the previous month. And February had started badly, with 8 pilots lost in less than ten days. As a result you saw only occasional pilots leaning against the bar, drinking their pint without a word, reading the previous day's London papers, brought by the duty Anson. One or two small groups in a corner were perhaps talking shop in a low voice, while a few more sitting on the ground by themselves, their glasses between their legs, read their letters. Occasionally one would burst in, pick up his chocolate and cigarette ration, hurriedly drink a glass of beer and go upstairs to bed without saying a word.

By 11 o'clock there was scarcely a soul. The barman dozed on his stool, a belated pilot still sipped his whisky, his back to the stove. The last B.B.C. programme could still be heard faintly through the heavy smoke-laden atmosphere.

*   *   *

4 o'clock. The beam from an electric torch seared your eyes through the lids and a hand shook your shoulder.

"Time to get up, sir."

The M.P. ticked a name on his list and noiselessly went off in his gumboots to wake up the other pilots on dawn "readiness." It was cold, you felt empty headed. Painfully you left the warmth of the blankets; you put on your battledress, your pullovers, your flying boots, smoking a cigarette which made you feel slightly sick. Your Irvine jacket on your back, muffled up in a Balaclava, you went down to the icy dining-room. The frosted window panes gave back a pale reflection of the electric light bulbs. A half-asleep mess waiter brought grilled sausages and scalding tea, which you swallowed sitting astride the benches. Late comers tore down the stairs, banged the doors, put a sausage between two pieces of bread and margarine, swore as they swallowed the hot tea, and rushed out to join their comrades in front of the entrance. The lorry was already there, the N.C.O. pilots sitting inside, smoking.

As flight commander I was entitled to the use of a jeep and a man from the transport section had brought one round for me. Accompanied by my two section leaders, my hands still numb with cold, I drove off, keeping my eyes on the red tail lamp of the lorry in front of me. There was ice on the road and as, since that 1st January show, headlights were not allowed, I had difficulty in following it.

An icy wind blew over the airfield, lifting the snow in damp clouds which pierced us to the marrow.

In the Dispersal hut the timekeeper had lit the stove and the kettle was beginning to sing on the Primus. Outside JJ-B—my aircraft—was so close that it seemed that its wing tip rattled against the boards of the hut. The wind found its way in in spite of the carpets hanging on the walls.

It was like being at a meeting of sleepwalkers. My pilots were doing two, and often three, very tough operations a day, and sometimes were 10 hours on "readiness." They went to bed worn out and got up still tired. Numbed by the cold, their eyes heavy with sleep, they took down their parachutes, checked their helmets, staggered out and hauled themselves up on the slippery wings to get their planes ready.

The mechanics also led a dog's life. In that cold you had to have a night crew every 20 minutes to start up the engines and warm them up to 110°. It would have been catastrophic to let the oil in those sleeve-valve engines get too cold, as it was impossible to get the frozen oil feeds cleared. As a result the engines had to be run-up day and night.

0445 hours. The timekeeper rang through to Group Control to report that six Talbot aircraft were in a state of immediate readiness and would be called Blue Section. He then read out the names of the pilots with their call-signs and their positions in the section. He then passed me the telephone. It was Lapsley at the other end.

"Hallo, Pierre; got you up early this morning! The weather's pretty lousy but the controller doesn't want to relax the state of readiness as one or two jets might very well try to slip through to take photos of our lines under that blasted cloud cover. All right? Cheerio; be on your toes, just in case."

I hung up and went outside, shivering, to look round and see that everything was in order. Dawn was just breaking. The Flying Control lorries were picking up the night-flying flarepath.

With these low clouds, this sleet now coming down incessantly, not much chance of flying. Brr. . . . I nipped inside again. Complete silence in the hut. Sunk in their armchairs the pilots were all asleep. I took the opportunity of going through the order books, the RT procedure and the last battle reports, stuck up on the door.

The timekeeper noiselessly refilled his stove. The damp wood gave off an evil-smelling yellow smoke. I ended up by dropping off myself.

I was woken up with a start by the noisy arrival of the rest of the pilots, Squadron Leader Fairbanks at their head. A glance at my watch—already 8:15.

Fairbanks, an American who had joined up in the R.C.A.F. in 1941, was a tall fair, extremely pleasant fellow with delicate features like a girl. I got up and introduced myself. He had a frank firm handshake. In spite of his rather dreamy blue eyes he was an ace fighter pilot and a D.F.C. and bar adorned his chest. He had shot down 14 Huns, 12 in the previous month, including 2 jet Messerschmitt 262's.

He gave me a cigarette, we drank a cup of tea. I gave him the latest gen, and handed him the "Met." report, which needed no comment. We sat down and had a yarn. As usual we found we had a host of friends in common.

Fairbanks' tactics were very interesting and required a good deal of nerve. What a pity Jacques wasn't there! This would have been up his street. Broadly speaking, this was Fairbanks' technique.

The most frequented Jerry airfield was at Rheine, where a great many fighters were based. It took 8 minutes to get from Volkel to Rheine, thanks to the Tempest's colossal speed. Therefore Fairbanks had got into the habit of going there roughly once a day, generally round about 5 p.m. with only a section of four, sometimes even only a pair. When he got to the Rheine neighbourhood he kept just under cloud base—an average of 3,000 feet at this time of year—circling the airfield sometimes for as long as a quarter of an hour. Now and then, in spite of the flak, which was extremely dense and accurate just there, he dived to ground level, stayed on the deck for a few seconds then climbed back into the clouds fast. He used these few seconds to watch for enemy aircraft in the circuit. He almost always managed to establish contact with a flight of Messerschmitts or Focke-Wulfs which he immediately attacked hell for leather, taking advantage of the element of surprise. Usually he shot one down and ran for cloud cover. To be objective it must be pointed out that these tactics had enabled him to run up a remarkable personal score. On the other hand, he often lost his number two's.

"I'll make a milk-run to Rheine this evening if the weather clears a bit. If you'd like to see how I operate all you have to do is to come with my section as a reserve and you'll get the idea. I must get my hand in again; after seven days' leave you get a bit rusty."

TEMPEST VS. FOCKE-WULF

This afternoon the sky was an absolute death trap. We had been looking for trains in the Bremen area without much success. Fairbanks was leading a section of 6

Tempests—myself No. 2, Mossings No. 3, Inglis No. 4, Spence No. 5 and Dunn No. 6. I had pointed out before we started that his section was lop-sided—3 young inexperienced pilots was too many. All the same we attacked a train in a marshalling yard. We were met by dense and accurate flak. Spence was hit in the port wing, and only just had time to jettison his blazing auxiliary tank. Fairbanks had dived to the attack rather steeply and I had had trouble in following him; the 40-odd shells I had scattered in the general direction of the locomotive couldn't have done it much harm. I had climbed up to the clouds again very quickly, with tracers all round me; it was obvious that my nerves couldn't take flak any more.

Fairbanks then led us in zigzags for 10 minutes as far as Osnabrück. Giving up hope of finding another train he set course 260°, which brought us back over the Ruhr. Two hundred Lancasters were carrying out a big daylight raid. There was a good chance of meeting a few Messerschmitt 109's round here.

The sky was still pretty bad. There was a thin translucent layer of ten-tenth's cloud at 10,000 feet and below a medley of small cumuli, between which we wended our way. Just the kind of position where you can't see anything but anyone can see you. Control called us:

"Hallo, Talbot leader? Canary please!"

"Hallo Kenway, Talbot leader answering. Canary coming up in 10 seconds."

Canary was the cover name for the special secret apparatus which Tempests were equipped with. It sent out a certain radar signal when you pressed a yellow button on the right of the cockpit. This signal had the property of duplicating a radar echo and of changing its colour in cathode tubes. This enabled the controller, with much greater precision than the old I.F.F., to identify such and such a formation from several others on a crowded screen.

"Hallo Talbot leader, Kenway calling—there are Huns around coming back from the Ruhr. Can't give you anything definite yet!"

I released the safety catch and checked my reflector

sights. Hell! The bulb had burnt out. Feverishly I took off my gloves, fumbled in the little rack where the spare bulbs were clipped, and unscrewed the base of the sight.

"Look out for Huns coming down at 3 o'clock!" I swore under my breath and looked up, in time to see about thirty Focke-Wulfs peeling off less than 6,000 feet above and diving on us. Instinctively I stopped messing about with the sights and turned to face the attack with the other five aircraft. The base of my sight dangling on the end of the electric wire caught me full in the face, my gloves fell under my seat and a 30 mm. shell exploded in my starboard wing, riddling my fuselage with fragments. A poor start!

Fw Ta 152

A "long-nose" Focke-Wulf practically touched me and passed beneath me with a half roll.

Everything seemed to have got pretty confused.

"Good-bye chaps, I've had it."

It was poor Spence's voice—his Tempest was spinning down, coughing oil and flames. Poor Spence, so proud of his new-born baby.

Now things really began to hum. The Focke-Wulfs, cleverly divided in groups of five or six, attached themselves to each of us. Without my gun-sights, I fired away haphazardly and unsuccessfully at a Jerry who jigged in front of me for a moment. I was disarmed and could take no further part in the show. I warned Fairbanks, who didn't answer, and decided to remove myself. My engine was beginning to heat alarmingly.

In front of me two Focke-Wulfs had collided and their entangled remains were slowly falling, throwing off a hail of flaming fragments. A parachute opened and disappeared at once into a cloud.

Followed by four Huns, I did a vertical climb and waited with my nose pointing up into the sky for the controls to slacken . . . an anxious moment . . . no drop in the speed . . . my Tempest began to vibrate . . . nothing for it! I kicked violently on the rudder bar . . . the sky swivelled round . . . half roll . . . I was upside down . . . I pulled the stick back. . . . What a ropy effort! I obviously wasn't handling my Tempest very well.

One of the Focke-Wulfs had followed my manoeuvre with the greatest of ease and his shells whizzed close by my hood. I now dived vertically. With my 7 tons I quickly reached 500 m.p.h. on the indicator and left the Focke-Wulf far behind. I must straighten out quickly as my damaged wing was vibrating and the skin, ripped by the shrapnel, was tearing dangerously. I crossed the Rhine at less than 150 feet, to the accompaniment of frenzied flak. Besides, I had chosen my spot badly and found myself on the left bank at ground level in the middle of the Wesel pocket. And what flak! Even the machine guns were taking a hand. I now understood why everybody made a detour over Goch. I missed Volkel in the mist and found myself Heaven knows where over the Dutch countryside. All the windmills, all the canals and all the towns looked alike—the map was no help. I asked Desmond for a fix and he brought me back plumb on the base with his first vector.

I made a very poor landing, as my flaps would only

come halfway down and I was afraid they might pack up in the middle of my approach.

Inglis and Dunn had just landed, Mossings was in the circuit. Fairbanks and Spence had been shot down. Inglis and Mossings had each damaged a Hun and Dunn had scored hits on three. The violence of the scrap had prevented the results from being verified.

The mess was rather gloomy that night.

A TRAGIC LANDING

Through the dirty window-panes I was looking at Yellow Section of 274 Squadron returning from an armed reconnaissance. Only three aircraft in the circuit out of four . . . and even then one of the three seemed to have been badly damaged by flak.

Desmond called me on the 'phone and asked me to come at once to the Control Tower. Just as I jumped into the jeep the two first Tempests landed in formation. A cluster of red Verey lights for the guidance of the third rose from the A.C.P.'s* trailer. Desmond was on the balcony of the tower, microphone in hand. Without bothering about the stairs I joined him quickly by shinning up the outside ladder. "It's Alex," he said, handing me his field-glasses, "give him some advice."

Poor Alex must have caught a packet from a 37 mm., and one of the legs of his undercart was dangling pitifully, the wheel half torn off. That leg must be gotten up at all costs; he would never succeed in landing on his belly like this.

"Hallo Alex! Pierre here, try to get your port leg up!"

---

*Aerodrome Control Pilot.

No answer. I said it again, forcing myself to speak slowly and clearly. A few seconds later, at last, Alex's voice answered in the loudspeaker, hesitant and gasping: "Sorry, I can't."

"Try again," I insisted.

The row of his engine at full throttle, the propeller in fine pitch, brought everybody out. I could see people climbing on the roofs of the huts and crowding at doors and windows. Hibbert and Brooker arrived, anxiously following the evolutions of the plane as it dived, climbed, waggling its wings to try and free that blasted wheel. Finally after a dive an object detached itself from the plane, but there was still the oleo-leg.

"Alex, try your CO_2 bottle!" It was his last chance. With my glasses I could see the leg begin to come slowly up in jerks, almost into the cavity in the wing.

"Hallo Pierre, I have used up my CO_2 and the leg isn't fully locked yet."

His voice was trembling. Poor kid! How well I understood his panic, all alone up there, struggling with all that complicated machinery which had now become a death trap. I could almost see him, drenched in sweat, out of breath, desperately hammering at the undercart lever, still pushing on the CO_2 bottle lever although it was empty.

The ambulance started up and moved to the far end of the runway, keeping its engine ticking over. The fire tender followed; the crew on the running boards looking like deep-sea divers in their asbestos suits. The M.O.'s jeep arrived. Alex called me back.

"O.K. Desmond, coming in for belly-landing. Switching off."

"Christ! Clostermann, tell him to bale out!" shouted Brooker. Too late, he had switched off his radio.

The Tempest began its approach. I slid down the side of the ladder and leaped into a jeep. The fire tender got into gear and moved up to the front. People started running along the perimeter track. The Tempest lost height and quickly grew bigger. The brilliant disc of the propeller suddenly broke up as Alex switched off.

He levelled out perfectly. Tail and flaps down, he approached the brick runway.

I trod on the accelerator, pursued by the fire tender's bell and the siren of the ambulance.

The Tempest was about to touch down—the transparent hood flew off through the air. Now! A terrific scraping noise, the propeller buckled up and the 8 tons fell at 200 miles an hour. With a crash like thunder the plane bounced a good 30 feet into the air before our horrified eyes, turned over and crashed on to its back, tail forward, in a sheet of flame. Bricks filled the air. A muffled explosion, a blinding light and, straightaway, terrible 20-yard tongues of flame, mingled with twisting spirals of black smoke scored with vivid flashes.

I jammed on the brakes 50 yards from the furnace and jumped out, while the fire-truck literally hurled itself into the flames, spitting carbonic foam through its six high-pressure nozzles. The fire crew leapt off, armed with axes, followed by the medical orderlies.

Thirty yards away the air was so hot that it burned your throat like spirits. White sparks began to spurt from the blaze as the ammunition caught. The dry crack of the explosions and the whistling of the fragments filled the air.

One of the firemen, trying to forge into the inferno, collapsed. He was hooked out from behind, like a blackened, smoking log. He climbed out of his asbestos suit bespattered with molten aluminum, staggered, and fell on his face, vomiting. The flames roared, the smoke stung our eyes. The firemen went on pouring gallons and gallons of milky liquid which splashed, turned into steam and ran over the bricks.

The heat was getting less all the same and the shattered carcass of the Tempest began to show through the tongues of fire—the disembowelled engine showing its copper viscera besmirched with earth, the skeleton of the tail-plane, the fuselage broken up into three stumps, the wings ripped by the explosion of the belts of ammunition.

The fire was now almost vanquished. A vague shifting red glow could be seen beneath the boiling foam.

Wading in up to our knees, we rushed in. The horrible stench of burning rubber caught our throats and made us retch. A fine white dust of powdered aluminum fell. Then the sound of axes breaking into the remains of the cockpit.

"Easy, chaps, easy!"

The gauntleted hands tore off the tangled fragments, threw back bits of white-hot metal that fell sizzling on the grass, and then . . . I don't know what impelled me to press on, closer.

Delicately, they eased out an inchoate red and black mass, to which scraps of charred cloth still adhered. The parachute and harness straps had burnt away, but underneath the bleeding crust you could imagine the white-hot metal buckles which had gnawed their way through to the bone.

I felt the sweat congeal on my back. Completely unnerved, my legs gave way and I sat down in the slush of foam and cinders and, bent double, retched and retched.

*   *   *

The next day, same tragedy all over again with another pilot, who also tried to bring in his Tempest on its belly.

*   *   *

25th February, 1945

Another poisonous day. Snow, wind. Visibility nil; flying was quite impossible. However, G.C.C. maintained two sections of Tempests at immediate readiness —one from 486 and one from 56—together with a section of Spit XIV's from 41 Squadron. These three sections had been taking it in turns, with no hope of flying, since dawn.

At about 1500 hours the weather cleared slightly, and the 6 Spits were scrambled. In this appalling cold they had a job getting their engines started and we looked at them through our windows, jeering. In the end one pair took off, followed at least three minutes later by the rest. A quarter of an hour later these last four came back and landed, not having been able to join-up in the clouds. They told us, however, that the first two had jumped a German jet aircraft.

We got the remainder of the story that evening in the bar, when the pilots of 41 were distinctly pleased with themselves and let nobody forget it. Flying Officer Johnny Reid, D.F.C., shortly after he had scrambled and as he was patrolling Nijmegen Bridge at 10,000 feet, had spotted one of the very latest and rarest Luftwaffe planes—an Arado 234—sneaking into our lines at ground level. Diving straight down, flat out, ignoring the risk of his wings coming off, Johnny succeeded in catching the bastard in a turn, fired at him point blank and gently landed him in flames less than 100 yards from Broadhurst's H.Q. at Eindhoven.

We were told that the A.O.C. was delighted, as a group of American journalists had witnessed the operation, and it was the first Arado 234 to be destroyed for certain.

After this episode the pilots of 41 revived the good old Spitfire *vs.* Tempest controversy, and pursued us with their jeers: "You Tempests," they said. "You Speed Merchants, you think you're the cat's whiskers, you and your 7-ton crates, your 4 cannon, you've never managed to catch one of those things. You needn't have browned us off for days on end with yarns about your mighty dives and your terrific cruising speed!"

We naturally retorted that this particular Hun must have been very keen to commit suicide. Besides we'd seen Reid's plane after he landed: his poor Spit's wings were buckled like a concertina, all the paint had come off the surfaces, the rivets had sprung and the fuselage was twisted. Good for the scrap heap! And we closed the discussion by a conclusive argument that always annoyed Spitfire pilots considerably, i.e. that our landing speed was almost greater than their cruising speed.

As I was an ex-Spit pilot myself, Frank Woolley tried to drag me in as umpire. For 10 minutes I spouted feeble explanations and mathematical formulae and everybody was satisfied. Drinks all round settled it; we drank to the midges and they drank to the flying buses and we all went to bed in the best of tempers.

TEMPESTS
VS.
MESSERSCHMITTS

Following on recent blows, particularly the shooting down of Fairbanks, Ops. and G.C.C. decided that only formations of at least eight aircraft might operate deep into enemy territory. In addition, two formations at a time would do sweeps following parallel courses and less than 60 miles apart, so that they could go to each other's assistance.

Leading Talbot, I was carrying out a sweep with 8 Tempests of 274 in the Hanover area. 486 was operating somewhere not far off. At about 1505 hours, after having a look at the airfields at Hanover and Langenhagen, I set course 320° for Wunsdorf, from which two squadrons of Messerschmitts usually operated. Over the radio I warned Mackie who was leading 486:

"Hallo, Railroad, switching from H for Harry over to B for Baker."

Wunsdorf with its two great runways in the shape of a St. Andrew's cross, seemed deserted, though the field looked in pretty good shape. Leaving Steinhuder Lake on my left, I came up towards Bremen.

1515 hours. We were within sight of Hoya, a night-fighter base. I decided on a 360° turn to have a look at the neighbourhood and to regroup my Tempests, who were scattered over about three miles of sky.

"Come on, Talbot, pull your fingers out, join up!"

During the turn I mechanically counted my aircraft. Hell! Where was the eighth? I waggled my Tempest about to look in the blind spot formed by my tailplane.

"Break port, Talbot!"

I just had time to shout it in the mike. There were the Wunsdorf "109's", 3,000 feet above, in impeccable formation; forty to fifty Messerschmitts.

"Climb flat out. Don't let your speed drop."

They had seen us. A second of indecision, and they were now immediately above us, waggling their wings. They split up into two groups, one turning left, the other right.

"Hallo, Railroad, better come and give us a hand."

It would be safer to have 486's help! It looked as if I was going to be caught, sandwiched between the two groups of Huns. Better try and get back toward Hanover and take no chances.

What were the Huns waiting for? They seemed to be anxious about something, to have smelt a rat. Now there were Blue 4 and Blue 3 lagging half a mile behind the rest of my formation.

"Join up, Blue Three and Four, for Christ's sake!"

I had better try and maintain contact without fighting until Mackie turned up. I could hear Kenway bringing him along by radar.

"Join up, Blue Three and Four!"

Those two idiots were going to spoil everything! There! About fifteen "109's" peeled off from the left-hand group and dived on them. Blue 3 must have gone haywire, he just didn't seem to see them coming.

"Talbot Blue Three, break!"

Oh what the hell! I would have to attack.

"Talbot, break port. Attack!"

At full throttle, I cut short my turn and raced to help the two laggards. The first "109" fired a burst at Blue 3, as it passed. With one wing torn off by the 30 mm. shells the Tempest went into a spin.

I veered towards this Messerschmitt, who also turned towards me. He skidded, and I saw that his huge airscrew spinner bore the white spiral of the shock units of the German Air Force. I fired my four cannon together

—one shell on his port wing . . . two more on the cowling . . . an explosion . . . the "109" passed 60 feet below me, dragging a trail of thick black smoke, and disappeared. My finger on the firing button, I flew straight on through the thick swarm of diving "109's." I daren't attempt the slightest manoeuvre, in case of a collision.

I kept on reminding my pilots to keep their speed above 300 m.p.h., for "109's" could turn better than we could at low speed, and you had to watch out for the 30 mm. cannon in their propeller—it didn't give you a second chance. The best technique was to do a spiral dive, work up to a speed of 450 m.p.h., do a straight vertical climb and then start all over again. The "109's" on the other hand, knowing that we dived faster than they did, tried to get us up to 16,000 feet, where our Tempests were heavy and our engines sluggish.

I made a false move and let myself get cornered by four aggressive "109's" who wouldn't let go. I outdistanced them on the way down, but when I levelled out they caught up with me and fired one after the other. This lift-like rigmarole might have a sticky end.

Most unpleasant, it was. You saw their propellers, the white trails at their wing tips, the big air-intake to their superchargers to the right of the cowling—then, suddenly, the staccato flashes of the 20 mm. cannon firing, with, in the centre, more sedate, firing in burst of three shells, the 30 mm., whose fat tracer shells seemed to weave toward you in a most uncanny way. At the end of a few minutes the air was criss-crossed with a jumble of straight smoke trails left by the tracers. My engine was overheating as usual.

Sergeant Campbell stuck desperately to my tail and faithfully followed all my most violent manoeuvres. His life depended on it. However, he received a hit and, in a turn, I noticed oil streaking his fuselage. I shouted to him over the radio to go on with his turn normally while I passed behind him to cover him.

Pulling hard on the stick I did a flick roll and he shot in front. This movement brought me cheek by jowl with a "109," slightly below him, at less than ten yards distance. The sun reflected by the hood prevented my seeing the pilot's face. It was one of the latest Messerschmitt 109 K's with the new wooden rudder. He opened up flat out with methanol injection and tried to do a barrel roll round me. He slowly passed, on his back, above my cockpit and, looking up, I could see yellow-edged black crosses. Trying to slip in his rear, I throttled back suddenly. But he was a crafty beggar and, before I had time to move a muscle, he swung away violently, then turned and let fly with his 30 mm. One of his shells bounced off my cowling, exploded, and riddled my wing with shrapnel. At that same moment there were two explosions on the "109's" wing and he, surprised in his turn, broke away and went into a spin. It was Campbell, who had just winged him and got me out of a spot. Just in time!

A dozen "109's" had removed themselves from the scrap and were circling amongst the clouds above us, waiting for easy prey.

A Tempest caught fire and the pilot, W.O. Alexander, baled out. Another emerged from the dog-fight and started tacking about aimlessly—it was that infernal Blue 4, fast asleep as usual. Followed by Campbell, whose engine was missing badly, I made towards him at full speed, firing a burst on a Messerschmitt on the way. By the merest fluke I hit him, and he sheered off hastily, spouting glycol through his exhausts.

We were half a mile from Blue 4 when 6 "109's" dived on him, 3 from each side. By a miracle he saw them coming, but in a panic he dived instead of climbing. The "109's," who had accumulated an adequate margin of speed, easily caught up with him.

"Turn starboard, Blue Four!" I shouted at him, so that he should pass under me and bring the "109's" within range of my guns. The Tempest, followed by 3 "109's," passed below and in front of me 50 yards away. One of the Huns opened fire. With a violent kick on the rudder bar I flicked off and engaged him at 45°. Concentrating on his target, he didn't see me coming.

Deliberately, I corrected my aim—four rings on the sight—a cautious glance behind me; Campbell was faithfully covering me. The shells from my four guns ripped the air: a flash under the Messerschmitt's belly, a shower of sparks; a jerk and he exploded into pieces, his wings torn off, his engine in flames. In the sky all that was left was a big cloud of black smoke and, down below, burning fragments framing a slowly falling parachute.

"Hallo, Talbot Red Leader, Red Two calling. Going home; oil pressure."

It was Campbell. His oil pressure packing up was not unexpected. Let's go home.

"Talbot aircraft, re-form!"

Just at that moment eight aircraft bobbed out of the clouds—a moment's flap. However, it was Railroad's Tempests. They immediately went for the Messerschmitts scattered about the sky. The Huns didn't stay to fight it out and began to make for the clouds, in pairs, in wide climbing spirals.

"Talbot, rendezvous over base, angels 10."

On my way I dived down to have a look at an aircraft burning on the ground: it was a Tempest, which had turned over, trying to belly-land in a field of young wheat. I·passed again to look at the registration letters. Christ, it was one of mine—JJ-Y—G——, who was Blue 1. No signs of the pilot.

I detached Red 4 to escort Campbell and bring him back to Volkel the quickest way, on course 265°. Then I came back via Osnabrück to cover them from a distance with my two remaining aircraft, plus a lost Railroad who had tacked on to us.

When I got to Volkel, Red 4 told me that Campbell's engine had packed up on him three miles from the Rhine, which he just managed to get across in a glide. He had apparently made a correct belly-landing near a field battery. Sure enough, after dinner Campbell turned up in a jeep with some artillery types. He was grinning all over his face, in spite of a bandaged head, a black eye and two stitches in his lip.

"RAT CATCHING"

The Messerschmitt 262's were becoming a distinct nuisance. These blasted jets were appearing on our front in ever-increasing numbers. Every day at dawn and at twilight they came over, singly, at ground level, to take their photographs. Every now and again, just for a change, patrols of six, or even twelve, came and machine-gunned or bombed our lines.

For Kenway's controllers they were a difficult proposition. Radar couldn't pick them up properly as the posts swept the 360 degrees of the horizon too slowly to follow and fix the echo of a "262" batting along at nearly 600 m.p.h. at tree-top level.

21st Army Group G.H.Q. didn't understand these technical subtleties and bombarded G.C.C. with peremptory notes, demanding immediate steps to have these armed reconnaissances stopped. Poor Wing Commander Lapsley cudgelled his brains to find some means of intercepting the "262's" with Tempests capable of only 490 m.p.h. Finally, he and Brooker worked out the "rat code" (later called the "bastard code" by the pilots).

The principle of the thing was as follows. Two pairs of Tempests were permanently kept at a state of immediate alert—i.e. the planes were actually in scrambling position on the runway, with the pilots ready strapped in their cockpits, their finger on the starter, engines warmed up, radio switched on.

As soon as a "262" crossed the Rhine towards our lines, Lapsley sent out a warning in clear from his control post straight to the pilots, as follows:

Me 262

"Hallo, Talbot Leader, scramble, rat, scramble, rat!"

The engines were immediately started up, 3 red Verey lights went up to clear the circuit and give the
rat-catchers priority. The quarry being too speedy for
any attempt to catch it to be worthwhile, the two Tempests immediately made for Rheine/Hopsten, the jet-
fighters' base. Exactly 8 minutes from the sounding of

the alarm the Tempests would be patrolling the approaches of Rheine at 10,000 feet, and trying to catch an Me 262 returning from his trip, when he would have to slow down to let down his undercart and his flaps before landing.

In one week we brought down eight "rats" in this way. I was out of luck and missed two, who slipped through my fingers. The second one provided a complete triumph for the Volkel ack-ack boys. The "rat-scramble" had just been given out. I was taking off, followed by my No. 2, when the "262" whizzed over the field about a hundred yards behind me. By the merest chance, and by an extra-special dispensation of Providence, the two Bofors of posts S.E.4 and 5 were pointing in the right direction with the crews in position. Each gun fired one clip, with the odds about a million to one, and the Me 262 stopped a 40 mm. and disintegrated into the air.

The Germans soon found the answer to "rat catching." The Me 262's were told to return home at full speed and at ground level—which made them very difficult to spot, owing to their camouflage—and not to slow up until they got to the flak lane. Once there, they could land at leisure and in complete safety. In line with the main east-west runway at Rheine, over a distance of 5 miles there were 160 quadruple 20 mm. mountings in a double line. These could put up an impenetrable curtain of steel and explosive, under which the Jerry could slip and land perfectly peacefully.

In one week we lost 3 Tempests which tried to attack an Me 262 in this flak lane. There was no point in persisting. Strict orders came out, absolutely forbidding any attack on a "262" within a radius of 6 miles of Rheine; which considerably reduced our chances of bringing any down.

* * *

On the 7th of March, 3rd Corps of the 1st American Army reached the Rhine at Remagen and by an extra-ordinary stroke of chance found the Ludendorff bridge intact. The 9th Armoured Division seized it in double quick time and General Bradley began to exploit the bridgehead. Within a couple of days this enclave on the right bank of the Rhine had become such a threat to the Germans that they made desperate efforts to cut the bridge. The Lufwaffe was hurled in and the American fighters, who had no suitable bases within reasonable distance, were soon overwhelmed. The R.A.F. was called in to help and, as Tempests were the only aircraft with a sufficient range to cover Remagen while operating from Holland, this task too fell to our lot.

I led the first of these protective missions, at twilight. Our 8 Tempests flew up the Rhine, through Cologne, and reached Remagen, where we were greeted by virulent American ack-ack. The Yanks were in such a state of nerves that, even after we had made the usual recognition signals and they had been acknowledged, they continued to let off an occasional burst of Bofors at us. By the third salvo, which didn't miss me by much as I collected some shrapnel in the wing, I felt I didn't particularly want to go on giving these gentlemen target practice. I got my formation to do a 180° turn to make for home, when horrors!—We found ourselves face to face with an absolute armada of seven or eight Arado 234's escorted by thirty or so Me 262's, diving down on that miserable bridge.

At full throttle I fell in behind them. Just as I was opening fire on an Arado 234 at over a thousand yards' range, forty "long-nose" Ta 152's emerged from the clouds on my left. To hell with it! I warned my formation over the radio and kept straight on. The speed shot up frighteningly—420 m.p.h.—450—475. I was hurtling down at an angle of about 50°; the 7 tons of my plane, pulled by 3,000 h.p. had terrific acceleration. The Arado levelled out gently, insensibly, following a trajectory which would bring it down to the level of the Rhine a few hundred yards short of the bridge. I was 800 yards behind, but I daren't fire. At this speed, I felt that firing my guns would certainly wreck my wings. Still behind my Hun, I flew into a frightful barrage of 40 mm. and heavy M.G. I saw the two bombs drop from the Arado quite distinctly. One of them bounced over the bridge and the other hit the bridge road. I passed over the bridge, 40 yards to the left, just as it exploded. My plane was whisked up like a wisp of straw and completely thrown off her balance. I instinctively closed the throttle and pulled the stick back. My Tempest shot up like a bullet to 10,000 feet and I found myself upside down right in the clouds, sweating with funk. A violent vibration—my engine cut out, and a shower of mud, oil and ironmongery fell on my face. I dropped like a plummet and then my plane went into a spin. A spin in a Tempest is the most dangerous thing on earth—after one turn, two turns, you get thrown about helplessly, you cannon into the walls of the cockpit in spite of the harness straps.

In a complete flap, I wrenched at the hood release; it came away in my hand. I tried to get up on my seat to bale out, but forgot to unstrap myself and succeeded only in giving myself a terrific bang on the head. When I came out of the cloud I was still in a spin—there was the ground, less than 3,000 feet below. I pushed the stick right forward and opened the throttle wide. The engine coughed and suddenly fired again, practically jerking itself out of the fuselage. The spin turned into a spiral; I gently tested the elevators, which responded all right—the fields however were rushing towards my windshield. I levelled out at less than 100 feet.

A close shave. I raised my helmet and felt my hair soaked with sweat.

I pinpointed my position quickly. I was on the right bank of the Rhine to the north of the American bridgehead. I set course 310° for home and over the radio gave my patrol a rendezvous over Cologne at 13,000 feet. Just at that moment Kenway called me:

"Hallo, Talbot Leader, Kenway calling. What's your position? Over to you."

I replied briefly: "Hallo, Kenway, Talbot Leader answering, my approximate position is 20 miles north of Remagen, along Rhine. Out."

It was Lapsley personally controlling at Kenway to-day, I could recognize his drawl.

"O.K., Pierre. Look out, there are a couple of rats around. Out."

Right, I'd keep my eyes open. I was O.K. for juice and decided to do a quiet 360° turn under the clouds to try and spot the two rats in question.

A few seconds later some ack-ack tracers started coming up along the Rhine and I made out two long slender grey trails weaving just above the ground.

It was a "262." It looked superb with its triangular fuselage like a shark's head, its tiny arrow-shaped wings, its two long turbines, its grey camouflage spotted with green and yellow. This time I wasn't too badly placed, I was between him and his base. Once again I dived hell for leather, to accumulate the greatest possible speed. He hadn't seen me yet. A slight turn on the ailerons and I got up to him at a tangent. I was making careful allowance for speed and bullet drop when suddenly two long flames spurted from his jets. He had seen me and opened up. I was in perfect position, 300 yards away. I fired a first burst. A miss. I increased the correction and fired again quickly, for he was gaining on me. This time I saw two flashes on his fuselage, then one on the wing. The range was now 500 yards. An explosion on the right turbine which immediately vomited an enormous plume of black smoke. The "262" skidded violently and lost height. Our speeds evened out, with about 600 yards between us. The smoke got in my way and I missed him again. Curious red balls floating in this smoke dazzled me. Jesus! My two port cannon jammed. I aimed more to the right to correct the skid, and my two other cannon jammed too. The Me 262 flew on on one engine. I was mad with rage. There seemed to be a leak in my pneumatic system—no pressure showing on the gauge. I was simply livid with fury. I went on after the "262" in the hope that his second turbine would overheat.

After a few moments it was my own engine which began to heat. Regretfully I gave up, swearing to have that idiot's scalp who had written in the Air Ministry technical bulletin that an Me 262 couldn't fly on only one turbine.

Through all this I had clean forgotten my section, which must be getting somewhat restive over Cologne. Over the radio I handed over to MacCairn and we returned to Volkel separately at nightfall.

I was in a vile temper. Just to improve matters one of my tires burst as I landed. I had to wait in an icy wind until it was changed before I could taxi to the parking place and get off to dinner.

TRAIN-BUSTING

In the grey dawn a column of smoke began to rise amongst the long wisps of mist over the monotonous snow-covered plain. Then another a little farther along the black line which meandered through the immaculate whiteness of the countryside.

"Train, 2 o'clock, Talbot Leader!"

The four Tempests slid down to 3,000 feet in the frozen air and their polished wings caught the first gleams of a dingy dawn. We obliqued towards the second train and instinctively four gloved hands, benumbed by the cold, were already pushing the prop lever to fine pitch. We could now make out the locomotive and the flak truck in front of it and the interminable mixed train dragging painfully behind.

Without dropping our auxiliary tanks, we went into a shallow dive at full throttle . . . 350 . . . 380 . . . 420 . . . 450 m.p.h. The blood throbbed in my parched throat —still that old fear of flak. Only about a mile or two now. I began to set my aim for about 20 yards in front of the locomotive.

Now! I leant forward, tensed. Only 800 yards. The

first burst of tracer—the staccato flashes of the quadruple 20 mm. flak mounting—the locomotive's wheels skidding with all brakes jammed on. 500 yards. I was skimming over the snow-covered furrowed fields. Rooks flew off in swarms. My cannon roared—the engine driver jumped out of his cabin and rolled into the ditch. My shells exploded on the embankment and perforated the black shape which loomed in my sights.

Then the funnel vomited a hot blast of flame and cinders, enveloped in the steam escaping from the punctured pipes. A slight backward pressure on the stick to clear the telegraph wires, a quick dive through the smoke, then, once again, the sky in my windshield, covered with oily soot. Pulling hard on the stick I broke in zigzags. Live coals seemed to fly round my plane, "le Grand Charles," but whether they were flak or ricochets from my No. 2, I couldn't say. The usual fiery white puffs began to hang in the air.

A glance backwards. The locomotive had disappeared, shrouded in soot and spurting steam. People were scrambling out of doors and tearing down the embankment like agitated ants.

Red 3 and Red 2 caught up with me, while Red 4 was still disentangling himself from the very dense flak spouting from the three flak trucks. I made my section do a wide climbing turn and we set course for the second train. It had certainly been warned by radio. It had come to a standstill and the smoke now rose vertically from it. I waggled my wings, unable to make up my mind. No point in attacking this one, as the flak crews must be expecting us, all set.

"Hallo, Talbot, no use, chaps, they've got the gen. Break away to starboard, one, eight, zero!"

Christ! Red 4 had gone crazy! "Talbot Red Four, don't attack!"

The Tempest kept on down just the same, pointing at the locomotive.

"Come back. Break, you fool!"

The flak opened up, and I could see the trails of smoke from Red 4's wings as he fired. Then an almost imperceptible explosion along the fuselage, the Tempest slowly turned over, still keeping on its course. Almost on its back now, it just missed one of the trucks and crashed by the line. I could have sworn I heard the explosion. The inevitable mushroom of heavy black smoke, shot with burning petrol vapour immediately rose from the scattered debris.

"O.K. Talbot, going home."

On the way home we attacked three more trains.

*   *   *

Another tragedy when we landed. My No. 3 had been winged by flak and was therefore landing first. A hundred yards from the airfield the duty Anson, doing a long flat approach, suddenly emerged under him. The two pilots couldn't see each other and blindly converged towards one another. Red 3 had obviously switched off his radio as he didn't hear the runway controller's desperate call. At the last moment the Anson sheered brutally off, but too late. The tangled remains of the two planes blazed in front of the control trailer. Seven dead. The Anson was bringing five new pilots to reinforce the Wing.

WALTER NOWOTNY

Walter Nowotny was dead. Our adversary in Normandy and in the German skies had died two days before in the hospital at Osnabrück as a result of burns. The Luftwaffe, whose hero he was, would not long survive his death, which was as it were the turning point of the aerial war. That evening in the mess his name was often on our lips. We spoke of him without hatred and without rancour. Each one of us recalled his memories of him, with respect, almost with affection. It was

the first time I had heard this note in a conversation in
the R.A.F., and it was also the first time that I heard,
openly expressed, that curious solidarity among fighter
pilots which is above all tragedies and all prejudices.
This war has witnessed appalling massacres, towns
crushed by bombs, the butchery of Oradour, the ruins
of Hamburg. We ourselves had been sickened when our
shells exploded in a peaceful village street, mowing
down women and children round the German tank we
were attacking. In comparison our tussels with Nowotny and his Messerschmitts were something clean, above
the fighting on the ground, in the mud and the blood, in
the deafening din of the crawling, stinking tanks.

Dog-fights in the sky: silvery midges dancing in
graceful arabesques—the diaphanous tracery of milky
condensation trails—Focke-Wulfs skimming like toys
in the infinite sky. We too, of course, were involved
in less noble fighting: that strafing of trains in the grey
dawn of winter mornings when you tried not to think of
the shrieks of terror, not to see your shells smashing
through the wood, the windows shivering in fragments, the engine-drivers writhing in the burning jets
of steam, all those human beings trapped in the
coaches, panic-stricken by the roar of our engines and
the barking of the flak; all those inhuman, immoral
jobs we had to do because we were soldiers and because
war is war. We could rise above all this to-day by salut-
ing a brave enemy who had just died, by saying that
Nowotny belonged to us, that he was part of our world,
where there were no ideologies, no hatred and no fron-
tiers. This sense of comradeship had nothing to do
with patriotism, democracy, Nazism or humanity. All
those chaps that evening felt this instinctively, and as
for those who shrug their shoulders, they just can't
know—they aren't fighter pilots. The conversation had
ceased, the beer mugs were empty, the wireless was silent as it was past midnight. Bruce Cole, who was
neither poet nor philosopher, let fall these words:

"Whoever first dared paint markings on a plane's
wing was a swine!"

*   *   *

In May 1944, Jacques and Yule had had a pretty lively encounter with Nowotny over Le Havre. Many a time in Normandy, with 602 Squadron, we had had a bone to pick with him. He had machine-gunned our strip in the morning of 21st June, he had shot down over Bazenville three Dakotas ferrying loads of petrol and, a few days later, had had a scrap over Arromanches with a mixed formation of American Lightnings and Norwegian Spitfires which had lost three P-47's and two Spits, while one "109" crashed 100 yards from our mess.

At that time Nowotny was already the great ace of the Luftwaffe and was in command of the three fighter squadrons at Dreux. His sorties were easily identifiable as he always led his Me 109's in a Focke-Wulf 190.

Nowotny had cropped up again, in command of JG-52 at Rheine/Hopsten, when we got to Germany. Since the 1st January show the Luftwaffe had had, roughly speaking, no central direction and Wings were left to their own devices. Apart from vague directives from above the commanders on the spot had complete discretion. Each group of units in the Luftwaffe gravitated round a main airfield to which several satellites were attached. These autonomous units had their own staffs, their own operational control, their own supply, flak and repair echelons and were only remotely dependent on G.H.Q.

At Rheine/Hopsten Nowotny was in sole charge of Jagdgeschwader 52, which was dispersed on various satellites: Nordhorn, Plantlünne, Neuenkirchen, Lunen, Hesepe and Bramsche. JG-52 effectives comprised about 75 Me 109's, 75 Focke-Wulf 190's and about 100 jet Messerschmitt 262's. A Staffel of Junkers 88 nightfighters was attached to it. This represented, with the tactical reserve, about 400 fighter planes under the orders of this twenty-two-year-old Lieutenant Colonel.

He was credited by Allied Intelligence with 60 confirmed victories on our front and about 100 on the Russian front. He had succeeded in making himself respected everywhere. On the occasion of the shooting of 47 Allied pilots who had tried to escape from captivity, he had addressed a violent protest to Hitler himself, the echoes of which had reached even us.

On 15th March last I was leading a section of four Tempests in a rat scramble over Rheine/Hopsten at 8,000 feet. Suddenly we saw at ground level a Messerschmitt 262 without any camouflage, its polished wings glittering in the sun. It was already in the flak corridor and about to put down. The barrage of tracers was already up to cover its approach. In accordance with the new orders I decided not to attack in these conditions, when, without warning, my number 4 dived vertically towards the small bright dot which was nearing the long cement runway. Hurtling through the air like a bullet Bob Clark miraculously went through the wall of flak without being hit and fired a long burst at the silvery Me 262, which was in the final phase of its approach. The Messerschmitt crashed in flames just on the edge of the airfield.

A fortnight later we learnt by cross-checking captured documents and prisoners' reports that that Me 262 had been piloted by Nowotny. Everyone had gone to bed. Bruce Cole, Clark, Brooker and I had stayed up and we were glancing at an illustrated article on Nowotny in a review called *Der Adler* which we had found at Goch. There was his picture, taken on the day he received the Iron Cross with swords, diamonds and oak leaves—the highest German military distinction. A face like that of a tired child, with a trace of sadness and a determined mouth and chin.

"All right now," suddenly said Brooker, "time to go to bed. What a pity that type wasn't wearing our uniform?"

THE RHINE

Brooker had been keeping the Wing hard at it all the week. His 3 squadrons had lost 17 pilots. We had destroyed 24 German planes and 52 locomotives.

In 274 Squadron we were reduced to 11 pilots and 16 planes. We couldn't possibly keep it up. Group Support Unit could very quickly provide us with new aircraft but Tempest pilots didn't grow on every bush. On the 20th March in the morning the duty Anson had brought us four Sergeant Pilots and one Warrant Officer. The last of these five new recruits got himself killed on the 23rd. The old stagers, worn out by their three sorties a day, were already hard put to it to save their own skins, let alone look after the newcomers. These poor kids, fresh from O.T.U., had had just about three or four hours flying time on Tempests. Frightened by their machines, which they flew with great difficulty, they got themselves massacred by the flak and the Messerschmitt 109's.

Brown was one of these four Sergeant Pilots. As soon as he arrived at Volkel, at about 10 a.m. I had been obliged to put him through a firing test on one of our new Tempests before midday. He had then gone off to lunch on the mess with his kit and, before he could even unpack, he had been called back to Dispersal for an op.

Led by Hibbert, in a section of four, he had come up against a dozen Focke-Wulfs and, by the greatest luck, had succeeded in damaging one and getting home. But Hibbert and Humphries had been shot down.

That same evening, while my pilots went off for tea I had kept him with me for an immediate alert. Ten minutes later we were scrambled over Wesel at 10,000 feet. We arrived just in time to see a jet Messerschmitt 262 disappearing in the clouds. After a second's disappointment I broke, instinctively. Four Focke-Wulfs were on top of us and poor Brown went down like a torch on the banks of the Rhine.

The pilots' nerves seemed all in pieces, witness the uninterrupted succession of stupid accidents which were occurring—smashed undercarts, taxi-ing accidents, burnt-out brakes, punctures, bad landings, scrambles with propellers at coarse, etc.

The Wing couldn't go on like that. Between 15th February and 15th March we had had 31 pilots killed or reported missing. Out of all the pilots who made up 274 Squadron in Fairbanks' time, only two officers, a sergeant and myself survived. All Brooker could do was to show the categorical orders from G.C.C.—we must hold on until the Rhine was crossed.

* * *

24th March, 1945

First covering sortie at 3 a.m. over Wesel which was being attacked by the 1st Commando brigade. A thick pall of dust and smoke still hung over the town, which had been bombed by 186 Lancasters during the night.

In the airfield circuit there was a frightful mix-up of Tempests and Spitfires all flying round together at 300 m.p.h. Your nerve had to be good to last out 10 minutes' worth of this chaos of dancing green and red lights in which you had to try and form sections up in battle order. Nothing to report.

At 10 o'clock we took off again to escort the 669 aircraft and the 429 gliders from England which were carrying the Sixth British Airborne Division. It was an apocalyptic spectacle. Thousands of white parachutes dropped through an inferno of heavy, medium and light flak, while Dakotas crashed in flames and gliders rammed high-tension cables in showers of blue sparks.

The Typhoons were attacking every German flak emplacement with rockets. We were directed by the advanced radio control posts against Panzer columns coming up as reinforcements.

The Luftwaffe fighter force, broadly speaking, didn't interfere at all. The massive bombardment of Rheine and the tactical airfields the previous day had knocked it out temporarily.

We machine-gunned an armoured train near Ringer-berg and a convoy of panzers at Bocholt in the streets of the town itself. It was a hair-raising business. We came down at roof level, all four cannon spitting fire. Tiles flew all over the place, flak shells exploded along the walls, lorries burned, the panic-stricken inhabitants ran in every direction and sheltered in doorways. Danny got a direct hit from a 37 mm. and crashed at 450 m.p.h. into a huddle of houses near the church.

After lunch, a third mission. I led a flight from 56 Squadron. We flew over the Bielefeld viaduct, pul-

Bielefeld Viaduct

verized some days before by fourteen block-busters. The craters were more than 100 yards across. Our main objective was to bring to a halt all road traffic in the

Bielefeld-Altenbecken-Arnsberg triangle, and so I divided my planes into two pairs, each to act independently of the other.

I machine-gunned two lorries carrying troops—the poor devils didn't hear me coming owing to the noise of their engines. After two runs all that was left on the road were two flaming chassis and some bodies torn to shreds lying on the road. My No. 2 had lost contact and I found myself alone. I then fired a few shells at a locomotive sheltering in a marshalling yard and was greeted by terrific 20 mm. flak. One of my wing tips was torn off.

I circled over the rendezvous point for 10 whole minutes, waiting for my planes, and we went back to Volkel without Reg, shot down near Arnsberg by a free-lance Me 109.

1850 hours, 'phone call from Lapsley. He wanted a very experienced patrol of 4 planes to keep an eye on Rheine. It seemed that the Germans were going to try to evacuate their jet planes towards the interior, taking advantage of the last minutes of twilight. G.C.C. particularly wanted me to lead the patrol as our planes would be coming back after dark. Perhaps I felt flattered, anyway I accepted without giving myself time to think. Old Lapsley probably thought that quite normal—he had known me at Ashford in 1943, in Normandy in '44 and, as usual, he was banking on my willingness to take anything on. Yes, but after 40 sorties in 20 days my willingness had slightly cooled off.

Swallowing my pride I rang up the mess to try and get hold of Gordon Milne and get him to take my place. The orderly at the other end of the wire spent five minutes trying to find him and the time I was supposed to take off drew near. Oh well, to hell with it! I rang up the Flight Sergeant mechanic.

"Hallo Ron, stick JJ-B on the board, I'll fly her."

I was very careful to choose a really good team: that extraordinary type Tiny, an Australian, was my No. 2, Torpy my No. 4 and Peter West No. 3. There were few instructions to pass on, it was a kind of roving free for all.

1910 hours. We were a few miles from Rheine, which was covered by scattered cumuli dragging their rain-swelled bellies. It was already getting dark and a long trail of milk-white mist hugged the Hopsten hills, hiding the Dortmund-Ems canal and its shattered locks.

Rheine seemed to have been very badly bombed —its three main hangars had collapsed with the familiar outline of the control tower flanked by its formidable flak emplacements had disappeared. It almost made me feel sorry—curiously enough—to see Rheine where so many of our friends had been brought down and where we had had so many scraps with JG-52, in such a state. It seemed now to be the scene of intense activity. In the woods and along the dispersal tracks we could see lights running hither and thither and those two long bright trails were probably the turbines of a Messerschmitt 262 about to take off. Probably quite a number of kites had already sidled off in the shadows.

"Hallo, Pierre, bloody silly, can't see a thing."

I told Peter to dry up, but he was quite right, you couldn't see a thing. I decided to do a wide circuit over the airfield at 1,000 feet and then go home. My reflector sight was badly regulated and was dazzling me. After a lot of fiddling about I managed to turn it down until all I could see in the windshield was a dull red round filament.

A last look round. Suddenly, distinctly, two slender violent streaks, as of a twin-engined aircraft's exhausts, showed up to the left.

"Look out, Talbot Red! Attacking 9 o'clock!"

It was a Junkers 88 night fighter. In the darkness it was impossible to judge proportions and distances and he looked enormous in my sights. I fired a haphazard and rather ragged burst into the black moving shape and broke. Christ, what a fluke! Three quick explosions like Morse dots, and then a sheet of flame poured out of the punctured tanks in the starboard wing, lighting up the long fuselage with its black cross. Then, very distinctly, superimposed on this luminous mass I saw the outline of a Tempest. A nightmarish fraction of a second, and a dazzling light filled the sky. It was my No. 2, who had blindly followed me and, without having a chance to move a finger, had crashed straight into the stricken Ju 88.

Slowly the cascade of flaming debris from the two entangled aircraft scattered and settled in Mettingen forest. In a few seconds the night had swallowed up the scene.

Stupefied, panic-stricken, I lost for a moment all control over my plane and zigzagged about blindly, a few feet from the ground.

"Look out, Pierre, flak!"

Christ! I was flying over a grey strip pock-marked with craters and framed by buildings in shambles; by the light of the first tracer bullets I could see men running round in twos and threes, and a "long nose" Focke-Wulf, whose engine was ticking over.

It was Rheine. I had blundered straight into those terrific flak defences. In the night an impenetrable luminous web wove itself all round me. Glowing coals rippled towards me, lightning flashed angrily below the clouds, through the trees, round my wings. Desperately I opened the throttle wide and climbed, hanging on my propeller.

Suddenly, two stinging smacks—Bang! Bang!— shrapnel screaming through the aluminum plates, the stink of molten metal, burnt rubber and cordite. I was sick with funk and the thought flashed through my brain —This is it! This is the end! So this is what it's like.

I felt the blood thumping in my right leg. My toes were screwed up in a glutinous mess. My plane began to vibrate, shaking me, toppling my artificial horizon. No friendly voices in my earphones now—my radio was no longer a lifebuoy to a drowning man, it was a medley of cracklings and whistlings. I bit my tongue hard. My wits gradually collected themselves.

I reduced throttle and the vibration diminished. My tail-plane must have caught a packet. An icy draught whistling through the cockpit finally woke me up. All was calm. The moon had risen and seemed to be rolling over the Dutch landscape submerged in clouds. I must get home quickly—feel the ground beneath my feet, see friendly faces.

I set course on the conflagrations along the Rhine. I followed the course of the Twente canal, laboriously gaining height. For 10 minutes I concentrated on my instruments. They seemed to have gone haywire. Those faithful allies—altimeter, turn and bank indicator, pressure and temperature gauges—were now mocking me from behind their smashed dials.

Nijmegen and its new suspension bridge. The Rhine caught the last glow of the Arnhem fires and seemed to be clotted with blood. I tried my six wave-lengths in turn, I called Kenway and Desmond—no answer. With my burnt-out circuits, no radio, no recognition lights, I was obviously going to get myself shot down by our ack-ack. I instinctively checked my parachute straps. I followed the Meuse and at Gennep picked up the railway line leading to Volkel.

The airfield was in darkness and the main runway scarcely visible. Jesus! What were they waiting for to light the flare path? Couldn't those idiots at Flying Control recognize the sound of a Sabre engine? I did a dive over the control tower and wagged my wings. What the hell, surely those ack-ack types could tell the outline of a Tempest!

Suddenly, like a Christmas tree, Volkel lit up. At last! I passed over the field again slowly, waggling my wings to show I was in difficulties. I saw the headlights of the ambulance and the searchlight on the crash wagon.

I was going to land on my belly. I couldn't bale out because of my wounded leg and on top of that the left-hand runner of my hood had been buckled by a shell fragment. I pulled the lever to jettison it but nothing happened. The pain had now crept up to my hip, I couldn't feel the rudder bar any more. . . . I was very tired. Mechanically I began my approach—a quick one with 45° of flap. The plane answered sluggishly. I concentrated all my remaining strength on bringing her in. Suddenly fear, naked fear, caught me by the throat. I wrestled with all my strength against the vision of Alex and his burning kite on this same runway —switched off and leveled out between the two rows of flares. At all costs I must keep calm! A lump in my throat threatened to stifle me . . . careful . . . the brute mustn't stall . . . the flares passed by on either side . . . I gingerly tried to put her down . . . a bit more yet . . . here was the first of the eight red lights which showed the end of the runway . . .

Now or never! I rammed down the nose to lift the tail and, with the aileron, deliberately stuck one wing in to take up some of the shock—like that perhaps I wouldn't turn over.

My poor Tempest, in spite of its 7 tons, was like a straw in a gigantic vice . . . a first, terrific, shock . . .the machine bounced up, hurling me against the side of the cockpit . . . the hood flew off . . . the wings were crushed like tissue paper . . . the metal plates were torn apart . . . I crossed my arms in front of my face . . . a fearful scraping screech, like Judgement Day . . . a jerk of such violence that the straps of my Sutton harness snapped. I was hurled forward, my face smashed into the sights . . . a sheet of red light . . . jaws gone . . . a taste of blood . . . tooth enamel grating in my mouth . . .

A sudden stunning silence . . . a whiff of hot air in my face: the first shell going off in the flames.

A knife hacked at my shoulder, through the parachute straps, clumsy fingers caught me by my torn sleeves—"my leg, look out!" the heat ate into my lungs . . . hands painfully wrenched me out of the shattered cockpit . . . foam extinguishers were gurgling, the fire pump in full swing. People were shouting. I was dragged on to the damp grass and wrapped in a blanket. Millions of dazzling red and green stars pressed in to my eyes under the lids. The freezing air made me feel ill . . . a smell of ether—a sharp pain in the arm . . . oblivion.

I woke up again four hours after the morphia injection. My head felt empty and heavy and ached horribly. I tried to talk, but my lips were paralysed. The whole of my face except for one eye was in bandages. Was I in Eindhoven hospital? A night light showed white walls, a bedside table, a carafe, and, in a saucer, a small, rusty metal object on a piece of gauze.

"Ah, vous voilà réveillé," it was Doc Everald, who always insisted on speaking French in spite of his appalling Scots accent.

"Well, next time, try to land better. And don't go collecting scrap iron in your legs!"

Christ, what about my leg! Suddenly I got it . . . it was a piece of shrapnel I had picked up over Rheine. I felt more annoyed than anything else.

In any case it was going to be worth a week's peace and quiet to me! I was hungry and I was sleepy. The latter won and I fell peacefully asleep.

On the 30th March, six days later, I came back to Volkel in time to go to Warmwell in the duty Anson to choose a beautiful brand-new Tempest with the new Rotol airscrew. Two days later I was posted O.C. "A" Flight, No. 3 Squadron in 122 Wing (at B.112 Rheine).

CLOUDS, SNOW AND
FOCKE-WULFS

What a morning! We had been on "readiness" since 4:30 a.m. My team was exhausted and all those tired youngsters stood the cold badly.

7:30 a.m. Orders and counter-orders had succeeded each other and everything seemed to be going wrong this morning. It had started when the diesel generators had packed up, putting out the flare path just as the first of three Spitfire XIV's of 41 Squadron, Yellow Section, was landing. The one behind him had stalled

from a height of 30 feet, crashed and caught fire. The
third, piloted by a young Pole called Kalka, had stayed
up over the field for about ten minutes; short of juice
and diverted too late to Eindhoven, the pilot had
baled out. Huddling round the door of the Dispersal
we had vaguely caught sight of his Spitfire in the clouds
with its undercart and flaps down; and the whirling
black shape of the pilot falling. We had seen the parachute opening and had followed it as the wind swept
it off. An hour later the jeep brought back his stiff body
wrapped in the frosted silk of the parachute. The poor
devil had fallen in the Meuse and its freezing waters
had given him no chance.

Just as the sullen day was unwillingly breaking, four
Tempests had taken off, led by Wing Commander
Brooker. An hour and a half later only two came back.

After machine-gunning a train in the Osnabrück region, with only half-hearted reaction from its flak,
the section had re-formed. Suddenly Barry had seen a
fine trail of smoke filtering from his chief's radiator.
Brooker had been unaware of the danger and now
waggled his wings to try and see. Even in the mirror
the smoke was scarcely visible. Then suddenly the Tempest shook and a long slender flame unrolled in its
slip-stream. The other planes moved quickly out of the
way and saw Brooker's gloved hands wrestling with the
catches of the cockpit cover. Suddenly his face was lit
up by a red glow—the fire had penetrated into the cockpit. The Tempest turned over violently, skidding on
its back.

Appalled, Brooker's mates had eyes for nothing but
his disabled machine. They did not see two shadows
silently steal out of the iridescent mist. Just an incandescent trail of tracers and a glimpse of big black crosses
on the wings of two Focke-Wulfs before they vanished
again. A second Tempest went into a spin and its flaming fragments joined Brooker's alongside the autobahn.

*   *   *

At 8 o'clock, for the fourth time that morning, G.C.C. put us on immediate readiness—then countermanded it 10 minutes later. Every time we had to get out into the freezing cold, haul ourselves and our heavy parachutes up on to the slippery wing and take our gauntlets off to connect our helmets to the oxygen and the radio. We got back round the stove as fast as we could, our nerves on edge. We had another look at the map of the sector, with its black web of railway lines, which we were going to have to fly along at ground level, looking for those dangerous trains with their trigger-happy flak.

I kept an eye on my pilots—not a word passed between them, just an occasional sign for a smoke or a light.

Suddenly the telephone in the orderly's cubby-hole tinkled thinly. Everyone was as if rooted to the spot, tense and dry-mouthed.

"Back to normal state, 15 minutes readiness."

Shouts of rage, kicks at the unfortunate coal bucket —the feeling was not of relief so much as being tricked. I took my bad temper out on B——, one of the new pilots, who was timidly hiding his freckled, frightened face. The clot had dropped his parachute on a patch of oil yesterday or the day before and had failed to report it. Oil eats into tight folds of silk more surely than fire —a parachute in that state wouldn't stand up to the jerk of opening out, even at medium speed.

At 9:30 I took my chaps along to the mess for a second breakfast. In this weather I couldn't leave them on an empty stomach from 4 a.m. till lunch time. I had scarcely started on my porridge when the mess sergeant called me to the phone. My mouth full, I answered Lapsley's instructions—a patrol, Osnabrück—Münster—Bremen, with eight aircraft, priority for train strafing, naturally. Take off 0955 hours. O.K. I rang up Dispersal to warn them.

* * *

The weather had got worse, as foreseen. It was beginning to snow. The flakes stuck to the windshield and to taxi on to the runway we had to have a mechanic on the wing to guide us. With one hand he clung on to the freezing metal, slipping and with legs dangling, and with the other he showed us the way and wiped his streaming eyes.

My plane was continually skidding on the wire mesh of the taxi-ing strip. Surely they weren't going to let us take off in this weather? I switched on my radio and called Desmond:

"Hallo, Desmond, Talbot Red Leader here; pretty sticky—any gen?"

"Hallo, Talbot, Desmond answering. Scramble!"

We had now reached the intersection of the taxi-ing strip and the brick runway. The mechanics jumped down and started running back, bent double by the gusts, after the usual thumbs-up. My seven aircraft followed beautifully and took up their positions in pairs on the runway.

B——, nervous and upset, couldn't manage to line up properly next to me. He was maltreating his brakes and correcting with far too much throttle. I took off my oxygen mask and smiled at him encouragingly. If he panicked, with this cross-wind, he'd hit me when we took off.

The snow was now falling thick and fast. We could scarcely see as far as the end of the runway. I gradually opened the throttle and turned left as soon as I was airborne. I saw B——'s Tempest slip under my tail-plane and skim the bare trees and the housetops.

On the runway my Nos. 3 and 4 were moving, trailing behind them the snow raised by their propellers, while behind them the first pair of Blue Section was getting under way.

After climbing through the frost-laden clouds for ten anxious minutes, we emerged, drenched with sweat, 7,000 feet above Münster. The black roads crossed and recrossed round the snow-covered houses. The wind whisked away the smoke and steam from the factories. The town seemed dead.

The cathedral was surrounded by bombed areas—blackened frames of houses, gaping cellar holes, mounds of debris right up to the square. Serried rows of lorries and a few tanks were parked in the shadow of the towers.

On the other side of the canal jammed with ice-bound barges were the almost deserted marshalling yards. Bomb craters everywhere, burnt-out tank trucks and, in a corner near a turntable, two trains side by side, protected by automatic flak platforms. The flak crews were no doubt following our every move through their telescopic sights.

Suddenly I had an uncanny feeling that there was an 88 mm. battery in the vicinity.

"Talbot Red, quick, 180° starboard!"

I don't know why, but without waiting for the regulation second or two between command and execution, I at once did a tight turn. My planes, taken by surprise, started a rather ragged turn too. Just behind my tail and between me and B—— —who had luckily lagged behind—appeared three flashes followed by tufts of black smoke. B——'s plane disappeared for a moment.

An anonymous voice cried into the radio: "Christ, that was bloody close!"

*　　*　　*

My section were flying superbly. To be at the head of a formation was for me a constantly renewed source of naïve pride. On my left, impeccably spaced, Red 3 and Red 4. Close on my right was B——, Red 2. Five hundred yards farther away was Blue Section, Mac-Cairn at their head, with his four aircraft in close formation.

The sky, under a very high vault of absolutely smooth cloud, was the clear luminous grey that you find only in winter. My Tempests were as if etched against the backcloth of cumulus. A bank of cloud drew near, fantastically floating on a layer of warmer air at 8,000 feet. I had the curious impression of hanging motionless between the grey stratus and the snowy plain while these indefinite, immaterial, flat-bottomed masses glided towards me. Enough of that! Was I going to pass above, or below them?

Calmly and methodically, I scanned the horizon

all round me; I questioned the sky, dividing it up into neat strips by an upward and downward movement of my head. Nothing in the air.

Nothing on the ground either. I did catch a vague glimpse of a row of lorries parked along an autobahn —but I looked away again. I didn't want any fuss with flak before our auxiliary tanks were empty.

The radio was strangely quiet. We must be the only Kenway fighters in the air. Hardly surprising, in this weather. I felt a childish impulse to go romping among the clouds with my patrol.

"Priority for trains . . . priority for trains. . . ."

I could still hear Lapsley's voice on the telephone in my conscience. Naturally I wouldn't see any trains above a bank of clouds. I hoped to God there wouldn't be any trains down below either.

"Hallo, Talbot Squadron, keep just below cloud base." We glided thirty feet below the translucent plateau.

*   *   *

Suddenly the radio rang with yells and curses. I jumped, surprised—thousands of pins seemed to be pricking my tongue, the back of my hands and my ankles.

"MacDuff Squadron BREAK!"—"Help!"—"Look out, Focke-Wulfs above!"——

"MacDuff Leader, you've got one of the bastards on your tail!"

A dog-fight going on somewhere. Automatically my planes had taken up battle formation. From the waggling of the wings I could guess that seven pairs of eyes were tensely scanning the sky.

I didn't know "MacDuff"—probably a squadron from 84 Group. I anxiously asked Kenway what was going on. Between two strings of shouts from the Mac-Duff boys, Kenway replied:

"Hurry up, Talbot Leader, there is a big do over Rheine, steer 275°."

No need to warn my patrol, they had heard it too.

We turned due west at full speed, our sights switched on, safety catches released. A glance at the map—less than fifty miles, so we would be over Rheine in 5 minutes, probably too late.

"Talbot, over to Channel C for Charlie—keep your eyes peeled!"

We changed frequency, as B was cluttered up by MacDuff. Like all raw No. 2's, B—— began to lag. I was just about to call him up when I heard him excitedly shouting:

"Talbot Leader, aircraft just above the clouds, quick, they're Huns!"

Jesus! I looked up and saw, through the translucent layer, a dozen indistinct silhouettes each surrounded by an iridescent halo. I jettisoned my auxiliary tanks, changed to fine pitch, went through the emergency gate, and climbed vertically through the clouds.

I emerged into the clear sky hanging on my propeller, less than 300 feet below some Focke-Wulfs flying round in apparent disorder. In the luminous circle of my sights sprang the under surface of a wing, the outline of an undercart, the black crosses and the pale blue belly of one of the Huns. I pressed the button and kept my finger down, shaken to the bones by the continuous discharge of my four cannon. A rending crash—a large metal plate fell off the "long nose" Focke-Wulf, which did two flick rolls, vomiting a sheet of flame and fragments, I just managed to avoid it. His tail, threshing the air, passed less than five yards from my rudder. Having lost speed, I desperately tried to complete my loop. Carried away by my reflexes I had got my plane into the most vulnerable of all positions, and that Focke-Wulf had not been alone! I found myself on my back, stupidly hanging by my straps, like a fly in a spider's web. I pushed the stick hard to the left but nothing happened. My Tempest shuddered violently, then stalled and dropped like a stone.

Bang! a blinding explosion just in front of my eyes burst my eardrums. I let go of everything and instinctively covered my face with my two arms. The smell of ozone and indiarubber from a short-circuit mixed with the acrid smell of cordite, filled my nostrils. Jolted about, my heart in my mouth, hanging upside down, I tried in vain to get my feet back on the rudder bar—my legs weighed a ton! One of the smashed instruments on the panel was hanging on the end of its wire in front of my nose, and I could see blue sparks on my contact box and hear their crackling in my earphones. It couldn't be anything else but a 30 mm. hitting my wing root.

Panting, I mechanically straightened out 1,500 feet below the clouds and my flooded engine started up again after a few noisy backfires—bloop! bloop! Bang!

What again! This time it was a 20 mm. in the fuselage. I felt the impact like a hammer-blow through my back plate. Frantically, with both hands I put my aircraft into the steepest possible turn. The Focke-Wulf, spotted with green, flashed before my windshield, a white feather at either wing tip, and climbed vertically back into the clouds.

My radio was now dead, pulverized by that last shell. I hesitated—what ought I to do? I saw, emerging from the base of the cloud, in a shower of flaming fragments, a limp shape hanging on a half-opened parachute. Was it one of mine? Then I saw a Focke-Wulf dive vertically down at full throttle. The small glittering object hurtled towards the ground like a bullet—a fiery bubble burst on the snow, and the smoke bellied out immediately, mushroom shaped, but was soon swept away by the wind. A few little black crosses fading in the distance—then the sky was empty.

* * *

I was on patrol near the Elbe with Peter West, Longley and Don. We had machine-gunned a train in a small marshalling yard, without much result.

There was a lot of very accurate flak and Don's machine was hit. He baled out from his burning Tempest with some difficulty and landed on top of the flak battery.

Not much likelihood of being a prisoner long, as

things were going. His chances of being alive to see the end were now better than ours!

As we passed we machine-gunned a few panic-stricken lorries on minor roads.

The three German airfields we saw seemed to have been deserted by the Luftwaffe. No trains running in the neighbourhood, either. No point in courting suicide for the sake of puncturing a few locomotives in well protected yards.

Germany seemed just lousy with flak. It was everywhere, even in the most unexpected places. You sometimes hit upon a peaceful country lane with a few lorries trundling along, you made your approach and whoof! the sky was full of 20 mm. tracers.

German military road convoys now had to stick to round-about routes, which had been carefully worked out in advance and were covered for the whole of their length by light flak batteries. The game was no longer worth the candle—there was no point in stupidly risking a Tempest for the fun of merely pulverizing one Wehrmacht lorry.

Five other sections of four Tempests were also carrying out armed reconnaissance in the area, more for the look of the thing than anything else, as there seemed to be no interesting targets left. I stayed on the qui vive all the same, on principle: you never knew when you mightn't come across some free-lance Focke-Wulf.

Apart from that I knew jolly well my pilots were not on top of their form. They had been worked to death for the last month and they had probably reached the stage of nervous depression when you don't much mind having to risk your neck over something but you don't actually look out for an opportunity of doing so. What confirmed my opinion was that whenever I came down below 2,500 feet to have a better look at the sunken lanes my two team mates started zigzagging as if the entire German flak was after them. They came down with me unwillingly and hastened to get back to a safer height. Luckily it didn't prevent Peter West from keeping his eyes open.

"Look out, Filmstar Red One, aircraft 4 o'clock!"

"O.K. Filmstar Red, breaking starboard and climbing."

An aircraft became visible at tree-top level, approaching rapidly. A curious one, which I couldn't identify. He only saw us at the last moment, because we were just below the cloud base, in the shadows. He broke very quickly and for a moment I had a full view of him. He was obviously a Jerry—he had black crosses on the wings—but what an odd sort of bird!

Throttle full open, I tried to cut inside his turn, but he was moving astonishingly fast. Longley was better placed and fired at him, but without effect. The strange aircraft completed his turn and flew off at full speed. He really was an extraordinary looking customer. His tail-plane was cruciform, and it looked as if he had not only a normal propeller in front but on top of that a pusher propeller right in the tail, behind the rudder. His front engine was an "in line," with a cowling like a DB 603 in a Focke-Wulf Ta 152C with a ring-shaped radiator; the other engine was buried in the fuselage, behind the pilot. The two long grey trails in his slipstream showed he was using a supercharger, and the thread of white escaping from his exhausts showed he was using GM-1. I toyed with the idea of bringing my supercharger into action, but even with 3,040 h.p. we wouldn't be able to get him. We were doing nearly 500 m.p.h. and he was easily gaining on us.

I took a film of him, on the off-chance that there might be signs of jet-propulsion, but with this wan light the negative would be too under-exposed to show much. Longley kept after him for a bit, but he soon gave up. He fired one burst at extreme range, but the tracer bullets harmlessly bespattered the countryside.

"Hallo, Red Four, keep your ammo. No use shooting at the bastard."

As a matter of form we pushed on as far as the Elbe. It was raining there and the visibility was very bad. We flew over a German pontoon bridge, maintaining itself with difficulty against the violence of the current. Not a soul about, but bags of flak. We moved on hastily. A lousy day, we must get back.

I pored over my maps, trying to pinpoint our position, my two Tempests close by on either side. As our juice was getting low, I finally made up my mind to ask Kenway for a course, but just then the wavelength was pretty crowded. Filmstar Blue Section were using it. From what I could gather from their infernal chatter they had cornered some unfortunate Ju 88 somewhere near Steinhuder and were massacring him.

For almost a minute the air was full of a yapping as of hounds at the kill, then all was suddenly silent. The Ju 88 must be burning away in some field or other. As I called Kenway I made a mental note that I would tear them off a strip for their RT discipline.

Back at Rheine in the I.O. trailer we argued over our mysterious plane's identity for nearly an hour. In the end it was decided that its characteristics seemed to coincide with those of the Dornier 335, the latest

Dornier Do 335 (Pfeil)

German fighter. As it was the first time this type had been met on ops., I did several sketches from what I could remember for TAF H.Q. I wrote a report for the Intelligence services on its probable manoeuvrability and performance.

I spent the rest of the afternoon putting my papers into some sort of shape. What a bind that sort of thing was.

Longley had gone off again on an armed reconnaissance with one of our sections. When he landed we heard that they had met—but this time they had shot it down—another extraordinary plane.

He told me that, as they flew along a stretch of the Berlin-Hamburg autobahn that was in course of construction, just where it hugged the shore of Neu-Ruppin lake they had seen a plane just over the water. This plane, with its undercart and flaps down, seemed about to land on the autobahn. In spite of the flak, Longley had shot it down.

It was a Heinkel 162, or "Volksjäger," jet-propelled. This seemed to confirm reports we had of the mass production of He 162's in underground factories near Neu-Ruppin. But up till now nobody had understood how these planes were tested. The only airfield nearby was the one at Ruppin itself, and care had been taken to bomb it and make it unusable. In addition, the bi-weekly photo cover had never once in the last three months revealed the presence of a single aircraft on this field.

We now had proof that a section of the autobahn, 3 miles long and 60 yards wide and perfectly straight, was being used as a trial runway. The machines were probably parked in camouflaged shelters in the woods on either side of the autobahn.

Life was full of surprises. The Jerries had succeeded in turning Germany into a regular conjurer's shop.

FLAMES IN THE DUSK

20th April, 1945

G.C.C. were worrying us, as usual. They wanted us to fly a patrol that evening at dusk to cover the Bremen-Hamburg sector. This was because the Luftwaffe had been reacting in strength along the autobahn during the last few days. S.S. planes had been shooting up and bombing our advanced columns, considerably hampering their progress and their supply echelons.

We were quite agreeable, in principle, to flying a patrol, but G.C.C. couldn't seem to understand that Rheine/Hopsten had only one runway in good order, and a very short one at that, and no night-flying installation whatever. G.C.C. were also forgetting that the Jerries operated immediately after sun-down (if there had been any sun). Looking for small groups of Focke-Wulfs in the air in the mists that rose from the marshes of the Elbe and the low clouds which reflected the last glimmer of daylight was like looking for a needle in a haystack.

Besides, the aircraft situation was very tight. "Chieffy," after we had made some diplomatic enquiries, hinted at only nine machines available—ten at the outside—during the next 20 hours. In the end we decided on a compromise; Bruce Cole kept six Tempests for normal armed reconnaissance, and I get the rest myself. As I didn't know my new pilots very well yet, I chose MacIntyre and Gordon, to see how they coped with a difficult job.

We took off at 1936 hours. Gordon had difficulty in starting his engine and we lost 10 minutes of precious twilight circling round waiting for him.

At 1945 hours we set course for Bremen, flying at low level. Not much to be seen—in the distance a few vague bursts of tracers, dimmed by the summer lightning. Some houses on fire. In the vast pine forests a few fires glowed furtively.

We flew into driving rain which dragged down the clouds lower still. We went down to tree-top level. I could only just see Gordon's plane. The visibility was getting worse and worse. It was distinctly disquieting. The Huns were sure to come out, but I wasn't very keen on venturing at ground level over enemy territory in this sort of weather. I tried to pierce the mist. Hamburg, with its formidable flak defence, was somewhere quite close in the murk, straight ahead.

What the hell, let's go home!

"180° port, Filmstar, go."

I kept my eyes on the dead straight autobahn as best I could. It was the only reliable landmark in this gloom, even though its white surface had been partially camouflaged by patches of tar. It marked our front line positions approximately.

It was about 2030 hours. The rain came down with redoubled vigour. We roared over British and American armoured columns, producing considerable panic. Those stupid "pongos" never seemed to learn how to distinguish our aircraft from the Jerries'.

We flew over a squadron of Churchills scattered over a field, and the men ran all over the place, jumping for the shelter of the tanks, or under the caterpillar tracks or in the ditches. As they had been machine-gunned every evening recently in this part of the world—usually just about this time—they were taking no chances. Besides, we were probably the first R.A.F. fighters to operate round about there so late in the day.

Lousy weather. You might pass within five hundred yards of a regiment of Focke-Wulfs and not see them. All the same, I kept a sharp lookout.

2035 hours. Out of the corner of my eye I saw somewhere behind my tail a red and green Verey light come up from our lines, followed immediately by an eruption of tracers, which disappeared into the clouds. Christ, something was up—Jerries, perhaps! I started a left-handed turn and warned the other two:

"Look out, Filmstar White—180° port, and keep your eyes open!"

Just at that moment I felt a violent impact under my seat and at the same time a burning pain in my leg. Tracer bullets were whizzing up past my Tempest.

That really was too much! Those "pongo" morons not only were shooting at us, but for once their aim was accurate. I broke and went into a tight turn, and poured some pretty varied invective into the radio. As they couldn't hear me anyway it was rather a waste of breath. The other two Tempests followed me in my turn, hotly pursued by increasingly heavy bursts of ack-ack. We waggled our wings, switched on our navigation lights, went right through the whole recognition rigmarole, all to no avail. As a last resort I was just going to let down my undercart when, like a shoal of fish passing under a skiff, thirty Focke-Wulfs appeared. They were hugging the ground and the rapid shapes seemed to slip through the trees, pursued by the flashes of their delayed-action bombs dropping on one of our tank parks.

"Focke-Wulfs 2 o'clock, Filmstar. Attacking!"

I heeled over and, at full throttle, dived towards the Huns. Just as my finger was hovering on the firing button something made me look round: a dozen Focke-Wulfs in close formation were emerging from the clouds, a few yards from my team mates. In the meantime the ack-ack was increasing in fury—so was the rain. The Focke-Wulfs—they were magnificent "long noses" with the white spiral round the spinner—broke in every direction.

The visibility had by now got even worse, which didn't prevent two of the Huns from making a frontal attack on me—so close that I was left quite unnerved. My chief concern was not to get involved in a collision in the gloom. That really would be too stupid. In any case I hadn't had a genuine target yet.

Suddenly the radio blared. Gordon, in the hell of a flap, started shouting incoherently. He had just been hit by our ack-ack and a Focke-Wulf in quick succession. One of the Tempests—presumably his—was dragging a long trail of grey smoke and climbing straight for the clouds, followed by four Focke-Wulfs. Poor Gordon.

"Look out, Pierre, break! Break!"

Before I had even had time to realize this was meant for me, I had pulled hard on the stick—but too late. I was hit somewhere under my petrol tank. The impact was so violent that my feet jumped off the rudder bar. An acrid smoke filled the cockpit with the stench of cordite. A square wing bearing a black cross swept past in a flash only a yard or two away, and the Focke-Wulf's slipstream was so violent that this time the stick was wrenched out of my hand.

Instinctively I completed a roll and levelled out just above the tree-tops. The nausea of fear gripped my throat as a short bright flame licked my feet.

Fire! I felt the heat through my boots, quickening the first stabs of pain in my wounded right leg. I bent down and fumbled with my glove, trying to locate the course of the flame.

Bang! Bang! Two more shells smacked into my plane. This time my engine missed a beat—so did my heart. I hurled my Tempest into a violent skid which jammed me against the side of the cockpit, and at the same time reduced throttle. Then I slowly opened full out—the engine responded normally. Stick right back, I climbed back to the cloud base. All around me in dismaying confusion were Focke-Wulfs machine-gunning, climbing, diving, turning.

In the half light one turned towards me, rapidly waggled its short wings and engaged me. I turned at once to face him, fired a burst from three-quarters front, but evidently missed him, and passed like a whirlwind just a foot or two below him. I immediately brought the stick hard back, and put on full left rudder. My Tempest shuddered, showed signs of stalling, but completed an astonishingly tight turn all the same, two white "contrails" at its wing tips. The Focke-Wulf seemed nonplussed—began to turn to starboard—skidded—righted itself—then turned to port.

That was a boob: now I in turn was in a good position, at less than two hundred yards range. Quickly, before he had time to complete his manoeuvre, I corrected 10°—two rings of my sight. One long burst from my four cannon—lightning flashes lit up and seemed to bounce off his grey fuselage and his wings. Fragments were tossed about in a cloud of rapidly thickening smoke—the cockpit flew off and went spinning down, and I saw the pilot, his arms glued to the fuselage by the speed, trying to bale out.

Then the Focke-Wulf veered sideways at less than 150 feet, righted itself for a moment, hit the ground, bounced up, mowed down a pine tree in a shower of flames and sparks and finally crashed into a sunken lane. There was a terrific explosion which threw a lurid light like a magnesium flare for several hundred yards around.

The weather now seemed to be clearing a bit. Gaps appeared in the wall of mist, revealing a broad strip of moist, yellow horizon throwing a wan light over the pine forests and the marshes.

On the left a fire was raging; it was our tank park blazing, its tank trucks and its ammunition lorries in flames. Four Focke-Wulfs were flitting round like big moths, occasionally spitting a stream of bullets into the inferno. I daren't attack them—I could feel the others prowling round in the shadows.

Aha! I spotted a lone plane skimming over the tree-tops in the direction of Bremen, whose tall chimney stacks looked positively mediaeval outlined against the dying sky.

Engine temperature 125°, oil pressure down to 55. Regretfully I opened the radiator and closed the throttle to 3,500 revs. Even then I went on gaining on the Focke-Wulf, who was probably making for home, his magazines empty.

We were now over Bremen, and he was still about a thousand yards ahead. This business might take me rather far; I closed the radiator again and opened the throttle flat out. My "Grand Charles" responded at once. We were now over the first docks on the Weser.

We roared between the shattered remains of the big transporter bridge. On either side rose the charred hulks of the warehouses; the few cranes and derricks still erect rose up like black skeletons.

Suddenly a salvo of flak shells blossomed between the Focke-Wulf and me—brief white flashes, mingled with brown balls which passed by on either side of me. More kept appearing miraculously out of the void. The automatic flak now chimed in and the orange glow of the tracers was reflected in the black oily water, from which overturned hulks emerged, like enormous stranded whales.

I concentrated on not losing sight of my Focke-Wulf —luckily he was silhouetted against the dying glow in the sky.

For a moment the flak redoubled in intensity. There was a sudden clang behind my back—then suddenly the tracers were snuffed out and disappeared. . . . A bit suspicious! A glance behind me explained this curious phenomenon: on my tail were six Focke-Wulfs in perfect close echelon formation—exhausts white hot—pursuing me at full throttle.

With one movement I broke the metal thread to enable me to go to "emergency" and shoved the throttle lever right forward. It was the first time I had had occasion to use it on a Tempest. The effect was extraordinary and immediate. The aircraft literally bounded forward with a roar like a furnace under pressure. Within a few seconds I was doing 490 m.p.h. by the airspeed indicator and I simultaneously caught up my quarry and left my pursuers standing.

I had soon reduced the distance to less than 200 yards. Although in this darkness my gun-sight rather dazzled me, I had him plumb in the middle and I fired two long deliberate bursts. The Focke-Wulf oscillated and crashed on its belly in a marshy field, throwing up a shower of mud. He miraculously did not overturn. Without losing any time I climbed vertically towards the clouds and righted myself to face the others.

They had vanished in the shadows. They must have turned about and left their comrade to his fate. I flew back over the Focke-Wulf I had shot down. The pilot was limping off, dragging his parachute and quite dazed by the shock. I bespattered the remains of his machine with shells and they caught fire at once. That made two!

It was now pitch dark. With my engine set to cruising speed (I had to cool it down and go slow on the juice) I slowly regained height, setting course south.

Minutes passed. I was trying to pick out a landmark when my engine cut out violently. A shower of sparks passed on either side of my cockpit. With beating heart I saw that the flame was intermittently reappearing beneath my feet. My hydraulic fluid tank, punctured by a piece of shrapnel, had leaked under my feet. The liquid had soaked one of the wires and produced a short between the pedals of the rudder bar. An acrid smoke caught my throat through my oxygen mask.

To add to my discomfort an Allied ack-ack battery took this opportunity of opening first and surrounding me with a dozen 76 mm. shells.

I decided to bale out immediately if the fire got worse, and quickly checked my straps. I gained height to have a good margin of safety and called Kenway to my assistance. Kenway luckily answered at once and gave me a course on Rheine. After ten difficult minutes, during which Kenway mothered me like an anxious hen, I finally made out two rows of luminous dots winking on the ground. A white Verey light came snaking up. Rheine at last.

Should I bale out? Ought I to risk landing on my belly?

My experience of 24th March ought to have put me off. But, stronger than my will, was that old pilot's instinctive reluctance to sacrifice his machine; I wasn't going to write off good old JF-E, which I had chosen at Warmwell so lovingly, without a struggle.

My hydraulic system was certainly out of action—no more fluid in the pipes—and I wasn't going to try and get my undercart down and find myself with a wheel half in and half out. Desmond finally helped me to make up my mind by telling me that the fire was getting worse, that the flames were visibly getting bigger. On top of that my engine was cutting out more and more frequently.

"Hallo, Desmond, Filmstar Leader calling, landing now."

My voice probably wasn't very steady. Before switching off I heard Desmond wishing me good luck. I made a very straight approach, fast enough to give me a margin, jettisoned my cockpit hood and, well in the middle of the flare path, put my aircraft down.

Terrific row ... sparks ... jerks and jolts. ...

To my great surprise everything went off very well this time. After thirty yards of scraping and bouncing my Tempest stopped, lying slightly crooked between the two rows of lights. The ambulance and the fire tender arrived at once and I lost no time in jumping out of my kite.

My pilots came and picked me up in a jeep and I was surprised to meet the two reporters from *Aeronautics*, Montgomery and Charles Brown. They were still pale with emotion. They soon went back to the bar, while I went off to make out my report. I began by expressing to Higgins—our liaison boffin—just how well disposed the recent events had made me feel towards the Army. The most comic part of the proceedings was that MacIntyre, who had got back first, reported that he had seen Gordon disappear in the clouds belching oil and smoke. Actually Gordon was there as large as life, having managed to get back somehow. He thought *I* was dead!

So we all three had occasion to rejoice. Result of our trip: two Focke-Wulfs destroyed by me, another damaged by Gordon—one reparable Tempest (mine) and two others category B damaged but also repairable by our maintenance services on the spot. Not a bad balance sheet.

INTO THE INFERNO OF FLAK

The Germans had thought up a new mode of operation
for their fighter aircraft. All their large airfields had
become rather unhealthy since our troops had crossed
the Rhine—they had been bombed on a large scale.
The Luftwaffe no longer had enough planes to be able
to afford the luxury of having them uselessly destroyed
on the ground. Now the Jagdgeschwaders and the Jabos
no longer had any fixed bases.

All along the right bank of the Elbe, carrying out
Plan 1943 for the aerial defence of the Reich, the Todt
organization had built numerous secondary airfields,
designed for defensive fighter operations against large-
scale daylight raids by the Americans.

These bases were generally equipped with one good
permänent runway (asphalt or concrete), 1,000 to
1,500 yards long, and excellent auxiliary hangars. They
were ideal for the new "general post" technique. Three-
quarters of them were too far away to be bombed.
They were only fleetingly occupied and therefore there
was no justification for bombing them systematically,
particularly in existing circumstances. About fifteen
German fighter Wings—i.e. 1,200 ultra-modern fighters and fighter-bombers—led a nomadic existence between these bases. The motorized echelon moved off
during the night, the mechanics got the hangars ready
and the bowsers were hidden in the pine forests. The
aircraft came in at dawn and took off again from their
new home at about 10 a.m. for their operational trip.
After a few days—never more than a week—the Gesch-
wader again moved to another base.

Thanks to this technique the Germans succeeded in

harrying our troops pretty efficiently, especially in the morning and the evening. An increasing number of supply convoys rushed towards our forward armoured columns were being intercepted and strafed or bombed to a standstill by low-flying Jerry planes.

The Army complained bitterly to R.A.F. Tac H.Q. The latter passed the baby to 2 Group but there was nothing Group could do about it: its Mitchells and Bostons already had too much on their plate doing three sorties a day on tactical objectives, and maintenance was difficult. 2 Group in turn appealed to 84 Group, but the latter's fighter units were stationed too far to the rear to intervene.

In the end 83 Group found itself holding the baby. As usual it was our Tempest Wing which had this task palmed off on it as it alone was equipped with aircraft that were sufficiently fast (in theory) not to be massacred by flak; and it had sufficient radius of action to root out the Geschwaders from their most distant lairs.

We received from Intelligence plenty of gen on the new Jerry set-up, which was not calculated to increase our well-being.

In order to allow its fighters to operate in relative peace and quiet, the Luftwaffe had provided at least one Abteilung, i.e. battalion, of flak for each airfield. These Abteilungen were attached to the fighter Wings and generally comprised 3 batteries of automatic flak: one 37 mm. (9 single guns) and two 20 mm. (24 barrels in double or quadruple mountings). These Abteilungen followed the Geschwaders in their moves from field to field and were always the first on the scene. These formidable anti-aircraft defences manned by superbly trained crews and equipped with gyroscopic sights and predictors made any attack extremely dangerous. The defences were always on the qui vive, helped by relays of experienced spotters over a radius of six miles. As a result an Abteilung could and did within a matter of seconds put up an impenetrable curtain of tracer shells over the airfield it was defending. Any aircraft caught flying at low level had pretty slim chance of running the gauntlet of the 250 or so shells a second thrown up by the 33 barrels of the battalion.

All this didn't make us feel so good. Since our experiences over Rheine no one had the slightest wish to try conclusions with airfield flak again. I still had my morbid flak complex and as a result was in a poor position to improve my pilots' morale.

* * *

The two first airfield shoot-ups laid on by G.C.C. as a result of the new situation drew a blank: the airfields were deserted.

As a result of these checks G.C.C. thought up a new scheme to produce quicker action between the spotting of an inhabited "Einsatz" (the name given by the Luftwaffe to these new fields) and an attack on it. The Canadian reconnaissance Wing (49 Wing) was to inform us direct, without going through G.C.C., of any interesting objective. We were to drop everything and go into action with whatever aircraft were available, at the same time informing G.C.C., which kept at our disposal a squadron of anti-flak Typhoons in immediate readiness.

* * *

The new scheme came into operation at dawn the next day. 56 and 486 Squadrons had carried out the two previous fruitless sorties and so it was my 3 Squadron which was on stand-by "readiness." The suspense was unbearable. I don't remember ever feeling more nervous, and the pilots, who weren't feeling too good either, told me I looked as happy as a dying duck in a thunderstorm.

When I had put up the dawn flying order, the seven chosen hadn't shown any marked enthusiasm, except Bay Adams, the Australian member of the party, who was quite imperturbable and feared neither God nor the Devil. Our nervousness finally infected even the mechanics. Every other minute the crew-room door would open and an anxious face ask whether there was anything doing yet.

12 o'clock struck. The situation was becoming intolerable. The weather was very stormy. I had absolutely forbidden any mention of the word flak—penalty at £1 fine. You could have cut the silence in the room with a knife. We had been on "readiness" since 0355 hours. The consumption of tea and cigarettes was frightening, the floor was carpeted with cigarette ends. In the end I shut myself up in the office with Adj. near the telephone and tried to take my mind off it all by writing to my parents. I tore up three letters and gave it up.

"Adj., I'll take the jeep and pop over to control to have a look at the last 'Met' report. If anything happens in the meantime, fire a white Verey light." I had just got into the jeep when I heard the phone go. I jumped out again. In Dispersal everyone was on his feet looking anxious. It was 49 Wing. I dictated to Ken Hughes:

"Schwerin airfield—40 Messerschmitts seen by Spit Recco at 1140 hours, landing. About 100 A/C on base, 15 Arado two-seaters—refuelling point 500 yards S.E. of main hangar. Map 829 GA II—good luck!"

I glanced round at my pilots. For a moment no one spoke.

"Well, this is it!" sighed Wormsley philosophically.

"Quick, Adj., jump in the jeep and get hold of the I.O. and the German Airfield List, Volume 2," I said. Ken Hughes had already found Schwerin on the wall map—30 miles south-east of Lübeck—150 miles for us to cover.

Adj. came tearing back with Spy, and handed me the list open at page 829: Schwerin, a fine big airfield by a lake, west of the town of the same name. I put up a rapid sketch on the blackboard: the three runways forming a triangle, the probable location of the aircraft, from 49 Wing report.

The Jerries had landed at 1140 hours. It was now 1210 hours. Refuelling and re-arming the planes would take the Germans a good hour—we just had time to catch them before they flew off, dispersed or hid in the pine woods.

I gave last instructions, while Spy phoned through to G.C.C. to tell them what we were going to do and to ask for the rocket Typhoons to be laid on.

"We shall attack from north to south, all eight together, in line abreast, with a 200-yard interval between aircraft. Speed 530–540 m.p.h. Each pilot will pick out his target as he dives—no last minute change of direction. Open fire at 1,000 yards and continue till point-blank range. Stay as close to the ground as you can, count up to twenty, and then break fan-wise and climb at full throttle.

"Rendezvous with the Typhoons is at 1300 hours —late, I'm afraid, but they can't get there any earlier. The Typhoons will come down from 8,000 to 3,000 feet 30 seconds before us and they will shoot up any flak posts they can spot with their rockets. Because there is bound to be some flak." (Slightly forced smiles.)

"Remember that surprise, speed, and especially, flying at zero feet, are our best defence. No point in waggling your wings and pretending you're putting off the flak boys—you'll lose a few precious m.p.h. and risk sticking a wing on the deck.

"One last bit of advice: if you are hit and have to bale out, the best way, let me remind you, is this: stick right back—jettison the hood—curl up in a ball—wait a few seconds—jerk the stick right forward. You'll have nine chances out of ten of being thrown clear of the cockpit. Naturally I hope it won't come to that!

"Any questions? O.K. then, let's go!"

* * *

"Hallo, Kenway, Filmstar Leader calling—what about the Tiffie boys?" I was beginning to get anxious. We had crossed the Elbe and we could already see Schwerin lake on the horizon quite clearly. No sign of the Typhoons. A few moments later Kenway answered apologetically:

"Hallo, Filmstar Leader, sorry old boy, there's a cock-up about the Tiffies. Do the best you can without!"

A pleasant prospect! Without anti-flak Typhoons, we

were in for the hell of a time. My voice was probably not too steady as I got my patrol into attack formation. A big blue lake edged with pine trees, cut in the middle by a peninsula on which stood the town of Schwerin, a picturesque little town with renaissance steeples and varnished tiles, clinging to the rock. To the west a fine airfield, intact, complete with buildings and camouflaged hangars—not many like that left in Germany.

We were at 14,000 feet and kept straight on over to the left, as if we had no intention of attacking. I took a close look at the field: the small dark crosses parked just where we had expected them showed up on the bright grass of early spring. I particularly noticed one, two, four, seven flak towers, their shadows clearly projected on the perimeter track by the sun. . . .

"Look out Filmstar Leader, flak at 6 o'clock!"

Sure enough, 200 yards behind us five big black puffs from 88 mm. shells had appeared. O.K.! five more seconds and then I would attack. The objective was behind us and we were facing the sun. Fear caught me by the throat and stopped me breathing. Aerial combat against fighters had always found me calm—after the early stages—but flak was quite different.

"Drop your babies, Filmstar."

My stomach contracted and a wave of nausea swept over me—the advantage of a single-seater is that you can pass out with funk without anybody noticing.

"Quick, 180 port, go!"

This would bring us back facing the airfield, with the sun at our backs.

"Diving—full out, Filmstar!"

My seven Tempests were beautifully echeloned on my left although we were diving almost vertically.

"Smell of flowers," came Bay Adams' voice mockingly in the earphones. Flak! Christ, what flak! The entire surface of the airfield seemed to light up with flashes from 20 mm. and 37 mm. guns. There must have been at least forty of them. A carpet of white puffs spread out below us and the black puffs of the 37's stood out in regular strings of eight.

What flak! Physical fear is the most terrible thing

man can suffer—my heart leaped to my mouth, I was covered with sweat, with sticky, clammy sweat. My clenched toes swam in my boots.

We dived desperately into the smoke . . . explosions and tracers to left and right crossing over and under us . . . bangs round our wings and sinister dazzling flashes.

We were a mile from the perimeter, 150 feet from the ground. Men were running hither and thither.

"Lower, for Christ's sake," I yelled hysterically. The broad expanse of grass, carved by the grey runways, tilted up before my eyes and rushed towards me. We were doing over 450 m.p.h. First a hangar . . . a bowser . . . then the Messerschmitts, perched clumsily on their narrow undercarts, about thirty of them, with men crouching under the wings. Too far to the left, unfortunately, outside my line of fire.

A group of a dozen Arados loomed up in my sight. I fired, I fired frantically, my thumb jammed on the button. My shells formed a ribbon of explosion worming its way between the Arados, climbing up the fuselages, hitting the engines . . . smoke . . . one of the planes exploded just as I was over it, and my Tempest was tossed up by the burning gust. A Tempest touched the ground and the fuselage bounded up in a shower of fragments of smashed wings and tail-planes.

More hangars in front of me. I fired a second burst —it exploded on the galvanized iron doors and the steel stanchions.

"Look out, Red Two!" My No. 2 was coming straight for me, out of control, at terrific speed. His hood had gone. At 470 m.p.h., 20 yards to my right, he went smack into a flak tower, cutting it in two underneath the platform.

The wooden frame flew into the air. A cluster of men hanging on to a gun collapsed into space. The Tempest crashed on the edge of the field, furrowing through a group of little houses, with a terrific flash of light; the engine had come adrift in a whirlwind of flames and fragments scattered in the sky.

It was all over . . . almost. One, two, three . . . the tracer bullets were pursuing me . . . I lowered my head and hunched myself up behind my rear plating . . . twelve, thirteen, fourteen . . . I was going to cheat . . . a salvo of 37 burst so close that I only got the flash of the explosions without seeing the smoke . . . splinters hailed down on my fuselage . . . nineteen, twenty! I pulled the stick back and climbed straight up into the sky. The flak kept on.

I glanced back towards Schwerin, just visible under my tail-plane. A thousand feet below a Tempest was climbing in zigzags, the tracers stubbornly pursuing him. Fires near the hangars, columns of greasy smoke, a firework display of exploding magnesium bombs. The lone Tempest caught me up, waggled his wings and formed line abreast.

"Hallo, Filmstar aircraft, reform south of target, angels 10."

"Hallo, Pierre, Red Three here. You know, I think the rest had it!"

Surely Bay couldn't be right! I scanned the 360° of the horizon, and the terrific pyramid of flak bursts above Schwerin right up to the clouds, hanging in the still air. No one.

1304 hours. We had attacked at 1303 hours. The nightmare had lasted perhaps 35 seconds from the beginning of our dive and we had lost six aircraft out of eight. . . .

*   *   *

We crossed the Elbe again. I was beginning to relax and my legs stopped quivering. No point in thinking about the others. What good would it do?

One more trip done, 56 and 486 would do the next two. A day's respite perhaps.

Rheine again.

"Hallo, Desmond, Filmstar over base. May we pancake?"

Mechanically I lowered the undercart, reduced throttle. The usual sensation of being born all over again at the moment when your tires screech on the concrete.

* * *

G.C.C. had just sent along the photos of the Schwerin show. They were very clear. A Canadian from 49 Wing had taken them three hours after the shooting up of the airfield and had been greeted by some very trigger-happy flak. He had had to come down pretty low to get his obliques and had been badly wounded. By sheer grit and will-power he had succeeded in bringing back his damaged Spitfire XIV and his photos.

We scrutinized the photos very closely. The game really wasn't worth the candle. Two Messerschmitts had apparently been destroyed by a bowser exploding, and you could see, between two sections of the Focke-Wuff assembly plant, a tractor with another damaged one in tow. The only genuine havoc seemed to be in my group of Arados, five of which were clearly a total loss. However, that hadn't been the point of the trip, and it was pretty poor compensation for the loss of six Tempests and their pilots.

The flak really held too many trumps. I said as much in my monthly op. report and, for once in a while, G.C.C. took note. This type of show was given up.

* * *

The security chaps had just brought in a Luxemburg-er, caught hiding in a neighboring farm. He had been an observer in the Luftwaffe. I listened to his interrogation. The poor fellow wasn't feeling too happy and made no difficulty about answering Abund's questions.

He was an interesting specimen, having served in Lechfeld as observer in KJG40 from August 1943 to 25 September, 1944. Lechfeld was the centre for the new jet Messerschmitt 262's, and the prisoner was a bosom pal of Fritz Wendel's, Messerschmitt's chief test pilot.

According to him the 262's performance was as follows: maximum speed 610 m.p.h. at 23,000 feet, minimum landing speed 210 m.p.h. The 262 seemed to be equipped with a pressurized cockpit; anyway he had never seen Wendel wearing special flying clothes, although he had told him he had already been up to 42,000 feet.

All the aircraft of this type which the prisoner had seen had a white V painted on the grille of the turbine air-intake, followed by a number. He couldn't tell us whether this was a serial number. As the highest he had seen seemed to be V-15, the suggestion was that they were prototypes—V might very well stand for "Versuchs," i.e. "experimental."

We found a lot of secret documents in his kit, which were duly passed on to H.Q.

*   *   *

"Curly" Walker had got his D.F.C. and we decided to celebrate the occasion in the customary manner. On top of that it was his birthday, and his mess bill by the time we were through was enough to swallow up at least three months' pay. He was called Curly because of his round, prematurely bald cranium. He was 28, but looked 35. He was, with Ken Hughes, the senior surviving pilot in the squadron.

THE LAST TEST

3rd May, 1945

We had a very clear feeling that we were on the last lap. How long would German resistance last? If the Germans wanted to hold out on the Kiel Canal line, in the Danish islands and in Norway, they certainly could for at least another two months.

The evacuation of the Luftwaffe was taking place in pretty orderly fashion. All the airfields in Denmark were full to bursting point with transport and combat aircraft. In every bight, in every estuary, along the beaches, were moored entire fleets of Blohm und Voss and Dornier flying boats. Their petrol stocks would certainly allow them to carry out effective defence for some time yet—at least in theory. Every hour the retreating movement on Norway became clearer. The big naval convoy in Kiel, the endless stream of aircraft across the Skagerrak, the obstinate resistance of the ground troops, all those were sure signs.

By the same token our bomber planes in the 2 Group area were out-distanced and could not operate from their bases carrying effective loads. Nor could we, for the same reason, rely on any effective help from the Marauders of the American Ninth Air Force. Once again our poor 83 Group had to hold the baby.

This was confirmed by a phone message from Broadhurst, followed by one from Lapsley. As a sop we were told that all means would be taken to reinstate the airfields in the Lübeck area, once they were captured, so that our damaged aircraft should have somewhere to land. Belly-landing strips had already been installed at Ratzeburg and Schwartzenbeck and on the airfield at Lübeck itself. Ambulances were going to be permanently stationed there from 1300 hours that very day. If, by any chance, our troops were to occupy any airfields further north that were free of mines, the ends of the runways would be marked by "electric red" strips.

Maintenance was a hard problem. Each flight could only collect at most three or four planes capable of flying. In No. 3 Squadron alone we had seven planes in the hangars (flak, oil leaks, plugs to be changed, flak again and yet again). Ken Hughes' aircraft looked more like a gigantic sieve than anything else with its leading edges, its airscrew spinner and its radiator riddled with shell splinters. Johnny Walker had a hole two feet across in his tail-fin. My mechanics were just finishing rushed repairs to two holes the size of my fist in the fuselage of my "Grand Charles."

The personnel of the maintenance section hadn't half its equipment to hand, the hangars were open to the four winds, it rained into them and it was cold there.

We were short of ammunition and guns, as the convoys had not been able to catch up with our rapid advance. All these details of base organization were a big responsibility and the Squadron Leader Admin. of the Wing wasn't all that much help.

At this time I had been placed in temporary command of the Wing. I was still uneasy about my new rank and therefore felt rather edgy. My position—if it hadn't been for the sporting attitude of the British—might have been awkward because after all I was only a Sous-Lieutenant though I was in command of English officers much higher in rank. I knew that the Air Ministry were doing their best to rectify the position but in Paris nobody cared a damn. There they thought only about politics, and whether those who were still fighting got promotion was a matter of complete indifference to them.

All the same I had done three trips that day and I was completely creased. In the course of the morning the Wing had lost six pilots, including "Bab" Austin and Flying Officer Blee, the two best of the New Zealand 486 Squadron.

Charlie, senior engineer officer of the Wing, had a list of our available aircraft. We had 27—really 23—out of the 95 that we ought normally to have at our disposal. He could promise four more for 1700 hours. It was 1530 hours.

Ken Hughes, Johnnie Walker and my two Australians Torpy and Bay, with Longley as reserve, went on a short armed reconnaissance in the Flensburg area. Ken was a careful type and wouldn't get himself shot down without good cause.

I went on studying the morning's pilot reports, cooking up the Wing's report for G.C.C. with Abund. No way of glossing over our deficiency in planes. The pilots' morale wasn't anything to write home about either, and I registered a devout hope that we wouldn't be sent on any anti-shipping strikes.

Flak was looming ever larger on my pilots' mental horizon. You could sense how it obsessed them in every conversation, at meals, at the bar, during briefings.

To be convinced you had only to watch how sharply those who came back from a trip were questioned as to how dense the flak was, and where the posts were, by those who were about to set off. The word was on everybody's lips, all the time.

I chain-smoked cigarette after cigarette and drank innumerable cups of tea. My jaw and teeth still hurt from that lively landing on 24th March.

I had a somewhat lively argument with one of the liaison boffins from the Canadian 2nd Army—after that 20th April show I just didn't seem to cotton on to those khaki types. He didn't even seem to know what was going on on the ground. I had to go off and have a look at the teletypes myself to get up to date.

The ground situation seemed pretty confused—armoured thrusts towards Kiel and Elmshorn (north of Hamburg) against some strong nests of resistance supported by the airfields of Neumünster and Bad Segeberg and their satellites.

The Luftwaffe confined itself to covering the retreat

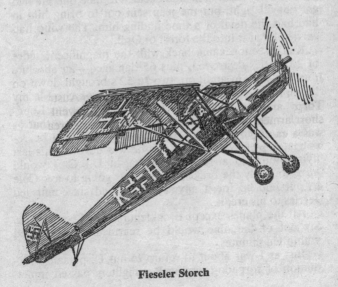

Fieseler Storch

of the ground troops and evacuating the staffs in Ju 88's and 52's, Heinkel III's and particularly Fieseler Storchs, which sneaked off while layers of mist covered the Poner Lakes area at dawn and sunset.

The rather low clouds (ceiling less than 3,000 feet) which had covered the base of the peninsula of Denmark for several days militated against interception patrols on our part. The flak was so dense that as soon as one of our planes emerged below the cloud cover it was immediately caught in a cross fire by the hundreds of automatic guns covering the arterial roads from Eutin to Kiel and especially the Neumünster-Rendsburg and Schleswig-Rendsburg autobahns.

All this was not very encouraging.

* * *

1720 hours. I went outside to watch 56 and 3 Squadrons landing on their return from a trip.

Poor Brocklehurst had been badly hit by flak as he was flying along the Flensburg autobahn. Rather than make a belly landing he had decided to bale out. He had got out all right, but the jeep sent out to bring him in had had the devil of a time finding him. The wind had carried him far into the forest of Orel.

Ken's section came back with the magnificent score of 23 lorries destroyed, plus 65 damaged—an absolute record—and, in addition, two Ju 52's brought down on the coast by Longley. Fine, that would look good in my report. On the other hand I was worried about Longley. He was getting increasingly rash. He knew that as soon as his tour of ops. was finished he would be repatriated to New Zealand, and he was devoting his last flying hours to an attempt to bag a D.F.C. I would have to apply the brakes a bit. I was going to ask Cole to put him up for it anyway as he had six confirmed Jerries to his credit.

All the planes except Brocklehurst's had come back. Six out of the nine would be rearmed and refuelled within ten minutes.

Just as I was about to return to our Dispersal, a formation of torpedo-carrying Beaufighters passed immediately overhead in a roar like thunder, coming from the north. There were swarms of them, about three Wings. They were on their way back from the monster shipping-strike organized against the notorious convoy at Kiel.

One of them had an engine on fire—there was the tell-tale trail of black smoke—and tried to land on our field. He went into a spin about 500 yards off and crashed with a terrific explosion near the bathing pool. The fire tender and the ambulance tore off.

"Christ, what's all the hurry?" murmured Peter West. "There can't be much left." How right he was. Ten minutes later the ambulance came slowly back, bearing the pitiful remains of the pilot and the observer.

We were still talking about it at dinner, an hour later in the mess, when Spy rushed up:

"Phone for you, Pierre."

Who on earth could be wanting me at this ungodly hour? I leapt into the jeep and tore off to the Intelligence Room.

Ops. on the phone:

"Take down the following, for immediate action: Grossenbrode air-naval base, reference N.54.22 E.11.05. Over 100 large transport aircraft loaded on beach and at anchor. Strong enemy fighter cover probable. Turn all available effectives on the designated objective. Strafe if possible. Actual method of execution left to your discretion. Inform Kenway of your plans at least 10 minutes in advance. I will try to give you anti-flak Typhoons. Do not rely on them too much. Good luck."

I said thank you and hung up. This sounded exciting, but I was furious. How delightful, after such a day, to be sent off again, at 8 p.m. on an objective like that!

I studied the wall map. Grossenbrode was about ninety miles as the crow flies but the "Met" reports said that Lübeck Bay and the Hamburg area were completely blocked. There was thundery cloud, with showers, up to 20,000 feet. We would have to make a detour to the north.

Tires screeched on the concrete. The jeeps were beginning to arrive, carrying bunches of pilots. What with their interrupted dinner and the heavy day they had had, they were not in the best of tempers. A few were munching improvised sandwiches.

Everybody there? O.K. I quickly outlined the situation. We hadn't enough available aircraft to fly as a Wing, in formation by flights. So we would fly in twice three flights, each of four planes echeloned to starboard. As Bruce Cole was on leave I would lead the first formation of 12 Tempests and MacDonald, from 486, the second. Like that I hoped my 24 planes would be under control.

I couldn't then and there give precise details as to how the strike would be carried out; I would give the necessary orders on the spot over the radio. It would be more a question of what turned out to be advisable than of a premeditated plan. In any case I had neither the necessary data nor the time to elaborate a plan of attack.

"Synchronize your watches. . . . It's 2007 hours. Engine start-up at 2015 hours. I shall take off as No. 1, will do a wide circuit over the airfield to let the 24 planes get into proper formation, and I shall set course on the target at 2025 hours. Any questions? O.K. then, get weaving."

For the other three in my section I chose F/Lt. Bone, F/O Dug Worley and young Sgt. Crow, whose third operational trip this would be. Not a particularly experienced trio, but I had no choice. I couldn't decently ask pilots who had already had three trips that day, and who were completely creased, to do a fourth and certainly pretty tough one.

*   *   *

2015 hours. "Grand Charles" was ready. The engine was already ticking over and Gray, lying on the wing, did a thumbs-up to show that everything was in order. The vast concrete expanse, framed by the great dark hangars, was alive with movement. As I strapped myself in I looked around. Engines ticked over, starter cartridges went off with a bang, mechanics rushed with maps or parachutes forgotten at the last minute. Pilots climbed awkwardly into their cockpits, festooned with Mae Wests and parachute harnesses.

2016 hours. "Chocks away." At 2025 hours, with the sun already low on the horizon and heavy cloud banks rolling eastwards, I set course north, slowly gaining height. The formation this evening was lousy—difficult to fashion a homogeneous team out of personnel from three different units.

"Come on, Filmstar, pull your bloody fingers out!"

Blue Section, which ought to have been on my left, was wandering about to my right, 1,500 feet above me. Yellow 2, 3 and 4 were trailing along more than half a mile to the rear. I was on edge and called them to order without mincing my words.

We flew round Hamburg to avoid the clouds of dirty smoke rising from the burning buildings. My aircraft at last decided to fly in formation.

We flew over Neumünster at 10,000 feet and got shot at, very sloppily, by an 88 mm. battery. We veered to starboard and set course 052°. The weather was deteriorating and I had to zigzag to avoid the blocks of cumuli which rose high in the sky like white towers.

"Hallo, Kenway, any gen.?"

"Hallo, Filmstar Leader, Kenway answering, nothing at all."

No signs of the recall I was secretly hoping for.

* * *

We were scarcely twenty miles from our objective when an impenetrable barrier of cloud blocked our way. I dived, followed by my formation, to try and find a way through underneath, but all we met was heavy rain and visibility zero. We quickly turned 180°, climbing, and then 180° again, bringing us back on our original course.

What was to be done? One plane by itself, or at a pinch a couple, might succeed in getting through, but for a compact formation of 24 to try it was not only a ticklish business, it was damned risky. I insinuated as much to Kenway.

"Hallo, Kenway, Filmstar Leader here. The weather stinks."

Kenway's answer was straight to the point and his tone of voice left no room for doubt.

"Filmstar Leader, press on regardless."

All right, then; "Cloud formation, go!"

I divided up my planes into independent sections of four, each one taking up box formation. We would have to try to get through the clouds on a set course and hope to join up again the other side.

We plunged into the storm and immediately lost sight of each other. Christ, it was pretty bumpy in there and I concentrated hard on my instruments, with an occasional eye open for my three unfortunate companions, who were keeping as close as they dared. The layer of cloud was luckily not very thick. After a very few moments we emerged over the Straits of Fehmarn, near Heiligenhafen. The sky was clear before us, all the way. My cockpit had got fogged up but now it cleared and I prepared to pinpoint our position.

"Look out, Filmstar Leader!"

In a fraction of a second the sky had filled with a whirling mass of aircraft . . . an unforgettable sight!

Below, to the right, the big airfield of Grossenbrode, with its seaplane base and its runways crawling with multi-engined aircraft. Beyond, a calm sea with a few ships at anchor. Behind us, a solid wall of clouds from which my Tempest sections were just emerging haphazardly and at various heights. All around us were massive groups of 30 or 40 German fighters on patrol. One of them had already seen us and was swooping down on Yellow Section.

In front of us, either on the ground or just taking off, were more than 100 enormous transport planes—theoretically my primary objective. In the air, about 100 enemy fighters. One group at 1,500 feet, another at 3,000, a third at 4,500 and two others on a level with us, i.e. at about 10,000 feet. Above us there were certainly one more, perhaps two. And I only had 24 Tempests!

My mind was quickly made up. Filmstar Yellow and Blue Sections would attack the fighters above us, and Pink, Black and White Sections, commanded by MacDonald, would engage the Focke-Wulfs below us. In the meantime I would try to slip through with my Red Section and shoot-up the airfield. I passed this on over the radio and then, closely followed by the rest of my section, I released my auxiliary tanks and went into a vertical dive, passing like a thunderbolt at 600 m.p.h. through a formation of Focke-Wulfs which scattered about the sky like a flock of swallows. I straightened out gradually, closing the throttle and following a trajectory designed to bring me over the airfield at ground level, from south-west to north-east.

All hell was let loose as we arrived. I was doing more than 500 m.p.h. by the clock when I reached the edge of the field. I was 60 feet from the ground and I opened fire at once. The mottled surface of the anchorage was covered with moored Dornier 24's and 18's. Three lines of white foam marked the wake of three planes which had just taken off. A row of Blohm und Voss's in wheeled cradles were lined up on the launching ramps. I concentrated my fire on a Bv 138. The moorings of the cradle snapped and I passed over the enormous smoking mass as it tipped up on the slope, fell into the sea and began to sink.

The flak redoubled in fury. A flash on my right, and a disabled Tempest crashed into the sea in a shower of spray.

Jesus! The boats anchored off shore were armed, and one of them, a large torpedo boat, was blazing away with all it had. I instinctively withdrew my head into my shoulders and, still flying very low, veered slightly to the left, so fast that I couldn't fire at the Dorniers, then quickly swung to the right behind an enormous Ju 252 which had just taken off and was already getting alarmingly big in my gunsight. I fired one long continuous burst at him and broke away just before we collided. I turned round to see the Ju 252, with two engines ablaze and the tail-plane sheered off by my shells, bounce on the sea and explode.

My speed had swept me far on—straight on to the torpedo boat which was spitting away with all her guns. I passed within ten yards of her narrow bows, just above the water and the thousand spouts raised by the flak. I caught a glimpse of white shapes rushing about on deck and of tongues of fire from her guns. The entire camouflaged superstructure seemed to be alive with them. Tracer shells ricocheted on the water and exploded all round over a radius of 500 yards. Some shrapnel mowed down a flock of seagulls which fell in the sea on all sides, panic-stricken and bleeding. Phew! Out of range at last!

I was sweating all over and my throat was so constricted that I couldn't articulate one word over the radio. Without realizing it I had held my breath through the whole attack and my heart was thumping fit to burst. I regained height by a wide climbing turn to port. What was happening? The situation looked pretty grim. A terrific dog-fight was going on above the airfield. Three planes were coming down in flames—I was too far to see whether they were friend or foe. Another, pulverized, had left a trail of flaming fragments in the sky and a fifth was coming down in a spin, followed by a white trail of smoke. Yet others were burning on the ground.

The radio was transmitting an incomprehensible chaos of shouts, screams and curses, mingled with the vibrations of cannon firing. Near the torpedo boat, in the middle of a patch of foam, the remains of a plane were burning and heavy black smoke curled up from the sheet of burning petrol.

What had happened to the rest of my section? Not a sign of them in the sky. I had seen a Tempest crash on my right when the attack began, presumably Bone's. The machine which had been shot down by one of the German ships was Crow's, I was sure. As for Worley, he was invisible.

I thought for a moment. Ought I to try to join in the fight against the German fighters raging above Heiligenhafen, or ought I to try a second run over the German base, taking advantage of the flap that was probably going on there?

Rather unwillingly I decided on the second course. I went down to sea level again and began to fly round Fehmarn Island at full speed. Suddenly I found myself face to face with three Dornier 24's, probably the three which had taken off from Grossenbrode a few seconds before our attack and whose wake I had seen. Do 24's are big three-engined flying boats of about 19 tons, fairly slow but well provided with defensive weapons.

Dornier Do 24

When I had recovered from my surprise I sheered off to keep outside their crossed fires, opened the throttle wide and zigzagged back towards them, taking photos. Then, keeping out of range of their machine guns, I drew a deliberate bead on the first one. After two bursts one of his engines was on fire and another was coughing. He tried a forced landing, but as on this side of the promontory the sea was rough he capsized and did himself considerable damage.

Immediately I made for the two others, who were skimming the water and attempting to get away. Long black trails escaped from their overworked engines. I felt almost sorry for them. With my 250 m.p.h. margin of speed and my four cannon, it was almost like potting two sitting birds. I chose the left-hand one, which was heavily laden and had lagged slightly behind the other. But this time, the bastard turned very cleverly at the last moment. Carried forward by my speed I found myself, like a fool, having to turn within point-blank range of his rear gunner who hit me with three bullets. Luckily they were only popguns of 7.7 mm. A side-slip brought me back into firing position and my shells ravaged his fuselage at less than 100-yards range. His wing tanks caught fire. The rear gunner shut up. Within a few seconds the machine was enveloped in flames. The pilot tried to gain height to allow his crew to bale out, but he was too low. Three men did jump, all the same. Only one parachute opened and that closed again at once, swallowed up by a wave. The big machine was nothing but a ball of fire rolling a few feet above the crests of the waves in a thick trail of black smoke. A few seconds later it exploded.

I looked for the third one. It had miraculously vanished into the landscape, probably behind one of the little islands in the strait. This business had brought me right round Fehmarn and I climbed to 10,000 feet. There was Grossenbrode behind the hill. I swallowed the lump in my throat, instinctively tightened my safety straps and once again dived for the airfield for another strafe.

This time I took them by surprise. The flak was otherwise engaged, firing rather haphazardly in the general direction of the swarm of German fighters and Tempests. I swept between two hangars and emerged over the airfield at full throttle. There were so many aircraft piled up there that I didn't know which to choose. Right in my sight there was a row of enormous transport Arado 232's. Before my shells exploded on the first two I had time to take in the curious fuselages, the big double-decker cabins and the 24-wheeled undercarts needed to support these gigantic machines.

A flak shell exploded within a few yards of my plane and shook it violently. Once out of range I broke away in a climbing spiral and found myself plumb in the middle of the scrap, which by this time was beginning to slacken.

I tried to rally my aircraft, but in that confusion it was difficult. The first thing I saw was a Tempest in a dive. It was spinning, increasingly fast. Then both the wings broke off . . . a few seconds later a bright flame leapt up between two hedges . . . no parachute.

Two Fw's tried to engage me in a dog-fight, but I quickly got rid of them by breaking away under them. JF-H, piloted by Bay the Australian, was in difficulties, its engine smoking. He was engaged with a Messerschmitt which was defending itself very cleverly, gradually reducing speed and beginning to get the upper hand. I roared towards the "109" and caught him by surprise, hitting him with at least two shells in the wing-root. The pilot, taken aback, instinctively reversed his turn and Bay, now in position, fired in his turn, hitting him again. Panic-stricken the Hun again reversed—I fired—he broke away—Bay fired—the Hun seemed to hang in the air for a moment, then one of his wings folded up in flames. The pilot managed to bale out all right, but his parachute screwed up.

At last my Tempests began to reform and, two at a time, cautiously withdrew from the scrap. The Huns gave ground and turned back one by one. They dived towards Grossenbrode, from which a column of smoke rose up in the sky—probably the two Arados burning.

A belated Focke-Wulf had slipped in amongst us and was desperately waggling his wings. Followed by Bay, I immediately went for him. A long burst—then suddenly my guns rattled noisily—no ammunition left. However, the Focke-Wulf had slowed down and was beginning to smoke, so I must have hit him after all. Bay fired in turn, point blank, and pulverized him. He burst like a ripe tomato. This time the parachute did open.

The sun had now slid down, over there, behind the Danish islands. My patrol reformed in the luminous twilight. I counted the planes; two, four, eight, ten, eleven—and then two others, lower down, laboriously catching up, probably damaged.

With navigation lights on we flew back towards Fassberg in the deepening night. Already the outlines of the landscape were becoming blurred. The warm evening air gently rocked my "Grand Charles." As we approached the airfield, undercarts and flaps down, I wondered what Mitchell, our engineer officer, would have to say when I brought him back thirteen planes out of the twenty-four.

THE DOOR CLOSES

Soon after that came the armistice, like a door closing. Eight days of bewilderment—an indefinable mixture of gladness and regret. Noisy jollifications, followed by long periods of calm, and, especially, a thick unaccustomed silence, which hung heavy on the airfield, on the tarpaulin-covered planes, on the empty runways. The snapping of the nervous tension was dreadful, as painful as a surgical operation.

That evening in the mess was like some extraordinary vigil over a corpse. The pilots were slumped in their chairs—no one spoke a word, or sang, or anything. Round about eleven o'clock Bay switched on the wireless. The B.B.C. was giving a running commentary on the scene in the streets of London and Paris, where the population was really letting itself go. All eyes turned towards the set, and in them you could read a kind of hatred.

It was so unmistakable, and yet so surprising, that I glanced enquiringly at Ken. I heard a crash of broken glass—someone had hurled a bottle at the set, at all this noise, at all those people shamelessly parading their sense of relief and deliverance before us.

One by one the pilots got up and eventually only Ken and I and the sleepy barman were left in the silent mess. From the smashed wireless still came a feeble whispering noise.

I again looked at Ken. No need of words, we both understood. Half an hour passed, an hour perhaps. And then, suddenly, I swear I felt they were all there, round us in the shadow and the cigarette smoke, like kids who have been unjustly punished.

Mackenzie . . . Jimmy Kelly . . . Mouse Manson . . . young Kidd . . . Bone . . . Shepherd. . . Brooker . . . Gordon . . . dark uniforms too, with tarnished gold stripes . . . Mouchotte . . . Mézillis . . . Béraud . . . Pierrot Degail—all those who had set off one fine morning in their Spitfires or their Tempests and who hadn't come back.

"Well, Pierre, that's that. They won't need us any more."

We went off to bed and I closed the door softly, so as not to awaken the barman, who had dropped off to sleep on his stool, and also so as not to disturb "the others."

*   *   *

It was only too true that nobody needed us any more, and we were made to realize it pretty quickly. Leaves cancelled, seats in planes reserved for superior officers; endless pin pricks, which may have been unintentional but rankled none the less.

I received a note from the Ministère de l'Air, countersigned by a general in the F.F.I., to the effect that, as an exceptional favour, I had been posted Lieutenant in the reserve.

On 12th May the big fly-past at Bremerhaven took place, and a tragedy—the aircraft in my section getting catastrophically tangled up, at less than a thousand feet. I recalled my parachute opening just before I hit the ground, the claps of thunder as the aircraft crashed, and myself running in a dream like a madman towards the four pillars of black smoke, stunned by the suddenness of the disaster. I saw one pilot's dislocated corpse at my feet, sunk in the ground with his unopened parachute. Then a body, in a pool of petrol, eaten by the flames, and twenty yards further on another plane, an inchoate mass in a blackened crater, with a ball of charred flesh and bone somewhere underneath the scrap metal.

Up above, the thirty planes of the Wing, scattered about the sky, flying over one by one, puzzled, waggling their wings, trying to make out what had happened.

*   *   *

The Wing left for Copenhagen. For a few days at Kastrup we were infected by the intoxicating feeling of liberation. Soon fear came back to grip me—dread of my own plane, with the Bremerhaven catastrophe dancing in front of my eyes; the kind of fear that distorts and destroys all one's reflexes.

The 1st of July came. If I had been able to read the signs I shouldn't have flown against my instincts. My "Grand Charles" had developed an oil leak, just as it had on 12th May. I refused to back out and again borrowed a plane.

My aircraft flew past impeccably, low over the crowd and the roofs bedecked with red flags with white crosses. Just as the gremlins which I had subconsciously been dreading seemed to have gone, I made that stupid error of judgment. After that everything happened that could: my undercart only half came down, my engine failed to respond just as it was most desperately needed. At 200 m.p.h. my Tempest ripped through the control trailer and disintegrated, shedding smashed fragments of wing, of engine and of tail-plane over a hundred yards. The ambulance picked me up unscathed, stunned, dimly comprehending that this was the last miracle, Fate's final fling.

*   *   *

27th August, 1945

I had applied for immediate demobilization and it had been granted. I had that morning gone to say my farewells to Broadhurst and to the R.A.F. The New Zealander Mackie was then commanding 122 Wing. I had made a point of going to H.Q. at Schleswig in my "Grand Charles." Coming back I had taken him high up in the cloudless summer sky, for it was only there that I could fittingly take my leave. Together we climbed for the last time straight towards the sun. We looped once, perhaps twice, we lovingly did a few slow, meticulous rolls, so that I could take away in my finger-tips the vibration of his supple, docile wings.

And in that narrow cockpit I wept, as I shall never weep again, when I felt the concrete brush against his wheels and, with a great sweep of the wrist, dropped him on the ground like a cut flower.

As always, I carefully cleared the engine, turned off all the switches one by one, removed the straps, the wires and the tubes which tied me to him, like a child to his mother. And when my waiting pilots and my mechanics saw my downcast eyes and my shaking shoulders, they understood and returned to the Dispersal in silence.

* * *

I sat next to the pilot of the Mitchell which was to take me back to Paris. As he taxied towards the runway he passed in front of the aircraft of the Wing, smartly lined up wing tip to wing tip, as if for an inspection. By them stood the pilots and the mechanics, waving.

Slightly to one side stood my "Grand Charles," my old JF-E, with its red spinner, the black crosses of our victories under the cockpit, compact, determined and powerful-looking with its big motionless four-bladed propeller, which would never again be started by me. It was like the turning of a page in a book.

To the accompaniment of the strident howl of its American engines, the Mitchell gathered speed and rose into the air. I glued my face to the window for a last glimpse behind our tail of Lübeck airfield, of the tiny glittering crosses on the grass, growing smaller and indistinct in the evening mist. The pilot, embarrassed, turned his head the other way.

It was all over. No more would I see my flight of Tempests line up behind my "Grand Charles," clumsy looking on their long legs, offering the yawning hole of their radiators to the wind from their propellers, with the trustful faces of their pilots leaning out of the cockpits, waiting for my signal.

But pride welled up within me when I thought of you, my planes, and above all of you, my dear R.A.F. friends, whom I had had the privilege of knowing and living amongst, with your uniforms the colour of your island mists.

* * *

The Big Show was over. The public had been satisfied. The programme had been rather heavy, the actors not too bad, and the lions had eaten the trainer. It would be discussed for a day or two more round the family table. And even when it was all forgotten—the band, the fireworks, the resplendent uniforms—there would still remain on the village green the holes of the tent pegs and a circle of sawdust. The rain and the shortness of man's memory would soon wipe out even those.

* * *

My surviving comrades from the Big Show have luckily not "understood"—nor have I—and it is our sole reward.

"We are the playthings of universal incoherence. We are individual stones in a mighty edifice, whose completed design we shall need more time and more peace to see in its proper perspective."

A. DE ST. EXUPÉRY,
"Pilote de Guerre."

BANTAM WAR BOOKS

Now there is a great new series of carefully selected books that together cover the full dramatic sweep of World War II heroism— viewed from all sides and representing all branches of armed service, whether on land, sea or in the air. All of the books are true stories of brave men and women. Most volumes are eyewitness accounts by those who fought in the conflict. Many of the books are already famous bestsellers.

Each book in this series contains a powerful fold-out full-color painting typifying the subject of the books; many have been specially commissioned. There are also specially commissioned identification illustrations of aircraft, weapons, vehicles, and other equipment, which accompany the text for greater understanding, plus specially commissioned maps and charts to explain unusual terrain, fighter plane tactics, and step-by-step progress of battles. Also included are carefully compiled indexes and bibliographies as an aid to further reading.

Here are the latest releases, all Bantam Books available wherever paperbacks are sold.

AS EAGLES SCREAMED by Donald Burgett

THE BIG SHOW by Pierre Clostermann

U-BOAT KILLER by Donald Macintyre

THE WHITE RABBIT by Bruce Marshall

THE ROAD PAST MANDALAY by John Masters

HORRIDO! by Raymond F. Toliver & Trevor J. Constable

COCKLESHELL HEROES by C. E. Lucas-Phillips

HELMET FOR MY PILLOW by Robert Leckie

THE COASTWATCHERS by Cmd. Eric A. Feldt

ESCORT COMMANDER by Terence Robertson

I FLEW FOR THE FÜHRER by Heinz Knoke

ENEMY COAST AHEAD by Guy Gibson

THE HUNDRED DAYS OF LT. MAC-HORTON by Ian MacHorton with Henry Maule

QUEEN OF THE FLAT-TOPS by Stanley Johnston

V-2 by Walter Dornberger

BANTAM WAR BOOKS

These action-packed books recount the most important events of World War II. They take you into battle and present portraits of brave men and true stories of gallantry in action. All books have special maps, diagrams, and illustrations.

☐	12657	**AS EAGLES SCREAMED** Burgett	$2.25
☐	12658	**THE BIG SHOW** Clostermann	$2.25
☐	11812	**BRAZEN CHARIOTS** Crisp	$1.95
☐	12666	**THE COAST WATCHERS** Feldt	$2.25
☐	*12664	**COCKLESHELL HEROES** Lucas-Phillips	$2.25
☐	12141	**COMPANY COMMANDER** MacDonald	$1.95
☐	12578	**THE DIVINE WIND** Pineau & Inoguchi	$2.25
☐	*12669	**ENEMY COAST AHEAD** Gibson	$2.25
☐	*12667	**ESCORT COMMANDER** Robertson	$2.25
☐	*11709	**THE FIRST AND THE LAST** Galland	$1.95
☐	*11642	**FLY FOR YOUR LIFE** Forrester	$1.95
☐	12665	**HELMET FOR MY PILLOW** Leckie	$2.25
☐	12663	**HORRIDO!** Toliver & Constable	$2.25
☐	12670	**THE HUNDRED DAYS OF LT. MACHORTON** Machorton	$2.25
☐	*12668	**I FLEW FOR THE FURHER** Knoke	$2.25
☐	12290	**IRON COFFINS** Werner	$2.25
☐	12671	**QUEEN OF THE FLAT-TOPS** Johnston	$2.25
☐	*11822	**REACH FOR THE SKY** Brickhill	$1.95
☐	12662	**THE ROAD PAST MANDALAY** Masters	$2.25
☐	12523	**SAMURAI** Sakai with Caidin & Saito	$2.25
☐	12659	**U-BOAT KILLER** Macintyre	$2.25
☐	12660	**V-2** Dornberger	$2.25
☐	*12661	**THE WHITE RABBIT** Marshall	$2.25
☐	*12150	**WE DIE ALONE** Howarth	$1.95

*Cannot be sold to Canadian Residents.

Buy them at your local bookstore or use this handy coupon:

Bantam Books, Inc., Dept. WW2, 414 East Golf Road, Des Plaines, Ill. 60016

Please send me the books I have checked above. I am enclosing $_____ (please add 75¢ to cover postage and handling). Send check or money order —no cash or C.O.D.'s please.

Mr/Mrs/Miss _____

Address _____

City _____ State/Zip _____

WW2—2/79

Please allow four weeks for delivery. This offer expires 8/79.

THE SECOND WORLD WAR

The full drama of World War II is captured in this new series of books about a world on fire. In addition to paintings, there are maps and line drawings throughout the text at points where they are most informative.

Bantam Book Catalog

Here's your up-to-the-minute listing of over 1,400 titles by your favorite authors.

This illustrated, large format catalog gives a description of each title. For your convenience, it is divided into categories in fiction and non-fiction—gothics, science fiction, westerns, mysteries, cookbooks, mysticism and occult, biographies, history, family living, health, psychology, art.

So don't delay—take advantage of this special opportunity to increase your reading pleasure.

Just send us your name and address and 50¢ (to help defray postage and handling costs).